Time Out LONDON SHOPPING GUIDE

Compiled by
LINDSEY BAREHAM

TIME OUT LONDON SHOPPING GUIDE

ISBN 0 600 20085 X

First published in Great Britain 1980
by Hamlyn Paperbacks

Hamlyn Paperbacks are published by
The Hamlyn Publishing Group Ltd,
Astronaut House,
Feltham,
Middlesex, England

Made and printed in Great Britain by Cox & Wyman Ltd,
Reading.

The map inside the back cover is reproduced by
kind permission of London Transport

CONTENTS

ACKNOWLEDGEMENTS

Special thanks to Irene Campbell and Jane Rackham of Sidekicks for research help and typing the manuscript. Thanks also for research assistance from Sally Bradbery, Susie Brown, Angela Coles, Suzie Crowley and Jill Trethowan.

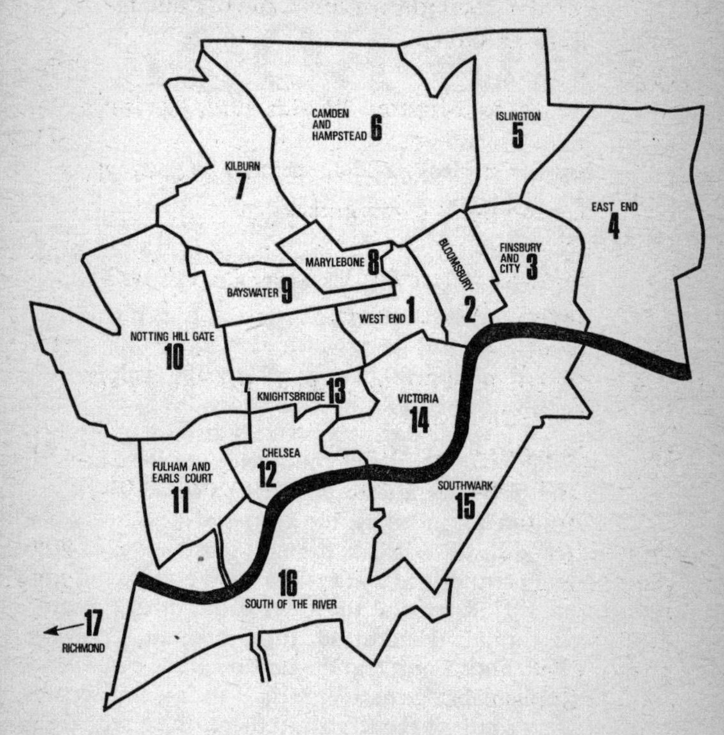

This map shows how we have divided London's main shopping areas. The numbers refer to the chapters.

HOW TO USE THIS BOOK

This shopping guide is based on the premise that if you want something badly enough, you'll cross London to get it. Once you've crossed London, made your purchase and have some time to spare, it's worth knowing about any other nearby speciality, unusual and interesting shops.

The centre and outskirts of London have been divided into several loosely defined areas which each incorporate one or more distinct shopping centres. With the help of the comprehensive contents list and the two indexes, planning a short visit or a whole day's shopping is made easy. To help you, opening hours, nearest public transport, local half-day closing and places for a restorative cuppa are all listed.

Having carved London up into a series of areas it was then particularly difficult to decide the most sensible way to order them. Finally we decided to start with the West End and work east through Holborn and the City; go north to Islington, then west through Hampstead; turn south to Bayswater, Notting Hill, Earls Court and Fulham; and head east again to Chelsea, Knightsbridge and Victoria. The last few sections look at areas south of the river, and those which are further out but considered worth visiting for one shopping purpose or another.

Assuming that readers will be shopping on foot, we have ordered the sub-sections to follow each other as sensibly as possible. Where possible chapters/areas link together. When they also link into other areas we have noted these at the end of the relevant introduction.

The selection of shops and street markets is entirely my arbitrary choice and is based on years of writing about London shops and pounding the streets to find places with either interesting or specialist stock, or those which offer outstanding value or a useful service. These shops are arranged by street within their area.

Some areas, notably South of the River, the East End and City have far fewer entries than, say, Notting Hill or Bloomsbury. These have been chosen to reflect the character of areas not noted for an abundance of good shops. However, in these areas new shops are opening all the time. If you know of a shop which you consider worthy of inclusion, in any area of the book, please write to me at the following address. It may be possible to include the shop in future editions of this book: Time Out London Shopping Guide, Tower House, Southampton St, London WC2.

Finally, two indexes list everything mentioned, by subject and under the names of the individual shops.

Lindsey Bareham
London, 1980

HELPFUL HINTS AND 24-HOUR SERVICES

Public Transport

Getting around London is notoriously time consuming and expensive. If you plan a day's shopping all over London one of London Transport's special tickets is a wise investment. They can be brought from any London Transport Enquiry Office, bus garage or tube station.

'Red Bus Rovers' give you one day's travel anywhere on all red buses (greater London) (£1.50 adult, 40p child as we went to press).

'Go As You Please Tickets' are for travel on both underground and buses for three-, four- or seven-day periods (£7.90/£9.90/£12.20).

'Central Tube Rovers' cover a day's tube travel in the area within the Circle line (plus Earls Court and Waterloo) (£2.20).

Moped

Hiring a moped or small motorbike is an ideal way of getting around London if you've got the nerve. Scootabout of Tachbrook St, Victoria (01–821 5177) say anyone able to ride a bicycle can manage one of their Puch mopeds. Larger bikes and mopeds can also be hired from Rent-A-Scooter in Kilburn (01–624 8491).

Bicycles

As London buses, taxis and motorists become more aware of the increasing number of bicycles on London roads, cycling is far safer than it seems. There are very few provisions for cycle parking but a bike can be locked to a parking meter – of which there is no shortage.

Always ride close to the kerb, and take care on main roads.

Bicycles can be hired for the day from the following places:
Bell Street Bikes, 73-75 Bell St, NW1 (01-724 0456)
Beta Bikes, 275 West End Lane, NW6 (01-794 4133)
Bicycle Revival, 28 North End Parade, North End Rd, W14 (01-602 4499) and 17-19 Elizabeth St, SW1 (01-730 6716)
Covent Garden Cycles, 41 Shorts Gardens, WC2 (01-836 1752)
Rent-A-Bike, Kensington Student Centre, Kensington Church St, W8 (01-937 6089)
Saviles, 97-99 Battersea Rise, SW11 (01-228 4279).

Car

Car hire isn't advised as a sensible way of shopping in London but the following is a cross-section of the many companies which keep small cars for hire.

It is virtually impossible to hire a car unless you are over 21, and most companies require a driving licence to have been held for a minimum of one to two years.
Avis (01-848 8733)
Budget Rent-A-Car (01-306 8266)
Central Car Hire (01-730 9138)
Godfrey Davis (01-828 7700)
Hertz (01-542 6699)
Kardrop (01-589 9244)
Portobello Mini Hire (01-727 2424)

Getting Free

If you have children a day's shopping may not be easy to organize. The following babysitter agencies hire occasional one-off babysitters. All have a minimum four-hour hire period, and fares are extra.
Solve Your Problems Ltd, 25a Kensington Church St, W8 (01-937 0906)
Babysitters/Childminders, 67 Marylebone High St, W1 (01-935 9763)
Babysitters Unlimited, 313 Brompton Rd, SW3 (01-730 7777/8)

Money Out of Hours

If you don't own a cash card, cheques can be cashed with a banker's card at the 24-hour banks at Heathrow and Gatwick airports. Chequepoint Services and Scotia Bureaux are essentially foreign exchanges but they will cash cheques with a banker's card. The following Chequepoint branches are open until midnight:

Chequepoint Services
89 Gloucester Rd, SW7 (01-370 5137)
130 Kings Rd, SW3 (01-589 7466)
58 Queensway, W2 (01-229 4268)
236 Earls Court Rd, SW5 (01-370 3238)
47 Old Brompton Rd, SW7 (01-584 6654)

Scotia Bureaux
15 Shaftesbury Ave, W1 (01-734 1400)
open until 21.00, 'til 23.00 Sat
152a Cromwell Rd, SW7 (01-370 6848)
open until 20.00 every evening
22 Leinster Terrace, W2 (01-402 6305)
open until 20.00 every evening
2 London St, W2 (01-723 9964)
open until 20.00 every evening

Shopping Out of Hours
Food
London is not a late night city; we only have one 24-hour shop and only a few areas of London have any shopping life after 18.00. Earls Court Rd, and Queensway leading into Westbourne Grove are the two most lively late shopping streets; both cater for their mixed ethnic and bedsitter community with numerous sub-quality mini-supermarket food shops. Other late food shops are dotted all over London.

Chalk Farm
The Chalk Farm Nutrition Centre, 41 Chalk Farm Rd, NW1 (01-485 0116) is open 9.00-21.00 seven days a week. They sell a wide range of health foods, Ceres breads and cakes, vitamins, natural drinks, grains and a wide variety of cheeses and yoghurts.
Marine Ices, Chalk Farm Rd, NW1 (01-485 8898) is open 11.00-23.00 seven days a week. They sell 18 different flavoured superb non-dairy ice-creams made with vegetable fats and fresh fruit.

Kilburn
Osaka, 17 Goldhurst Terrace, NW6 (01-624 4983) Mon to Sat is open 8.00 to 20.00. They sell unpackaged foods mainly from the West Indies, China, Japan and India – bulk sales preferred.

St Johns Wood
Five Star Foods, 5 St Johns Wood High St, NW8 (01-722 1248) is open 09.00 to 23.00 seven days a week. They sell a wide range of delicatessen and provisions.

West End
Late food shopping in the West End is centred around Chinatown. The following Chinese supermarkets sell food and cooking equipment:
Great Wall, 31-37 Wardour St, W1 (01-437 7963) open 11.00-2 am Mon to Sat
Loon Fung Supermarket, 39 Gerrard St, W1 (01-437 1922) open 12.00-21.00.

Knightsbridge
The Midnight Shop, 223 Brompton Rd, SW1 (01-589 7788) is open 'til midnight seven days a week. They sell general provisions including refrigerated meat and fresh vegetables.

Sloane Square
Partridges, 132 Sloane St, SW1 (01-730 0651) open 9.00-20.00 Mon to Sat; 10.30-19.30 Sun. A useful last minute food shop, Partridge sell delicatessen, cheese, fresh coffee and bread as well as numerous groceries.

Fulham
Luigi's, 60 New King's Rd, SW6 (01-731 4994) open until 20.00 seven days a week. An Italian delicatessen and grocery with an amazing number of Italian wines - 145 at the last count.

Hammersmith
Buy Late Foods, 99 Hammersmith Rd, W14 (01-603 2300) is a fairly ordinary self-service general food shop and is open from 9.00 until 22.00 seven days a week.

Bayswater
The 24 Hour Supermarket, 68 Westbourne Grove, W2 (01-727 4927) stocks most general provisions; both food and hardware. There are numerous other food shops open late in Westbourne Grove including a particularly good delicatessen called Corfutrade. Le Relais Basque, 28 Westbourne Grove, and its sister patisserie/bakery Maison Bouquillon at 41 and 45 Moscow Rd, W2, both stay open until 20.00.

Richmond
The Richmond Hill Delicatessen, 22 Richmond Hill, Richmond (01-940 3952) sells 60 different cheeses, home made pâté and high class groceries. They stay open until 21.00 seven days a week.

Other Things
Flowers can be bought from the refrigerated vending machines outside Chivers branches at 43 Charlotte St, W1 and 129 Tottenham Court Rd, W1.
Delightful *homeware* including bamboo furniture, kitchenware and numerous gift items can be bought until midnight Mon to Sat at the Inside Out Shop, 1 Neal St, WC2 (01-240 0331).
Jeans, jerseys and shirts at rock-bottom prices can be bought at Dickie Dirts, 59a Westbourne Grove, W2 (01-229 1466) until 23.00 seven days a week.

Chemists
Bliss Chemist, 54 Willesden Lane, NW6 (01-624 8000) and Boots, Piccadilly Circus, W1 (01-930 4761) are both open 24 hours.
John Bell and Croyden, 54 Wigmore St, W1 (01-935 5555) open their dispensary until 21.00 Mon to Sat and until 20.00 Sun.
All shops mentioned in this section are given detailed write-ups in the main body of the book.

Consumer Law

Anything sold as perfect must comply with the following conditions of The Sale of Goods Act. You stand a better chance of getting your money back if you can produce a receipt but it's not a legal requirement. Some shops will offer you a replacement or credit note but it's at your discretion which you choose. *Goods must be* 1) of merchantable quality, i.e. free of faults; 2) fit for the purpose for which they are sold; and 3) fit their description exactly.

1
WEST END

Oxford St, Bond St, Tottenham Court Rd, Regent St, Soho and Leicester Sq.

Land of London's leading department stores - John Lewis, Selfridges, D. H. Evans and Bourne and Hollingsworth (now re-launched as Bournes), Oxford St is a mecca to all tourists and day-trippers. It's also the place for chain shoe shops - (Lilley and Skinner, Bata, Sacha and Dolcis) - cheap and cheerful fashions - (C & A, Peter Robinson, Girl - and various covered souk-type markets; cheap home things, particularly lighting, at British Home Stores, and the internationally popular Marks & Spencer. Various streets running off both sides of Oxford St house interesting shops. On the south side Davies St is overtaken by the vast Grays Antique Market, while South Molton St houses an interesting mix of long-established specialist shops and extremely pricey but unique fashion boutiques. Bond St (most of which is actually called New Bond St) and its adjoining streets are the places for couture clothes like Gucci, Yves St Laurent, Zandra Rhodes and Ted Lapidus; leading shoe- and boot-makers such as Magli, Rayne, Ferragamo and Elliott, as well as jewellers like Asprey, antique shops, art galleries and other expensive delights. On the north side, St Christopher's Place is a relatively peaceful and little-known backwater off Wigmore St, which has several specialist shops.

Regent St, which intersects Oxford St, is slightly more exclusive with its main department store, Liberty's, renowned for beautiful fabrics, expensive hand-crafted goods and Oriental luxuries. In Regent St there is a giant branch of Boots the Chemist, the Scotch House (for Scottish woollen goods), department store Dickins and Jones, and Jaeger, Aquascutum and Austin Reed - classic clothes shops for men and women. Some of the backstreets behind Regent St bordering on Soho are worth investigating for long-established specialist shops, but the once famous Carnaby St has sadly declined.

Soho warrants plenty of time, with its superb French and Italian food shops. Charing Cross Rd is the place for books new, secondhand and antiquarian, from those on the most obscure specialist subject to the latest textbook. It's also a leading hi-fi/audio equipment centre, as is Tottenham Court Rd. This whole area is full of old-established traditional shops, Charlotte St and Goodge St being particularly good.

See also Marylebone, Camden, Hampstead and Victoria.

TRANSPORT

Oxford St
Tube Stations: Tottenham Court Rd, Oxford Circus, Bond St, Marble Arch
Buses: 12, 25, 73, 88

(New) Bond St
Tube Stations: Bond St
Buses: 25

Tottenham Court Rd
Tube Stations: Tottenham Court Rd, Goodge St, Warren St
Buses: 24, 29, 73, 134

Regent St
Tube Stations: Piccadilly Circus, Oxford Circus
Buses: 3, 6, 12, 15, 88, 159

Soho
Tube Stations: Piccadilly Circus, Leicester Sq, Tottenham Court Rd
Buses: 14, 19, 22, 38

Leicester Sq
Tube Stations: Leicester Sq, Piccadilly Circus
Buses: 1

Local opening hours

The majority of West End shops stay open until 19.00 or later on Thurs; some close at midday on Sat. Only Soho shops have no late opening, many close at midday on Thurs, some also close at midday on Sat. A small number of shops in this area close all day Sat.

REFRESHMENTS

Cranks in Heals
Tottenham Court Rd, W1. *Open 09.00–17.30 Mon to Sat; 09.45–17.30 Thurs.* Tea, coffee, soft drinks, pastries and vegetarian snacks.

Maison Bertaux Ltd
28 Greek St, W1. *Open 09.00–18.00 Tues to Sat; 09.30–13.00 Sun.* Long-established patisserie; coffee, tea, croissants, tarts and cakes.

Patisserie Valerie
44 Old Compton St, W1. *Open 08.00–19.00 Mon to Sat.* Long-established patisserie; coffee, tea, croissants, tarts and cakes.

OXFORD ST

Virgin Megastore
Virgin's largest and latest branch with a whole floor devoted to deletions and sale stock. Also all albums in the British catalogue at discount prices and hefty reductions on albums in their weekly top 50. Imports from America, Japan, Ireland, Jamaica, France, Germany and Holland plus all the punk music labels.
14–16 Oxford St, W1 (01-636 1771). Open 10.00–19.00 Mon to Sat.
Also at 2 Edgware Rd, W2; and 130 Notting Hill Gate, W11.

Anello and Davide
This is the fashion branch of the famous 60-year-old West End ballet and theatrical shoemakers. They keep enormous stocks of ready-made boots (classic designs are made to order) and shoes, and sell shoes for both men and women.
33–35 Oxford St, W1 (01-437 4042). Open 09.00–17.30 Mon to Fri; 09.00–13.00 Sat.
Also at 30 Drury Lane, WC2 (see page 41).

Dixons Discount Video Centre
Dixons specialize in home video equipment and usually demonstrate three different machines in their shops. They operate a price challenge; if you find the same machine cheaper elsewhere, they'll refund the difference.
88 Oxford St, W1 (01-636 8511). Open 09.00–18.00 Mon to Sat.
Also at Brent Cross.

Top Shop At Peter Robinson
An escalator leads down, curiously enough, into Top Shop, Peter Robinson's fashion basement. Their own disc jockey intersperses the music with best-buy news from the wide variety of fashion houses represented with small shops in this vast pulsating open-plan store. Women's clothes and all accessories.
Oxford Circus, W1 (01-636 7700). Open 09.30–18.00 Mon to Sat; 10.00–20.00 Thurs.

Harpers House
A vast neon sign boasts the presence of Pinto, one of three fashion houses who operate from Harpers House. Stirling Cooper (women only here) are upstairs, while the less familiar Pinto Sportswear is on the ground floor. Pinto clothes are young, casual, easy to wear, reasonably priced and are for

both men and women. The last of the three shops here is Succhi, which sells fashion footwear for men and women.
240 Oxford St, W1 (01-629 8574). Open 09.30–18.30 Mon to Sat; 09.30–20.00 Thurs.

Take Six
Moderately priced and (usually) well designed fashion clothes for men. Particularly good for off-the-peg suits, knitwear and shirts, plus a full range of accessories. This is their largest branch, there are others in Bond St and Kings Rd, SW3.
362–364 Oxford St, W1 (01-499 9909). Open 09.00–18.00 Mon to Sat; 09.00–20.00 Thurs.

HMV
HMV is the largest record shop in Europe. It's run on a self-service basis with informed back-up sales staff. The four floors house albums, pre-recorded (and blank) tapes and video tapes of all types from all over the world. They can get anything to order and offer 60 albums at discount prices every week.
363 Oxford St, W1 (01-629 1240). Open 09.30–18.30 Mon to Fri; 09.30–20.00 Thurs; 09.30–18.00 Sat.

Greenfields
Previously Millets, Greenfields sell everything for camping: a range of ridge tents, three types of frame tent and camping accessories. Also waterproof clothing, work wear, outerwear and casual wear including army jerseys, shetlands, Dr Martin boots and winter suedes, plus inflatable dinghies and accessories.
445 Oxford St, W1 (01-491 7381). Open 09.00–18.30 Mon to Sat; 09.00–20.00 Thurs.

Marks & Spencer
The largest branch of Marks & Spencer (for other branches see telephone directory) which regularly has queues of tourists and is reputed to have the highest turnover of any shop in Europe. Good for Shetland jerseys, blouses, underwear and children's clothes.
458 Oxford St, W1 (01-486 6151). Open 09.30–17.30 Mon to Fri; 09.30–19.30 Thurs; 09.00–17.00 Sat.

Wallis
Wallis, a smart middle- to upper-price range fashion clothes shop for women, has branches all over London. They are particularly good at copying haute couture fashions and selling them at High Street prices. Their sales staff are very keen; consequently browsing can be difficult.
490 Oxford St, W1 (01-629 2171). Open 09.00–18.00 Mon to Sat; 09.00–20.00 Thurs.

Theatreland
Mr Marcus has been supplying

the theatrical world with fabrics since 1928. The shop boasts a variety of glittery, glamorous and sparkling fabrics, like lamé and sequinned covered cloths, as well as plainer satins and cheap muslins. Also a full range of trimmings, haberdashery, and ballroom dancing records.
14 Soho St, W1 (01–437 2245). Open 09.00–18.00 Mon to Sat.

Distinctive Trimmings
(See page 123 for full details.)
11 Marylebone Lane, W1 (01–486 6456). Open 09.30-17.00 Mon to Fri.

Fern & Co.
A delicious smell of roasting coffee wafts into the street from this small, dark, wood-panelled shop with brass heaters and a spiral staircase. They stock ten brands of coffee including a superb Turkish blend, and nine blends of tea sold loose from giant black and gold tea caddies. There is also a full range of coffee-making equipment, spare parts, filter papers, coffee mills and coffee sugars.
27 Rathbone Place, W1 (01–636 2237). Open 08.00–17.00 Mon to Fri; 08.00–13.00 Sat.

Winsor and Newton
Everything required by the amateur and professional artist is on sale at Winsor and Newton. Easels, brushes, pencils, painting grounds, colours, oil paints, water colours, gouache and dry ground pigments. Also modern mediums including vinyl paints, acrylics and alkyd resins and quick-drying oil colours. They specialize in unusual products like glass paints and cater particularly for students and children.
51 Rathbone Place, W1 (01–636 4231). Open 09.00–17.30 Mon to Sat.

Blacks of Greenock
Old-established camping equipment firm; here on two floors. Sleeping bags, frame and individual tents, walking shoes, and a vast variety of camping accessories.
53 Rathbone Place, W1 (01–636 6645). Open 09.30–17.30 Mon to Sat.

D. Lewis Ltd
Lewis' are specialists in motorcycle leather and waterproof clothing. A wide range of colours is available in their leather clothes, many of which are designed for specific jobs like scrambling. They'll make up racing clothes and special colour combinations to order. They stock a full range of motorbike accessories like helmets, goggles and bits for DIY customizing.
120/122 Great Portland St, W1 (01–636 4314). Open 09.00–17.30 Mon to Sat.

The Irish Shop
Beautiful knitwear, clothes and

crafts from Ireland including the famous Waterford crystal and Belleek china.
11 Duke St, W1 (01-935 1366). Open 09.30–17.30 Mon to Fri; 09.30–18.00 Thurs; 09.30–16.00 Sat.

Warehouse Utility Clothing Co
Cut price women's fashion clothes, see page 138–9 for full details.
27 Duke St, W1 (01-487 5909). Also at 5 Harewood Place, W1; 19/21 Argyll St, W1 and 129 Queensway, W2. Open 09.30–18.00 Mon to Sat; 09.30–20.00 Thurs.

Justin de Blank Food and Drink Ltd
Really a café/restaurant serving superbly prepared seasonal savoury snacks, main dishes, salads, old-fashioned English puddings and fruit salads. At the front there's a small selection of Justin de Blank breads, butter and cheese, biscuits and vegetables; also a take-away food service.
54 Duke St, W1 (01-629 3174). Open 09.00–21.30 Mon to Fri; 09.00–15.30 Sat.

BOND ST

Janet Reger
Beautiful but incredibly expensive and ultra-feminine designer lingerie and nightwear in silk, satin-de-lys, crêpe and chiffon. Watch out for their genuine post-Christmas sale when up to 50% reductions are usually sold out within the first hour. Also at Knightsbridge.
12 New Bond St, W1 (01-493 8357). Open 10.00–18.00 Mon to Fri; 10.00–17.00 Sat.

Cameo Corner
Previously in Bloomsbury and now moved to these far smaller premises, Cameo Corner was established in 1903. They specialize in cameos, but also sell antique jewellery dating back to Roman times, plus Victorian, Art Deco and Art Nouveau pieces. They also undertake fine repairs, alterations and valuations.
22 New Bond St, W1 (01-629 0071). Open 10.15–17.00 Mon to Fri.

Smythson
Smythsons are stationers to the Queen and anyone else who cares about the quality of their writing paper. Aside from a variety of gift items and novelties they excel in their range of special stationery including superb, hand-made, water-marked writing paper and engraved visiting cards. They also sell a variety of diaries, bound in materials ranging from silk to crocodile; address and note books; and everthing from photograph albums and press cuttings books to menus and

guest registers. They are one of the few places left that sells sealing wax.
54 New Bond St, W1 (01-629 8558). Open 09.30-17.30 Mon to Fri; 09.15-12.30 Sat.

Fenwicks
Women's clothes for all occasions sold in department-store style. Also accessories, costume jewellery, hats, handbags, shoes and lingerie.
63 New Bond St, W1 (01-629 9161). Open 09.00-17.30 Mon to Sat; 09.00-19.30 Thurs.

Midas
Footwear on sale at Midas is always distinctive and is far cheaper than at many Bond St shoe shops. All styles are made exclusively for Midas and imported largely from France and Italy. This summer's range will have a strong Sixties flavour and for the first time will include a men's range. Also at Hans Crescent, SW3; and Marylebone High St, W1.
72 New Bond St, W1 (01-629 3633). Open 09.30-18.00 Mon to Sat; 09.30-19.00 Thurs.

Elle
Beautiful women's fashions from top French designers are displayed with elegance at Elle. There are clothes for all occasions with the emphasis on elegant, easy to wear ensembles. This branch also sells Italian fashions and a full range of accessories including lingerie.
92 New Bond St, W1; also at 23 Brompton Rd, SW3 (01-629 4441). Open 10.00-18.30 Mon to Fri; 10.00-19.30 Thurs; 10.00-17.30 Sat.

Ronnie Stirling
The Stirling Cooper team of designers are established trend-setters creating several new co-ordinating collections throughout the year. Designs can be plain and classic with a tailored look; there are plenty of T-shirts and ultra-feminine evening wear. Men's clothes (Jasper label) are neat and casual.
94 New Bond St, W1 (01-499 2675). Open 09.30-18.00 Mon to Sat; 09.30-19.00 Thurs.

Fiorucci
High fashion clothes; (see page 174 for full details).
133 New Bond St, W1 (01-491 4351). Open 10.00-18.30 Mon to Fri; 10.00-18.30 Sat; 10.00-19.30 Thurs.

Capt. O. M. Watts Ltd
Captain Watts is the man to visit for everything needed for small boat sailing – charts, barometers, compasses; the full range of clothing; sails, shackles, galley equipment. The basement specializes in rubber dinghies and outboard motors.
48 Albemarle St, W1 (01-493 4633). Open 09.00-17.30 Mon to Fri; 09.00-13.00 Sat.

Holland and Holland
Founded in 1835, Holland and

Holland are one of London's leading gunsmiths. They are particularly famed for their shotguns, double-barrel rifles and trap guns. 'Everyone gets regal treatment, from kings to bricklayers.'
13 Bruton St, W1 (01–499 4411). Open 09.00–17.30 Mon to Fri.

Culpeper
Named after the 17th-century herbalist Nicolas Culpeper, this seemingly very old-established shop in fact dates back only to the early 1920s. There's a delicious aroma of over 200 dried herbs, and the shop sells a wide range of herbal medicines, natural herbal cosmetics, pot-pourris, spices, scented pillows and gift items.
21 Bruton St, W1 (01–499 2406). Open 09.30–17.30 Mon to Fri; 10.00–17.00 Sat.

Roots
This Canadian company manufactures a range of natural (backward-sloping) walking shoes. They are extremely well made in leather with a hard wearing rubber sole. From sandals – the Mary Jane Root – to working man's boots – Work Roots.
4 Conduit St, W1 (01–493 4555). Open 10.00–18.00 Mon to Fri; 10.00–17.30 Sat.

Biba
The original Biba owner's sister runs this shop and designs all the clothes. She also created the shop's interior: bentwood clothes stands, Art Nouveau logo and communal changing rooms. The 'look' is familiar; dresses, tights, bags, shoes, jackets, umbrellas, jerseys and make-up co-ordinate in a range of 12 muted Biba colours. Prices seem very high.
23 Conduit St, W1 (01–491 3498). Open 10.00–18.30 Mon to Fri; until 20.00 Thurs; 09.30–18.00 Sat.

Grays Antique Market: Grays In The Mews/Grays In The Street
Jointly claimed to be the biggest antique market in Britain, (Bennie) Grays Antique Markets have around 400 stalls between them. Both are custom-designed with taste, and Grays In The Street features a delightful Japanese water garden in the basement. Both buildings have wholefood restaurant/cafés. Both markets feature furniture, paintings, clocks and watches, Oriental and European porcelain, rare books and prints, postcards, ivories and bronzes, swords and guns, tiles and stained glass, an extensive range of Victorian, Art Nouveau and Art Deco jewellery, buttons, early glass, rugs, Victorian games and toys and ephemera.
Grays In the Mews, 1–7 Davies St, W1 (01–493 7861); Grays In

The Street, 58 Davies St, W1 (01-629 7034). Both open 10.00–18.00 Mon to Fri.

Katrina Shoes
Katrina is a small footwear company which concentrates on being very up to date. They have new stock, all exclusive to the shop, every week and offer very competitive prices. Styles for both men and women.
2 South Molton St, W1 (01-493 5851). Open 10.00–18.30 Mon to Fri; 10.00–19.00 Thurs; 10.00–18.00 Sat.
Also at 124 Kings Rd, SW3.

Carolyn Brunn
Knitwear for all seasons with unmistakable chic, but decidedly easy to wear is the keynote of Carolyn Brunn's designs. The variety of styles at any one time is enormous and prices aren't too outrageous.
4 South Molton St, W1 (01-629 1708). Open 10.00–18.00 Mon to Sat.

Rider Footwear
Modelled on Parisian shoe shops, Rider display their range of shoes in a tasteful setting. Designers include Walter Steiger, Pancaldi, Soda Shoes, Barrows and Sacha of Paris. Styles are for men and women, include a full range of footwear and accessories, and are as trendy as possible. Wide price range.
8 South Molton St, W1 (01- 493 8953). Open 10.00–18.00 Mon to Sat; 10.00–19.00 Thurs.
Also at 231 Kings Rd, SW3.

Ideas
Unusual ceramics, gift ideas. (See page 105 for full details.)
10 South Molton St, W1 (01–491 4587). Open 10.00–18.00 Mon to Fri; 10.00–17.00 Sat.

Arte
This new, lively fashion shop specializes in trendy, sexy, high-fashion clothes for women. You'll find no demure, classic styles here! Prices vary enormously and new designs appear throughout the year. Virtually everything on sale is exclusive to the shop.
12 South Molton St, W1 (01-408 0870). Open 10.00–18.00 Mon to Sat; 10.00–19.00 Thurs.

Joseph
Superb, French, high-fashion clothes for women from leading designs and Joseph's own label. Expensive.
13 South Molton St, W1 (01–493 4420). Open 09.30–18.00 Mon to Sat.

Jacob Gordon Ltd
Since 1946 Jacob Gordon Ltd has been selling dress-making fabrics remarkably cheaply. They buy in large quantities and keep up a very fast turnover. Regular lines include plain and printed crêpe-de-chine; a large selection of woollens, wool

tweed and gaberdines, pure wool crêpes and georgettes; cottons; fancy silks; brocades, cashmere and cashmere/wool mixtures. Despite their smart address, prices are really low.
19 South Molton St, W1 (01-629 5947). Open 09.00-18.00 Mon to Sat.

Browns
The clothes, footwear and home things at Browns are always exquisitely simple, unfussy, subtle and stylish. Complete outfits from leading continental designers and Browns' own label are on sale and the idea is to give a 'total' look (including haircuts and conditioning at Molton Brown.) Prices are unfortunately astronomic. For both men and women.
23, 25, 26 & 27 South Molton St, W1 (01-491 7833). Open 10.00-18.00 Mon to Fri; 10.00-19.00 Thurs; 10.00-17.00 Sat.

Prestat
Originally a French firm making chocolates by hand, Prestat first came to London in 1908. There is a possibility they may move some time this year (undecided when we went to press) but for the moment they continue to make and sell their superb chocolates from here. Their speciality is truffles which they make in three flavours. They also have a strong following for their brandy cherries - reputedly soaked in brandy for 18 months!
24 South Molton St, W1 (01-629 4838). Open 09.00-18.00 Mon to Fri; 09.00-17.00 Sat.

Galaxy Shoes
Casual high-fashion footwear for women, never over-dressy and always easy to wear, can be found at Galaxy.
40 South Molton St, W1 (01-629 7040). Open 09.30-18.00 Mon to Fri; 09.30-19.00 Thurs; 09.30-17.00 Sat.

H. R. Higgins Ltd
Higgins sell 28 different varieties of coffee and a full range of coffee-making equipment from premises which are little changed since they opened in 1942.
42 South Molton St, W1 (01-499 5912). Open 08.45-17.30 Mon to Wed; 08.45-19.00 Thurs; 08.45-18.00 Fri.

Friends
Owned by Stephen Marks and French Connection, Friends sells designs from these two fashion houses. Stephen Marks designs tend to be classic with a tailored look, while French Connection specialize in a totally co-ordinating, easy to wear range of day and evening clothes.
For women only at this branch, men's shop at Kensington High St.
44 South Molton St, W1 (01-629 7095). Open 09.30-18.00 Mon to

Wed; 09.30–19.00 Thurs; 09.30–17.00 Sat.
Also at 170 Kensington High St, W8 & 193 Sloane St, SW1.

Ebony
Ebony is one of London's few high-fashion boutiques for men. Clothes are colourful and extravagant, mostly designed by leading British designers with a few French and Italian clothes, too. Although aimed at men, Ebony sells lots of their clothes – particularly their hand-painted silk shirts – to women.
45 South Molton St, W1 (01–408 1247/629 4721). Open 10.30–18.00 Mon to Sat; 10.30–19.00 Thurs.

Module
If you fancy a complete change of image to a sporty, casual look, Module is the place to go. Everything from shoes and socks to hats and gloves from French, Italian and New York designers, is on sale for men and women.
49 South Molton St, W1 (01–493 3619). Open 10.00–18.00 Mon to Sat; 10.00–20.00 Thurs.

Zero Four
Sporty, casual but elegant French and Italian clothes for children up to 12 years old can be found at Zero Four. They also sell their own hand-knitted jackets and dresses.
53 South Molton St, W1 (01–493 4920). Open 10.00–18.00 Mon to Fri; 10.00–17.00 Sat.
Also at Môme, Harrington Rd, SW7 (see separate entry).

Ace
Ace is where the flamboyant and wealthy buy their clothes. The shop caters particularly for theatrical and disco wear and their clothes are highly original. Many garments are one-offs or short runs with no repeats. Much is diamantéed, sequinned or hand-painted, on silk, chiffon, metallic silks and cottons. There are clothes for both men and women, together with complementary accessories, including the most expensive T-shirts in London.
51 South Molton St, W1 (01–499 1469). Open 10.00–18.00 Mon. to Sat; 10.00–19.00 Thurs.

Monsoon
Delightful range of flouncy, floating dresses, skirts, blouses and nightwear designed by Janet Wood and Gilli Thompson and made up in hand-block printed fine cotton fabric from Jaipur. All dyes are vegetable-based and the colours are rich and subtle. There are also silk hand-painted dresses, blouses and skirts from Calcutta; dresses from Afghanistan and hand-embroidered, hand-crocheted cotton clothes from Romania. This branch has occasional sales to shift slightly damaged stock.
67 South Molton St, W1 (01–499 3987). Open 10.00–18.00 Mon to Sat; 10.00–19.00 Wed.
Also at 35 Beauchamp Pl, SW3;

54 Fulham Rd, SW3; 24 Thackeray St, W8; and 1 Hampstead High St, NW3.

Crochetta

Crochetta design and manufacture a range of crocheted clothes in specially dyed yarns, silk, acrylics, cotton and viscose. Designs are for dresses, suits, jumpers and jackets, and tend to be classic styles that don't date. Colours are vibrant or pastel.
68 South Molton St, W1 (01-493 1500). Open 09.45-18.00 Mon to Sat.

Country Club

Opposite Kickers at the Brook St end of South Molton St, this men's and women's clothes shop specializes in classic French and Italian designs. Prices are very competitive for such a centrally located shop and they stock entire outfits, from shoes to hats with everything in-between. They also sell English classic tweeds and wide range of Italian knitwear.
34 Brook St, corner South Molton St, W1 (01-629 5262). Open 10.00-18.00 Mon to Sat; 10.00-19.00 Thurs.

TOTTENHAM COURT RD

Laskys

Established in 1917, Laskys, famed for its hi-fi equipment, is part of a 30-odd store chain. Equipment stocked by all branches includes hi-fi separates, music centres, record and tape care accessories, portables (including TVs), and video and blank cassettes. Most goods are below retailers' recommended prices; 14-day credit service if goods are not up to standard.
10 Tottenham Court Rd, W1 (01-637 2232); 257 Tottenham Court Rd, W1 (01-580 0670); 42 Tottenham Court Rd, W1 (01-636 0845). Open 09.00-18.00 Mon to Sat (branch at 42 Tottenham Court Rd open until 19.00 on Thurs).
Also at 152 Fleet St, EC2; 311, 346 and 382 Edgware Rd, W2.

Adrena

Known as the basket shop, Adrena used to be the only place in London to get Ibiza-style shoulder baskets. A fraction of the shop's stock of shoulder-and hand-held baskets are hung outside; inside many more are piled on top of suitcases and trunks. They also stock Moses baskets.
15 Tottenham Court Rd, W1 (01-636 5571). Open 09.30-18.00 Mon to Sat; 09.30-20.00 Thurs.

Western Warehouse Ltd

Large stocks of camping gear; bankrupt, salvage and government surplus clothes. Decent prices considering its location.
82/83 Tottenham Court Rd, W1 (01-580 2230). Open 08.45-

18.00 Mon to Fri; 09.30–12.30 Sat.

Buck and Ryan
Established in 1824, Buck and Ryan have been in their present premises for 12 years. They have a high reputation and are one of the country's largest specialist tool shops. They stock any hand or electrical tool for any trade, including carpentry, plumbing, building, engineering and decorating; together with screws, nuts, bolts, washers, etc., garden tools and ironmongery. Mr Tom Ryan says that they live up to their reputation: 'if you can't get it elsewhere, try Buck and Ryan.'
101 Tottenham Court Rd, W1 (01–636 7475). Open 08.30–17.30 Mon to Fri; 08.30–13.00 Sats.

Adeptus
Ten years ago talented designer Dimitri Petrohilos first put into production his idea for identical solid foam seats cut with no wastage from square blocks. Since then Adeptus has mushroomed from its original Chalcot Rd home to workshops all over London and the country at large. The range of designs for seats, sofas and beds all rely on Dimitri's systematic, economic and functional approach to seating problems, which achieves the right balance between comfort, durability, versatility and cost.
110 Tottenham Court Rd, W1 (01–388 5965). Open 10.00–18.00 Mon to Sat; 10.00–19.30 Thurs.
Also at 40 Chalcot Rd, NW1; and 244 Belsize Rd, NW6.

Chivers
Opposite Maples, the giant furniture store, flowers can be bought at any time of the night from a refrigerated vending machine.
129 Tottenham Court Rd, W1 (01–387 6996).
Also at 143 Charlotte St, W1.

Habitat
When Terence Conran first started Habitat he had a revolutionary effect on British decoration and furnishings. For the first time, modern, well-designed, functional and attractive furnishings, from a napkin to a sofa, were available at a reasonable price. At this branch: fabrics, rugs and furniture upstairs; kitchen equipment, china, glass, basketware and lighting downstairs. Larger branch at Kings Rd, Chelsea.
156 Tottenham Court Rd, W1 (01–388 1721). Open 09.30–18.00 Mon to Fri; 10.00–19.30 Thurs; 09.00–18.00 Sat.

W. J. Johnson and Sons
Johnson's is the oldest named firm in Tottenham Court Rd and has been on the same premises since 1801. They began trading as opticians but

have now become leading technical stationers as well. Two long slim floors are packed with drawing equipment, conversion scales, Letraset and dissecting instruments as well as papers, notebooks, pencils, etc. Their most amazing stock is over 1800 different types of graph paper.
187 Tottenham Court Rd, W1 (01–636 2855). Open 09.00–17.30 Mon to Fri.

Heals
When Heals first began trading in 1810 its main business was feather dressing. By the mid-1850s the store had diversified into bedroom furniture and upholstery, for which it is now recognized. Heals have a royal warrant for bedding, specialize in fabrics, and have good children's toy, kitchenware and gift departments.
196 Tottenham Court Rd, W1 (01–636 1666). Open 09.00–17.30 Mon to Sat; 09.45–17.30 Thurs.

Reject Shop
Following the success of their Knightsbridge branch, this spacious two-floor shop opened three years ago. Most stock is reject – ends of lines, samples, slight seconds, etc. – but the great advantage of this shop is that it deals with large manufacturers and can provide continuity of goods rather than one-offs. Furniture, basketware, glass, china and kitchen equipment, plus gift items. Particularly good for small presents at Christmas.
209 Tottenham Court Rd, W1 (01–637 5567). Open 09.30–18.00 Mon to Sat; 09.30–19.00 Thurs.

Paperchase
The shop for delightful wrapping papers, specialist papers, cards, stationery, paper toys and mobiles. Particularly good around Christmas for decorative ideas. Also at South Kensington.
213 Tottenham Court Rd, W1 (01–580 8496). Open 10.00–18.00 Mon to Sat; 10.00–19.00 Thurs.

Video City
Video City sell all the major brands of home video systems. They do repairs and servicing on the premises.
Lion House, 227 Tottenham Court Rd, W1 (01–580 7383). Open 09.00–18.00 Mon to Sat; 09.00–19.00 Thurs.

R.E.W.
R.E.W. have several other branches but this is their largest. They are the biggest video dealers in Europe and sell all the major manufacturers' stock. They operate hire and long lease services, and also give advice.
230 Tottenham Court Rd, W1 (01–637 2624). Open 09.30–18.00 Mon to Fri; 09.30–16.00 Sat.

Leon Jaeggi & Son
Jaeggi are specialist makers of the domestic equivalents of hand tools used in the catering industry. They are noted, too, for their range of copper ware and their imported French and German kitchen knives.
232 Tottenham Court Rd, W1 (01-580 1957). Open 09.00-17.30 Mon to Fri; 09.00-13.00 Sat.

Hand Loom House
The Gudka family have been importing and selling saris from India, Japan and the Far East for the past 12 years. Their range is extensive, with over 150 different designs using nylon, polyester, mixed fibres, cotton and silk. Prices range from under £5 up to £100.
243 Tottenham Court Rd, W1 (01-580 1771). Open 09.30-18.00 Mon to Sat.

The Games Centre
The Games Centre reckons to stock the largest selection of games and puzzles in the world. Their less unusual games include Arabic scrabble and world monopoly, and they specialize in card games for adults and children.
16 Hanway St, W1 (01-636 8278). Open 09.30-18.00 Mon to Sat.

Byzantium
Small tasteful shop selling authentic Greek knitwear, leather sandals in various designs, cushion covers, bags, beads, leather belts, shirts for men and women, and rugs.
1 Goodge St, W1 (01-636 6465). Open 10.00-18.00 Mon to Fri; 10.00-17.00 Sat.

Ryness
Ryness is a small chain selling commercial and domestic electrical accessories. Their speciality is lighting and they keep a wide and varied range at all branches.
37 Goodge St, W1; also at 326 Edgware Rd, W2; 54 Fleet St, EC4; 57 Camden High St, NW1 (01-278 8993 all branches). Open 09.00-18.00 Mon to Sat.

Nice Irma's Floating Carpet
Della and Dan Hirsch together with Anatol Orient import an exotic range of exquisite cushions, embroideries, wall hangings, bedspreads, brass lanterns and cotton and velvet fabrics from India and Afghanistan. Most of the fabrics are hand-loomed with hand-blocked designs, and the wall hangings and pieces of fabric (ideal for cushion covers) are hand-embroidered with inset mirror-work. Their printed velvets are especially unusual and attractive. Catalogue on request, 25p.
46 Goodge St, W1 (01-580 6921). Open 10.00-18.00 Mon to Sat.

W. R. Loftus
Large and spacious home-brewers' shop laid out supermarket style for easy perusal. All the staff at Loftus are home-brewing experts willing to offer practical advice as well as selling their own kit for beginners.
1/3 Charlotte St, W1 (01-636 6235). Open 09.00–17.30 Mon to Fri; 09.00–12.30 Sat.

Bartholdi
The Bartholdi family have been trading here for nearly 60 years and as far as I know are London's only Swiss butchers. They smoke and make their own sausages, keep a full range of delicatessen, specialize in Swiss cheeses (and carry a range of other European cheeses too), as well as selling preserves, biscuits, continental cakes and tinned groceries.
4 Charlotte St, W1 (01-636 3762/3). Open 09.00–18.00 Mon to Fri; 09.00–13.00 Sat.

Louis Mankin
An old-fashioned shop with an original wooden counter and a wholesale-looking window display which doesn't encourage trade. Largely a wholesaler who buys direct from the mill, Louis Mankin gets constant and changing bargains in natural fabrics. The shop is a reliable source of cheap heavy-duty denim, unbleached calico and hessian, shirting, and butcher's stripes in a variety of colourways. Also haberdashery without the plastic packaging, and strong jean zips.
20 Charlotte St, W1 (01-636 6978). Open 09.00–17.00 Mon to Fri.

Pollocks Toy Museum
The retail side of the shop (the other half is a museum) specializes in toy theatres in Victorian style, a variety of traditional toys and loads of miniature toys, to suit children and adults alike.
1 Scala St, W1 (01-636 3452). Open 10.00–17.00 Mon to Sat.

J. D. Beardmore and Co Ltd
Beardmores are famous and long-established door furniture experts. Their range of stock is amazingly extensive and includes antique-style door fittings; various styles of door furniture in china, glass and brass; and hinges, letterplates, castors and window fittings. They will match door handles.
3–5 Percy St, W1 (01-636 1214). Open 08.30–17.30 Mon to Fri.

Chubb
The head office/showroom/shop for the range of Chubb locks, security fittings for doors and windows, wall safes and deed boxes. The locks can be fitted by any competent carpenter but repairs to Chubb locks and installations can be arranged with their Bromley-

by-Bow branch in E3 who operate a fitting service. No key cutting is done at this branch.
68 Tottenham St, W1 (01-637 2377). Open 09.30-17.00 Mon to Fri.

G. Wood
Wood's buy clearing lines, discontinued lines and oddments of all types of dressmaking fabrics. From their basement premises a changing array of bargains can be had.
162 New Cavendish St, W1 (01-636 7488). Open 09.30-17.30 Mon to Fri; closed Thurs and Sat and 14.00-15.00 for lunch.
6175-14

REGENT ST

Liberty's
Arthur Lazenby Liberty opened his original drapery shop in the late 19th century. The current Tudor-style building was constructed from wood from the last two serving 'men of war' in the Royal Navy in 1924. The shop has always had Oriental connections and currently has a superb Oriental department in the basement. Also known for its fine Tana lawns, Varuna wools and Liberty prints (on the second and third floors) Liberty's is unrivalled for its fine silks and cotton dress and furnishing fabrics. Other departments of note: antiques; an extensive range of jewellery from high fashion/designer work to renovated old pieces; modern furniture and Oriental carpets.
Regent St, W1 (01-734 1234). Open 09.00-17.30 Mon to Fri; 09.00-19.00 Thurs; 09.00-17.00 Sat.

Pencraft Ltd
Pencraft probably stock the largest number of pens in London. They certainly stock most makes of pen, the majority of refills and all related equipment. They can engrave pens on the spot, do repairs (to old and new pens, even those not bought from them) and offer expert advice.
119 Regent St, W1 (01-734 4928). Open 09.00-17.00 Mon to Fri; 09.30-14.30 Sat.

Coles
The Cole family have been designing hand-blocked wallpaper prints for nearly 100 years. Their extensive range covers a myriad of styles but they are particularly hot on historical designs. If they haven't got what you're after (there are thousands of samples in their showroom), Coles will make up paper to customer's requirements or print one of their existing designs to match your colour scheme. As theirs is a specialized trade, Coles have a minimum order system and are pretty pricey. They market their own paint, called Hatfield, and

also feature some French wallpapers.
18 Mortimer St, W1 (01–580 1066). Open 09.00–17.00 Mon to Fri.

Ells and Farrier
E and F was established in 1920 essentially as bead wholesalers to the trade. They've always had a trade counter where all their beads are catalogued in books from which the customer's choice is made. It's a tiny, crowded shop, and all beads are weighed out by the ounce or sold by the skein. They also sell sequins, a range of large, garish costume-jewellery type beads, and a cheap and pretty basic beading loom.
The Bead House, 5 Princes St, W1 (01–629 9964). Open 08.30–17.30 Mon to Fri.

S. E. Cuming
Cuming's are bead wholesalers. They do have a trade counter and will sell to the public but only in quantities of 4 oz (100 grams) or more. Their entire range of glass and plastic beads and sequins is displayed.
64 Margaret St, W1 (01–636 1233). Open 09.30–17.00 Mon to Fri.

James Galt
Although Galt toys can be bought from most toy shops, this is the company's London retail shop. Here their entire range of educational wooden toys is on sale, plus a few lines from other manufacturers. Up to 15 years age range.
30 Great Marlborough St, W1 (01–734 0829). Open 09.00–17.30 Mon to Fri; 09.00–17.00 Sat.

Craftsmen Potters' Association of Great Britain
Situated on the site of William Blake's birthplace, the Craftsmen Potters Shop sells the pots of its members, all of whom have been scrupulously chosen. Special orders can be taken but a wide selection of both decorative and functional pottery is on sale. There are also regular exhibitions.
William Blake House, Marshall St, W1 (01–437 7605). Open 10.00–17.30 Mon to Fri; 10.30–17.00 Sat.

Cranks Health Food
Cranks Health Food Restaurant runs a small adjoining health food shop. Produce is vegetarian and natural: eggs are free range; bread wholewheat (baked round the corner in their bakery), flour stone-ground, etc. They sell a wide range of health foods (dried fruit, nuts, grains etc.), made-up salads and pies, but are particularly recommended for their tasty breads and rolls. They are licensed for wine and cider. At their grain shop all grains, beans, pulses, nuts, cereals and herbs are organically grown where possible and are weighed out from wicker bas-

kets. Best prices for bulk sales, which are encouraged.
Cranks Health Foods, 8 Marshall St, W1 (01–437 2915). Open 09.00–18.00 Mon to Fri; 09.00–16.30 Sat. Cranks Whole Grain Shop, 37 Marshall St, W1 (01–349 1809). Open 10.00–18.00 Mon to Fri; 10.00–16.00 Sat.

Just Games
London's first adults' specialist games shop with an enormous range of traditional and new board games, games for one person, jigsaws, playing cards and books.
1 Lower James St, W1 (01–734 6124). Open 10.00–18.00 Mon to Sat; until 17.00 Thurs.

SOHO

A. Myall and Sons Ltd
Essentially a wholesalers supplying many of Soho's Italian restaurants, Myall's don't display fish on the slab but keep it hidden in deep aluminium drawers. They will, however, sell fish singly to passers-by and are happy to gut and fillet it. They stock large quantities of fish in season, including live eels and trout.
23 Romilly St, W1 (01–437 4063). Open 08.00–15.15 Mon to Fri; 08.00–12.00 Sat.

G. Parmigiani Figli
This well ordered Italian delicatessen and grocery claims to keep the largest selection of Italian cheeses in London, with weekly deliveries from Italy. Other specialities include fresh pasta, salamis and mortadellas, parma hams, olives and olive oil, dried pasta and beans – in fact everything required for Italian cooking. There is also a range of Italian wines, liqueurs and aperitifs.
43 Frith St, W1 (01–437 4728). Open 09.00–17.30 Mon to Sat; 09.00–13.00 Thurs.

EMI Videogram Production
EMI are (at the time of going to press) restricted by the five-year TV agreement from releasing new films. They produce a catalogue and release a small list of classic British feature films from the EMI library.
5 Dean St, W1 (01–437 8651). Open 09.00–17.30 Mon to Fri.

Gamba
Theatrical shoe makers: famed for their ballet shoes, one-bars and tap shoes in all colours. Also smart, ready to wear men's and women's fashion shoes.
46 Dean St, W1 (01–437 0704). Open 09.00–17.30 Mon to Fri; 09.00–13.00 Sat.

Dark They Were And Golden-Eyed
They try to stock every science fiction paperback in print in Britain and America; as complete a stock of fantasy

books as possible; most popular horror publications and a vast selection of comics, mostly American; plus non-fiction; cosmology; music books and posters, and magazines.
9-12 St Anne's Ct, between Dean and Wardour St, W1 (01-734 9181 for mail order). Open 10.00-18.00 Mon to Sat; 10.00-19.00 Thurs.

Great Wall
This enormous supermarket in the heart of Soho's Chinatown sells everything necessary to cook Chinese and Japanese food, including a range of cooking pots and pans, bowls and chopsticks.
31-37 Wardour St, W1 (01-437 7963). Open 11.00-20.00 Mon to Sun.

Video View Ltd
Video View sell and hire out a range of sports events video cassettes, a range of highly praised language courses and various middle of the road concerts/shows. They operate a trade-in service when you get fed-up with your selection of tapes.
68/70 Wardour St, W1 (01-437 1333). Open 09.30-18.00 Mon to Fri.

Gramophone Exchange
Mr Rogers specializes in classical music of all kinds, from all countries, at Gramophone Exchange. He has a large second-hand department, lots of imports and as a sideline keeps a selection of 1925-35 records of musical comedy artists and bands.
80 Wardour St, W1 (01-437 5313). Open 09.30-17.30 Mon to Fri; 09.30-13.00 Sat.

J. Blundell and Sons Ltd
A trade counter where queues form to buy silver in the form of wire, chains, tubing, rods and sheets in a variety of gauges. You can also buy gold if you have a licence. They do a full range of findings (clasps for necklaces, earrings etc.) which are illustrated at the counter.
199 Wardour St, W1 (01-437 4746). Open 09.30-16.00 Mon to Fri; closed Wed and Sat.

P. Denny and Co
Denny's have been supplying the restaurant and allied trades with uniforms for over 100 years. Everything is soundly made in cotton (and therefore easy to dye) for very economic utility wear. Chefs' uniforms, waiters' and barmen's jackets and check trousers, boilersuits, aprons and overalls. Along with Garraulds, Edgware Rd, the best place for butcher-stripe cotton cooks' aprons.
39 Old Compton St, W1 (01-437 1654). Open 08.45-17.30 Mon to Fri.

Libraire Parisienne
Stocks a wide range of English and foreign newspapers and magazines.
48 Old Compton St, W1 (01-437 2479). Open 06.15–19.00 Mon to Fri; 06.15–17.00 Sat; 06.15–12.00 Sun.

Moroni and Sons
Virtually every foreign newspaper and magazine can be found here.
68 Old Compton St, W1 (01-437 2847). Open 07.30–19.45 Mon to Sat; and 07.30–13.00 Sun.

Hamburger
The name of what is reputedly London's first snack bar foxes everyone until they realize the reason. You won't find any hamburgers on sale at this Jewish deli/snack bar – the name originates from the owner's trip to Hamburg! You can eat at the horseshoe-shaped bar or take away Hamburger's freshly smoked salmon, sturgeon, cod roe, buckling, trout and mackerel. They also sell delicatessen food and cheeses.
1 Brewer St, W1 (01-437 7119). Open 09.30–17.30 Mon to Fri; 09.30–14.00 Sat; snack bar open 12.00–15.00.

Richards (Soho) Ltd
Richards keep a really extensive range of fish including rareties like sturgeon, sea urchins, sardines, monk fish and carp as well as the more ordinary mackerel and cod. There are also live and boiled shellfish – oysters, mussels, crayfish, lobsters, etc. The shop is extremely busy but worth the wait.
11 Brewer St, W1 (01-437 1358). Open 08.00–17.15 Tues to Sat.

Randall and Aubin (London) Ltd
Randall and Aubin tell me they were the first people to import quiche lorraine (in 1906) to this country. They are one of Soho's oldest and most favourite (if somewhat chaotic) shops with lots of specialities. Aside from cheeses, salamis and other delicatessen products, Randall and Aubin are French butchers. They are a useful source for those fiddly French dishes requiring superb meat (French butchers remove all nerves and most fat); they make superb sausages; and they sell bacon, pâtés and galantines (made on the premises) as well as fresh herbs, groceries and fruit and veg.
16 Brewer St, W1 (01-437 3507). Open 08.30–17.00 Mon to Sat; 08.30–12.00 Thurs.

Lina Stores
Lina's is another of Soho's superb Italian grocer/delicatessens. One counter is stuffed with parma ham, salamis, frankfurters, Italian and French cheeses; the other is filled with their own superb fresh pasta (cooked on

the premises), Italian confectionery and olives. More salamis, cotechinos and mortadellas hang from the ceiling and the window is piled with Italian bread and rolls. They also sell dark roast coffee, herbs in huge jars and Italian groceries, tinned and bottled.
18 Brewer St, W1 (01-437 6482). Open 08.00-18.00 Mon to Sat; 08.00-13.00 Thurs.

House and Bargain
Sells a good range of cut-price kitchenware.
31 Brewer St, W1. 09.30-17.30 Mon to Fri; 09.30-17.00 Sat.

The House of Floris
For 40 years Floris have baked wedding, christening and birthday cakes for everyone who's anyone. They will take orders for any shape, size and content. Floris regularly bake 40 different sorts of cake, pastries, and excellent bread and croissants. Their other speciality is handmade chocolates, of which there are 60 varieties, available in special presentation boxes.
39 Brewer St, W1 (01-437 5755). Open 09.00-17.30 Mon to Fri; 09.00-13.00 Sat.

House Bros
Established in 1864 and a family concern, House Bros can supply virtually any hand-tool, many of which can't be found elsewhere. They specialize particularly in high quality cutlery including the entire range of French Sabatier cooks' knives.
85 Brewer St, W1 (01-437 3857). Open 09.00-17.45 Mon to Fri; 10.00-12.45 Sat.

Space Saving Bed Centre
Beds that fold up into small spaces; cupboards, tables and strange-shaped pouffés can be found at this two-floor showroom for space-saving beds. The company sell linen for their most awkward shaped beds and a range of mattresses from leading manufacturers.
13 Golden Sq, W1 (01-734 4246). Open 09.00-17.30 Mon, Tues, Fri; 09.00-16.30 Wed; 09.00-19.00 Thurs; 09.00-13.00 Sat.

Clarks of Soho
Known for London's best dark rye bread, which is baked on the premises, and egg bread.
27 Peter St, W1 (01-437 6622). Open 08.00-17.00 Mon to Sat.

Joelson's
The Joelson family have run this Jewish grocery/delicatessen for over 50 years. Everything for Jewish cooking; including four sorts of salted herrings from barrels, chopped herrings, pickled cucumbers, sour and cream cheeses, sauerkraut, smatana, buckwheat and barley.
28 Peter St, W1 (01-437 5261). Open 08.00-18.00 Mon to Fri; 08.00-13.00 Sat.

Lonsdale Sports Equipment
On the face of it a general sports shop, but with an ex-boxer for an owner, Lonsdale specialize in boxing gear. Everything for pros and amateurs; they will hire equipment but do so reluctantly and rarely.
21 Beak St, W1 (01-437 1526). Open 09.00–18.00 Mon to Fri; 09.00–17.00 Sat.

Anything Left-handed
The only shop in the land specialising in goods for left-handers. Their extensive stocks include all kinds of kitchen equipment like potato peelers, tin openers, spoons and spatulas. They specialize in scissors, also keep pens and wristwatches. A boon for gifts for left-handed friends.
68 Beak St, W1 (01-437 3910). Open 10.00–17.00 Mon to Fri; 10.00–13.00 Sat.

Berwick St and Rupert St Markets
Berwick St Market has been thriving since 1788 and is a mixed fruit and veg, clothes, fabrics, haberdashery and shoe market. In the heart of Soho, it attracts a mixed clientele of strippers, actors, office workers, restauranteurs and locals. It is always lively, and particularly busy at lunchtimes. There are several cheap butchers in Berwick St. A small passage links Berwick St to Rupert St where a smaller, though fair-priced market takes place.
Berwick St, off Oxford St, W1. Open 09.00–17.00-ish Mon to Fri.

Fratelli Camisa
The Camisa family run this excellent Italian delicatessen. They are famed for two specialities – pasta and cheese. Their fresh pasta is made at the shop into spaghetti, tagliatelli and ravioli, which they sell extensively to Soho's Italian restaurants. Their range of cheeses, all in perfect condition, is enormous and includes most English cheeses, over 20 Italian cheeses, around 15 French cheeses and a smattering from Holland, Switzerland, Denmark and Norway. They also stock a full range of delicatessen items; take bulk orders and do private catering.
1a Berwick St, W1 (01-437 7120). Open 09.00–18.00 Mon to Sat; 09.00–13.00 Thurs; 09.00–18.30 Fri.

Z. Kopelovitch Ltd
Mrs Gilbert presides over *the* shop for lace and embroideries. Most of her best lace comes from France and many types are hand finished. This shop has been open for 70 years and Mrs Gilbert reckons to have the largest lace selection in England, including a cheap range.
83–84 Berwick St, W1 (01-437 6194). Open 09.00–17.00 Mon to Fri.

S. Ferrari and Sons Ltd
One of London's leading catering equipment shops, much frequented by the trade and particularly acclaimed for cutlery, notably a full range of Sabatier and other kitchen knives.
60 Poland St, W1 (01-437 6515). Open 09.00–18.00 Mon to Fri; half-day closing Sat.

Dugdale and Adams
Reputed to sell London's best imitation of a French loaf. Apart from the traditional baguette, the stock consists of white English loaves, all of which are baked downstairs.
3 Gerrard St, W1 (01-437 3864). Open 08.00–16.00 Mon to Sat.

Loon Fung Supermarket
Everything for the Chinese cook can be found here, including woks (Chinese frying pans), bowls and chopsticks. Unfortunately, as the labels are written in Chinese, some pre-knowledge is advisable.
39 Gerrard St, W1 (01-437 1922). Open 12.00–21.00 Mon to Sun.

Hong Kong Culture Services
Probably Chinatown's largest art and craft shop with a room devoted to Chinese records and cassettes. Also has a range of curious Chinese comics and periodicals.
46 Gerrard St, W1 (01-734 5037). Open 11.00–20.00 seven days a week.

Teletape Photographic
A full range of cameras, photographic and audio equipment can be found at this branch of Teletape. They help customers make up systems and manufacture speakers. Video and closed circuit TV systems are stocked at 76 Brewer St and Golden Sq branches.
74 Shaftesbury Ave, W1 (01-437 3287). Open 09.00–17.30 Mon to Sat.

LEICESTER SQ

Collet's Penguin Bookshop
Collet's attempt to stock every paperback in print.
52 Charing Cross Rd, WC1 (01-836 2315). Open 10.00–18.00 Mon to Sat.

Collet's London Bookshop
Literature by and for the Left, from Fabians to the newest, smallest splinter group; also a secondhand section, badges, posters and Leftist newspapers.
64–66 Charing Cross Rd, WC2 (01-836 6306). Open 10.00–18.00 Mon to Wed; 10.00–19.00 Thurs; 10.30–19.00 Fri; 10.00–18.00 Sat.

A. Zwemmer
Small crammed bookshop

specializing in art and architecture with an excellent coverage of cinema and crafts.
76–80 Charing Cross Rd, WC2 (01–836 4710). Open 09.30–17.30 Mon to Fri; 09.30–16.00 Sat.

The Theatre Shop
Owners of the next-door Phoenix Theatre opened this haven for theatre buffs in 1978. They stock an extensive range of theatrical memorabilia including a variety of records from musicals old and new, posters and programmes, many of which have rarity value. Also have a service providing details of all current plays in London and the provinces.
110 Charing Cross Rd, WC2 (01–836 4207). Open 10.00–20.00.

Foyles
Probably the largest and best known bookshop in Britain. Titles on most subjects but best for academic text books, philosophy, fiction, biography and social sciences.
119–125 Charing Cross Rd, WC1 (01–437 5660). Open 09.00–19.00 Thurs; 09.00–18.00 Mon to Sat.

Booksmith
Remaindered books, new paperbacks. (See page 125 for full details.)
148 Charing Cross Rd, WC2 (01–836 3032). Open 09.30–20.00 Mon to Fri; 11.30–20.00 Sat.
Also at 201 Kensington High St, W8; 36 St Martins Lane, WC2; and 33 Maiden Lane, WC2.

Eaton's Shell Shop
This delightful long-established shop in a side street by Foyles specializes in shells and rocks (they show a rock of the week in their tiny window downstairs, and natural raffia, bamboo and cane for D.I.Y. upstairs. They also stock made-up, split-bamboo blinds, raffia hats and slippers.
16 Manette St, W1 (01–437 9391). Open 09.00–17.00 Mon to Fri; 09.00–12.00 Sat.

Stamps
Previously at 77 Victoria St, SW1, Georges Korel runs Stamps – a must for stamp fanatics. Mr Korel buys and sells stamps from all over the world and deals mainly in bargain lots and collections. His shop is always crowded. He has recently opened a stamp section in Bryan Forbes' bookshop in Virginia Water, Surrey.
2 Irving St, Leicester Sq, WC2 (01–930 4727). Open 10.00–18.00 Mon to Sat.

Swiss Centre Shop
Swiss cheese, cooked meats, bread, pastries, tinned foods, groceries and, of course, chocolate, can be had from the shop on the ground floor by the main entrance of the enormous modern Swiss Centre. Gift

items like music boxes, fondue sets, soaps, handkerchiefs, etc., are sold in a separate shop at Wardour St, next to the cinema entrance.
New Coventry St and 10 Wardour St, W1 (01-734 1291). Open 09.30-18.00 Mon to Sat.

Boots Chemists
London's most central 24-hour chemist. Often blocked with junkies but emergency medicaments and prescriptions are available at all hours.
Criterion Building, Piccadilly, W1 (01-930 4761).

2 BLOOMSBURY

Covent Garden, Russell Sq, Bloomsbury, Holborn

Traditionally Bloomsbury is synonymous with the literary and publishing worlds and the many narrow streets surrounding the British Museum and London University house more specialist and academic bookshops than anywhere else in London. Many date back to the early nineteenth century, retain their original character and are owner-run.

There are also a great number of hotels in the area, which are interspersed with little pockets of specialist shops. There's Davenport's, the joke shop, Westaway and Westaway, which sells London's cheapest quality Scottish knitwear, both opposite the British Museum; with Smiths, the umbrella and walking stick shop, just around the corner. Mel Calman's cartoon Workshop is in Lambs Conduit St and Rhann's sells ties in Sicilian Ave. The area is not well served with food shops (Soho is only a stroll away) and the enormous Brunswick Shopping Centre has overshadowed what few there were. However, quality food shops cluster around Tavistock Place, Marchmont St and Red Lion St.

Since the fruit and vegetable market moved to Nine Elms, a radical change has come over Covent Garden and it has become the 'in' area. Many fashion, craft and homeware shops have been opened by young designers, and they rub shoulders with long-established specialist shops. It's an exciting area with a great variety to offer the shopper, mostly centred in Long Acre, Neal St, Monmouth St, Bow St and Russell St. There's a food street market, The Jubilee, in Southampton St.

See also Camden and Hampstead, Islington and Victoria.

TRANSPORT

Covent Garden
Tube Stations: Covent Garden, Strand, Charing Cross, Aldwych, Leicester Sq
Buses: 1, 6, 9, 11

Russell Sq
Tube Stations: Russell Sq, Euston Sq
Buses: 68, 188

Bloomsbury
Tube Stations: Russell Sq, Holborn, Chancery Lane, King's Cross
Buses: 8, 19, 22, 38

Holborn
Tube Stations: Holborn, Chancery Lane, King's Cross
Buses: 8, 22, 25

LOCAL OPENING HOURS

Few shops observe a mid-week half-day closing in Bloomsbury. Many stay open until 19.00 on Thurs but close at midday or early afternoon on Sat. Many shops in Covent Garden stay open until 20.00 or later six days a week.

REFRESHMENTS

Monmouth Coffee House
27 Monmouth St, WC2.
Open 10.00–18.00 Mon to Sat.
Freshly ground coffee in small seating area at back of the shop. Daily papers are available.

Cousin Jack's Cornish Shop
14 Drury Lane, WC2.
Open 10.00–18.00 Mon to Sat.
Tea, coffee, soft drinks, Cornish cakes, pasties and other Cornish fare.

Food For Thought
31 Neal St, WC2.
Open all day.
Vegetarian restaurant serving wholesome meals all day; and between 15.00 and 17.00 tea and home-made cakes.

Tuttons
11–12 Russell Sq, WC1.
Open all day seven days a week.
Continental-style brasserie with outside seating. Tea, soft drinks, hard drinks and snacks. No minimum charge.

COVENT GARDEN

Drury Tea and Coffee Co
This pre-war company today roasts all its coffees at its Waterloo branch. It sells 22 different blends of coffee, ground to order at the shops, which also keep around half a dozen blends and pure teas which they import direct. Shops also sell teapots and caddies, specialized honeys and jams, and chocolates and complementary gift-packaged items. Also an extensive range of coffee-making equipment and

beer and wine sold throughout their opening hours. Mail order price list on request.
3 New Row, off St Martins Lane, WC1 (01-836 1960). Also at 37 Drury Lane, WC2 and 3 Mepham St, SE1. Open 08.30–18.00 Mon to Fri.

Scottish Merchant
This small colourful shop has been selling first class Scottish knitwear for ten years. Their specialities are Hebridean sweaters, striped Shetlands, Fair Isles, lacy shawls and jerseys in heather mixtures. They keep a limited range of designer knitwear which is expanded at their new shop Tomlinson and Tomlinson (see Notting Hill).
16 New Row, WC2 (01-836 2207). Open 10.30–18.30 Mon to Sat; 10.30–19.00 Thurs; 10.30–17.00 Sat.

Bland and Sons
Established in 1840 when they made all their own guns and rifles. Today 99% are factory-made and the rest hand-crafted by Bland. All guns are displayed and a licence is needed to buy any of them.
21 New Row, WC2 (01-836 9122). Open 09.00–16.30 Mon to Fri; 09.00–12.00 Sat.

James Asman
James Asman started collecting jazz records at the end of the 1920s. Today he boasts a fine collection of new and secondhand records and is well-known as a leading jazz record dealer.
23a New Row, WC2 (01-240 1380). Open 10.00–18.00 Mon to Sat.

Theatre Zoo
The bizarre window of sad, grotesque and animal masks at this long-established shop are for sale and for hire. They hire out a wide range of animal costumes as well as the masks and sell masks, false feet and hands, moustaches and beards, make-up and hats.
28 New Row, WC2 (01-836 3150). Open 09.00–17.00 Mon to Sat; costume hire 09.00–16.00 Mon to Fri only.

Paradox
This tiny shop specializes in modern ceramics with a surrealist and/or unusual quality. Wide range of Lustre Welsh, including aeroplane tea-pots and doggy toast racks. Also bizarre one-offs and amusing and functional wooden furnishing accessories by Keith Gibbons. Reasonable prices.
24 Bedfordbury, WC2 (01-836 3852). Open 11.30–19.30 Mon to Sat.

Catz
Cherry Saltzer has capitalized on her love of cats by opening a shop entirely devoted to feline shaped or decorated objects;

literature; stationery; cushions and a host of gift items to suit all types of cat lover. Her tiny shop is crammed with cat teapots, ashtrays, posters, jewellery, calendars and novelty objects. Cherry is interested in seeing any old cat memorabilia with a view to buying.
25 Bedfordbury, WC2 (01-836 6513). Open 11.00–18.00 Mon to Sat; 11.00–19.00 July and August.

Ironmonger and Hall
Between them Jackie Hall and Gay Ironmonger design and sell a range of well-made, smart, classic style, up-to-the-minute clothes for women in entirely natural fabrics. They also specialize in making clothes for bands.
28 Bedfordbury, WC2 (01-240 0787). Open 10.30–18.00 Mon to Fri; 11.00–15.30 Sat.

Nostalgia
Nostalgia have been in the business of selling '30s and '40s clothes for some years. Partly because of their location they've always specialized in clothes with a theatrical flavour and always have a good selection of accessories: gloves, shoes, bags, scarves and fur stoles. Bargain basement downstairs.
29 Bedfordbury, WC2 (01-240 5238). Open 10.30–18.30 Mon to Sat.

Moss Bros
Everyone knows that Moss Bros is the place to hire men's clothes to suit all formal occasions and to buy 'everything for the man's wardrobe', but few people know about the Special Offer room. Here over 2000 garments are crammed on to rails and include cancelled orders, hire clothes which have seen the end of their run and clothes damaged by display etc. Fantastic bargains have been known in Crombie coats, suits, dress shirts, trousers and even bow ties.
Bedford St, WC2 (01-240 4567). Open 08.30 (for hire); 09.00–17.30 Mon to Fri; till 19.00 Thurs and till 13.00 Sat.

Royale Stamp Co
Stamps from all over the world are bought and sold at Royale but they specialize in stamps from Great Britain.
41/2 Bedford St, WC2 (01-836 6122). Open 09.00–17.30 Mon to Fri; 09.30–13.00 Sat.

Harris Publications Ltd
Harris sell everything required by a stamp collector: stamp albums, mounts, tweezers, magnifying glasses, books on stamp collecting and stamp magazines published by Harris who are part of The Stamp Collecting Group.
42 Maiden Lane, WC2 (01-240 2286). Open 09.00–17.15 Mon to Fri; 10.00–14.00 Sat.

Jubilee Market
The arrival of this enormous, half-open, half-covered market coincided with Covent Garden Market's move. Good for fruit and vegetables, farm-fresh eggs, cheddar and a limited choice of other cheeses, poultry, bacon (in bulk) and an occasional fish stall. Daily meat auctions and a bric-à-brac market on Mondays.
Southampton St, WC2. Open 09.00 to 16.30/17.00 Mon to Fri, see separate entry for Sat Craft Market.

Jubilee Market (Crafts)
This Saturday craft market was still in its early days as we went to press but the aim is to house 300 craftspeople with space to demonstrate the creation of their craft. Anyone interested in hiring a space should contact *London Crafts Centre, 173 Bermondsey St, SE1 (01–407 2040).*
Southampton St, WC2. Sats only.

The YHA Shop
This large shop run by the Youth Hostels Association stocks a wide variety of tents and equipment for camping, walking and affiliated healthy activities. Also books on exploratory sports like mountaineering, cycle touring, rambling, orienteering etc; and guide books, maps and Ordnance Survey maps. Free catalogue on request.
14 Southampton St, WC2 (01–836 8541). Open 09.30–17.30 Mon to Fri; 09.30–19.00 Thurs; 09.30–16.00 Sat.

Samuel French Ltd
A theatre bookshop which attempts to stock all plays and books on the theatre and related subjects that are in the English language. Also sound effects records, opera libretti and opera books. A 100-page catalogue of technical books which are sent worldwide by mail order is available on request.
26 Southampton St, WC2 (01–836 7513). Open 09.30–17.30 Mon to Fri.

Falkiner's Fine Papers
A small, trade-style shop where Gabrielle Falkiner supplies specialist papers for artists and craftsmen: bookbinders, caligraphers, picture-framers and fine printers. She doesn't mind browsers, who can flip through the book of samples, or selling small quantities.
4 Mart St, WC2 (01–240 2339). Open 10.00–17.30 Mon to Fri.

Harvest
Harvest opened four years ago to sell the work of British craftsmen, particularly those who don't like dealing with the retail world. They sell the work of potters, woodworkers, jewellers, brassworkers, printers and greetings-card makers. They cover a wide range from

very modest up to thousands of pounds, and all craftsmen represented are commissionable through the gallery. They hold irregular exhibitions, have a notice board for related information and don't mind browsers.
40 Tavistock St, WC2 (01-240 0694). Open 10.00-19.00 Mon to Fri; 10.30-16.00 Sat, often later.

Penhaligon
Originally in Bond St and founded in 1870, Penhaligons hand-make on the premises a range of perfumes, toilet waters, after shaves, shampoos, deodorants, bath oils and hair dressings to match their original recipes. Essentially a man's house but many toilet waters, soaps and shampoos are popular with women. Beautifully produced catalogue on request.
41 Wellington St, WC2 (01-836 2150). Open 10.00-18.00 Mon to Fri; 10.00-17.00 Sat.

Suttons Seeds Ltd
Suttons London seed supermarket with the bonus of visiting experts who hold gardening surgeries. Ring for details. All seeds are in Suttons catalogue.
33 Catherine St, WC2 (01-836 0619). Open 09.30-17.30 Mon to Fri.

Knutz
Dedicated shoppers may remember this as a children's clothes shop. Now they specialize in novelty toys (for adults) like metre-long rubber snakes, rats, wax egg candles, funky ceramics and tin toys.
1 Russell St, WC2 (01-836 3114). Open 11.00-20.00 Mon to Sat.

Project Hand Shop
Only the handicrafts from unexploited small co-operatives in developing countries are sold at Project Hand's shop at the Africa Centre. Everything is beautifully made and includes mohair rugs from Lesotho, basketware from Bangladesh, Ethiopia and Africa, pretty cotton purses from Nepal, beads, musical instruments and batiks. The stock changes and is added to all the time.
38 King St, WC2 (01-836 6941). Open 10.00-20.00 Mon to Wed; 10.00-22.00 Thurs and Fri; 11.00-20.00 Sat.

Dance Centre
A free, photographically illustrated booklet showing everything on sale at the Dance Centre's shop is available on request. Leotards with various necklines, footless and footed tights, cat suits, swimsuits, towelling and velour tracksuits, leg warmers, shirts and shorts are available in 23 colours. Also a range of dance shoes, Greek sandals and tap plates.
11-14 Floral St, WC2 (01-836

6544). Open 09.00–20.00 Mon to Fri; 09.00–18.00 Sat.
Also at 20 Wellington St, WC2.

All Things Bright and Beautiful
Wholesalers using the ground floor of their warehouse as a retail shop, largely for slightly damaged or 'special' lines. Much stock is reduced in price and includes bags, clothes, homeware, old Afghan rugs, basketware, leather and fashion accessories and clothes from Third World countries.
35/36 Floral St, WC2 (01–836 0641). Open 10.00–17.30 Mon to Sat.

Hobbs
French chefs have prepared specialities for this new gourmet food and drinks shop. Giant jars of preserved vegetables and fruits, olives, shellfish, etc. line the shelves; and there are smoked hams, white truffles and other luxury foods; *premier cru* wines; and whisky from the wood.
3 Garrick St, WC2 (01–240 5653). Open 10.00–19.00 Mon to Sat.

C. and W. May
The fancy dress hire section of Moss Bros where they specialize in English fancy dress.
9–11 Garrick St, WC2 (01–836 5993). Open 09.00–17.30 Mon to Fri; closed 1.00–2.00.

Arts Council Shop
Large, spacious, tasteful and new shop selling all merchandisable spin-offs from Britain's subsidized arts. Postcards, posters, slides, prints, books on dance, film, poetry, opera, music and theatre as well as a limited selection of first and second novels from British authors. Details of 'events' (poetry readings etc.) are posted in the window.
8 Long Acre, WC2 (01–836 1359). Open 10.00–19.45 Mon to Sat.

Stanfords
Stanfords is London's leading map shop. They keep the complete range of Ordnance Survey maps for the entire UK and several other countries. Also wallmaps, militaria maps, RAC maps, professional and nautical maps, atlas, globes and the *Observer* map range which includes Zoo Britain, Roman Britain and Art Britain.
12 Long Acre, WC2 (01–836 1321). Open 09.00–17.00 Mon to Fri; 10.00–14.00 Sat.

Harveys Auctions Ltd
Harveys auction antique and general furniture, pictures, silver, bric-à-brac and oriental furniture. Sales are held every Wednesday at 10.30 and viewing is between 09.30 and 15.30 the preceding Tuesday. Auctions average 300 lots.
22–23 Long Acre, WC2 (01–240

1464). Open 09.00–17.00 Mon to Fri for receiving only.

Paul Wu
Oriental clothes, jewellery, accessories, silk hand-embroidered dressing gowns for men and women, beaded slippers and a host of other beautiful (and pricey) delights from the Orient. Particularly good for basketware.
64 Long Acre, WC2 (01-836 8566). Open 11.00–18.30 Mon to Fri; Thurs until 20.00; 11.00–18.00 Sat.

Glasshouse
A shop selling the work of a group of young glassblowers who can be watched working at furnaces at the back of the premises. They also run evening and weekend basic and advanced courses. Glass objects for sale include plates; goblets and glasses; dishes and bowls.
65 Long Acre, WC2 (01-836 9857). Open 10.00–18.00 Mon to Fri; until 20.00 Thurs; 11.00–16.00 Sat.

Brodie and Middleton
Run as a family business for 140 years, Brodie and Middleton supply the theatrical and arts trades with powder colours, pigments, glitters, curtains, drapes, muslin and everything necessary to make scenery. They supply virtually every theatre in the country with what they describe as 'the magic of the theatre', though they also function as a retail shop. Glitters and pigments are weighed, not pre-packaged. Also an extensive range of paint brushes and a fabric fire-proofing service.
79 Long Acre, WC2 (01-836 3289). Open 08.30–17.00 Mon to Fri.

J. W. Bollom and the London Graphics Centre
Bollom's main feature is a wide range of emulsion and eggshell paints and they keep samples of their hessians and display materials at this shop. They deal mainly with designers and architects. Within Bollom's is the London Graphics Centre, which stocks an extensive range of artists' (including graphic artists') materials. They claim to be the largest Letraset dealer in the country.
107 Long Acre, WC2. Bollom's open 08.00–17.30 Mon to Sat; Graphics 09.00–18.00 Mon to Sat.

FRIDA
FRIDA stands for Fund For Research and Investment of Africa Ltd and in this spacious two-floor shop/gallery the work of unexploited and FRIDA-aided craftsmen from Third World countries is sold. They stock basketware, a variety of jewellery, traditional carvings and rugs old and new.
111 Long Acre, WC2 (01-836 5051). Open 10.00–20.00 Mon to

Fri; 10.00–22.00 Thurs; 11.00–17.00 Sat.
Also 191 Kensington High St, W8 (01–937 9379).

Video Cassette Recorders
All leading video cassette systems with a concentration on industrial video equipment. Short term hire available on everything.
112 Long Acre, WC2 (01–240 0126). Open 09.30–17.30 Mon to Fri.

Paxman
Paxman's are the only horn-makers and sellers in this country. Mr Paxman makes some of the 38 models on the premises but most are made in their factory. A wide range can be seen in the window and they are made from brass and yellow, golden and nickel silver. Prices from over £500.
116 Long Acre, WC2 (01–240 3647). Open 09.00–17.30 Mon to Fri; 09.00–12.30 Sat.

Howie
Opened in 1977, Howie was Covent Garden's first fashion shop to be decorated high-tech style. Clothes for men (downstairs) and women (upstairs) are unusual, ahead of fashion and all by English designers. They try to be fresh and amusing and keep a range of casually witty jewellery and unusual accessories. There's no heavy sales pitch and no sideways glances at those who prefer to look and ponder rather than buy.
138 Long Acre, WC2 (01–240 1541). Open 10.00–18.30 Mon to Fri.

Booksmith
Remaindered books, and new paperbacks. See page 125 for full details.
36 St Martins Lane, WC2 (01–836 5110). Open 09.30–20.00 Mon to Fri; 11.30–20.00 Sat.

George Parker & Sons
Parkers is one of Covent Garden's few surviving specialist shops. Established in 1851, they carry a stock of craftsmen-made saddles and saddlery.
12 Upper St Martins Lane, WC2 (01–836 1164). Open 09.00–17.00 Mon to Fri; closed Sat.

Coleson
Until the Neals Yard Bakery opened, Coleson's was Covent Garden's only bakery. Bread is mainly white and crusty (a nice contrast to the wholewheat loaves at Neals Yard) and is delivered daily from the shop's Leather Lane bakery. Also rolls, cakes, pastries, sandwiches and hot snacks. *1 Monmouth St, WC2 (01–836 2066). Open 07.30–15.00 Mon to Fri.*

Paper Rainbow
Small but good range of

wrapping papers, stationery (now their own range with greetings to suit all occasions), and gift items like money boxes, china and Crabtree & Evelyn soaps.
17 Monmouth St, WC2 (01-240 3664). Open 10.00-18.00 Mon to Fri; 11.00-17.00 Sat.

Russell and Chapple
Don't be put off by the trade look to this shop; inside is a mine of useful ropes and twines, artists' and theatrical canvasses, coconut matting, green baize, hessian and deck-chair covering.
23 Monmouth St, WC2 (01-836 7521). Open 08.30-17.00 Mon to Fri; closed 13.00-14.00 for lunch.

Monmouth Coffee House
Anita LeRoy and Nick Saunders sell very cheap coffee beans in 1lb-, 3lb- and 7lb-quantities. Beans are roasted on the premises, they do no grinding, but coffees can be tried in their coffee shop at the back of the premises. Prices get better the larger the quantity. Enquiries for green beans welcome.
27 Monmouth St, WC2 (01-836 5272). Open 10.00-18.00 Mon to Sat.

Cheong-leen Supermarket
Everything needed by a Chinese cook is on sale here including cooking equipment and medicaments. It's London's oldest Chinese supermarket, is meticulously clean, and they'll take bulk orders.
4-10 Tower St, WC2 (01-836 4378). Open 10.00-19.00 Mon to Fri; 10.00-18.00 Sat; 12.00-17.00 Sun.

Collectors' Corner
Collectors' Corner is the place to hunt down obscure operatics and classical records. They import from all over the world and many recordings are unavailable elsewhere. There is also a small secondhand section.
63 Monmouth St, WC2 (01-836 5614). Open 10.00-18.00 Mon to Fri; 10.00-13.00 Sat.

William Page & Co Ltd
Page's cater mainly for the hotel and restaurant trade and much of their cooking equipment is ideal for large households. All culinary devices imaginable.
87-91 Shaftesbury Ave, W1 (01-437 8888). Open 09.30-17.30 Mon to Fri; 09.30-16.30 Sat.

Collet's Record Shop
Collet's are jazz and folk record specialists. They sell both new and secondhand discs; their jazz selection ranges from Jelly Roll Morton to Cecil Taylor and their folk covers British, American and ethnic groups from all over the world.
180 Shaftesbury Ave, WC2 (01-240 3969). Open 10.00-18.00 Mon to Fri; 10.00-16.00 Sat.

Arthur Beale

Ship's chandlers Arthur Beale were originally rope-makers on the banks of the Fleet River some four centuries ago. Their speciality is still rope, wire, rigging and splicing but they are well known for their wide range of nautical items more geared to sailing than motor boats.

194 Shaftesbury Ave, WC2 (01-836 9034). Open 09.00–18.00 Mon to Fri; 09.30–13.00 Sat.

Neals Yard Wholefood Warehouse

When Nick Saunders converted this old warehouse and stocked it up with sensibly packaged and easily accessible dried foods, Covent Garden dwellers and workers were delighted. All foods can be bought in small or large quantities and are progressively cheaper the larger the amount. Grains, pulses, nuts, dried fruits, seeds, flours, cereals, pasta, salt, tea, jam, a range of honeys and freshly-made peanut butter are laid out on shelves made from varnished joists discarded at the demolition site. Recently they have started to run a bakery where freshly ground whole-meal bread and flour can be bought. The latest venture is a dairy for making cheese and yoghurt.

2 Neals Yard, WC2 (01-240 1154). Open 10.00–18.30 Mon to Sat. Also Bakery, 6 Neals Yard.

Inside Out

Inside Out is a vast open-plan shop on two floors. It is essentially a homeware shop known for its extensive range of cane and bamboo occasional furniture, blinds, basketware, china and glass. They also sell kitchenware, cookery books, preserves, chutneys, teas, bath oils, soaps, essences and other gift items. At Christmas the the shop is devoted to small gifts.

1 Neal St, WC2 (01-240 0331). Open 10.00–midnight Mon to Sat (basement closed from 18.00).

Neal St Shop

This small, heavily-stocked two-floor shop always attracts a lot of browsers and people looking for a novel present. Christina Smith, who runs this and the New Neal St Shop, buys extensively from China and at this shop specializes in antique (Chinese) and modern jewellery; painted paper kites; baskets and wicker bowls of all sizes; colourful felt puppets and toy kits for children; imaginative and decorative household items and a wide range of other items, ideal for children and adults. The New Neal St Shop sells plants, plant holders, herbs, gardening and cookery books, dried flowers and leaves. They also import basketware from China (down-stairs) and have a delightful changing section of novel gift ideas including bone spoons and

prettily presented French sweets.
29 Neal St, WC2 (01–240 0136). Open 10.00–17.00 Mon to Fri; 10.00–16.00 Sat; hours extended at Christmas.
New Neal St Shop, 23 Neal St, WC2 (no phone). Open 10.00–17.00 Mon to Fri; 10.00–16.00 Sat. Hours extended at Christmas – details posted on door.

(Bead) Warehouse
What used to be one of London's liveliest and most colourful ethnic shops was re-opening as a specialist bead shop after several months' closure as we went to press. Aside from an extensive range of beads including millefiori beads from Venice, multi-coloured striped beads from Pakistan, glass flower beads from Czechoslovakia and porcelain beads from China, Warehouse also stock everything for jewellery makers – findings, wires, cords and threads. Discount on orders over £25.
39 Neal St, WC2 (01–240 0931). Open 11.30–18.00 Mon to Fri; 11.00–17.30 Sat.

Copper Shop
Extensive range of English manufactured copper goods from jelly moulds to mixing bowls, saucepans, omelette pans, fish kettles, preserving pans and hand-made coal scuttles of several sizes and shapes. Mail order catalogue on request.
48 Neal St, entrance Shorts Gdns, WC2 (01–836 2984). Open 10.00–18.00 Mon to Sat.

Clive Shilton
Clive Shilton makes a stunning range of (usually) leather accessories which includes shoes and boots (custom-made and from stock), occasion bags, briefcases, small leather goods and jewellery. His designs, which frequently incorporate a shell shape, use leaf and geometric patterns on the finest quality suede, kid, calf skin and satin. Everything is hand made, so it goes without saying that prices are very high.
58 Neal St, WC2 (01–836 0809). Open 10.00–18.00 Mon to Fri; 10.00–19.00 Thurs; 10.30–17.30 Sat.

Mayfair of London
Jacqueline Cooper runs this tiny shop where she sells men's shirts at 20% off normal prices. Makes include Van Heusen, Tern, Inigo Jones, Chard and La lionne.
60 Neal St, WC2 (01–240 2785). Open 10.00–18.30 Mon to Fri; 10.30–18.00 Sat.

R. I. Harding & Co
Despite Mr Harding's window display of some of the earliest cameras, he will only undertake modifications, adaptations and repairs to modern cameras. He offers a highly personal and specialist service, doing all the

work himself on the premises.
61 Neal St, WC2 (01-240 2860). Open 09.00–17.30 Mon to Fri.

Kites
London's first specialist kite shop and now reckoning to have the largest range of kites under one roof in the world. Also everything necessary to build the simplest and most complicated kites, plus books.
69 Neal St, WC2 (01-836 1666). Open 10.00–18.00 Mon to Sat.

The Badge Shop
Des Kay's shop is a haven for badge lovers and his variety is staggering. He has an instant badge-making machine on the premises for one-off specials, he undertakes commissions and he has a collection of the earliest and rarest badges known.
18 Earlham St, WC2 (01-836 9327). Open 11.00–19.00 Tues to Fri; 12.00–18.00 Sat.

Robert Bruce
Robert Bruce is the only fruit and veg. dealer who has survived Covent Garden's move to Nine Elms. He's essentially a wholesaler but operates a large semi-open shop bang outside Covent Garden tube station. The shop always keeps a superb selection of fresh and unusual fruit and vegetables. Bulk buying can be negotiated but otherwise prices are variable – bargains can be obtained on regular 'gluts' of fruit such as avocados, pineapples, mangoes, etc.
19 James St, WC2 (01-240 0194/836 5834). Open 08.00–19.00 Mon to Fri; 08.00–18.00 Sat.

The Vintage Magazine Shop
The Vintage Magazine Shop is divided into three sections. In the basement they keep '50s, '60s and '70s rock papers, photographs, US and English comics; upstairs is the cinema shop and alongside that is theatrical and general ephemera dating back over 100 years. Changing stock regularly includes 1912 to pre-war comics, *Picture Post*, newspapers, sheet music and glamour mags.
2 and 4 Earlham St, WC2 (01-836 2926). Open 10.00–19.00 Mon to Sat.

Blackman Harvey
This long-established framer, who will undertake all kinds of picture framing, also runs a print centre which keeps a selection of modern graphics and reproduction prints of all periods.
29 Earlham St, WC2 (01-836 1904). Open 09.00–17.30 Mon to Fri; 09.00–16.00 Sat.

British Craft Centre
The BCC was set up (it is indirectly goverment-aided via the Crafts Advisory Committee) to promote and sell British

crafts. It holds regular exhibitions of members' work upstairs in a spacious, well-lit gallery, and some pieces are available for sale downstairs, but it is advisable to make direct commissions. Many craftsmen don't bother to apply for BCC membership because so much red tape, time and expense is involved.
43 Earlham St, WC2 (01-836 6993). Open 10.00-17.30 Mon to Fri; 10.00-16.00 Sat.

Corner House Bookshop
This aptly-named bookshop keeps titles on radical education, the women's movement, language and literacy, culture and communications, plus non-sexist children's books, Third World education pamphlets and an enormous range of magazines and pamphlets on related subjects. They are the only London outlet for *WHERE*, published by the Advisory Centre for Education.
14 Endell St, WC2 (01-836 9960). Open 10.00-18.00 Mon to Sat.

Detail
The work of around 20 young jewellery and object designers is on sale at this newish shop, which goes in for synthetic materials in bright, shocking colours. Stock ranges from relatively ordinary ponytail clips, earrings and bracelets all under a couple of quid, to joke jewellery and special, pricey pieces. Amongst their stocks is Susannah Heron's mass produced range.
49 Endell St, WC2 (01-379 6940). Open 11.00-19.00 Mon to Sat.

Salvi
Salvi offer a full service to harpists; from their extensive display of Italian-made harps (£2,400-£5,900!) to individual strings. Also all accessories, books, records and sheet music. They don't mind curious browsers.
55 Endell St, WC2 (01-836 0788). Open 10.00-16.00 Mon to Sat.

The Golden Orient
Mr Undeem has been selling his range of Indian herbs, spices, groceries, nuts and whole foods for a good 20 years. Ground spices are sold loose; a wide range of Indian pickles, ghee, large polythene bags of dried prawns, dried fruits, soy flour and honey can be bulk-bought.
6 Shorts Gdns, WC2 (01-240 2658). Open 10.00-17.00 Mon to Sat.

Covent Garden Cycles
With such a central position, this bicycle shop could hardly fail to succeed. Service and advice is friendly and informal from young guys very keen on cycling. They keep bikes from leading manufacturers (includ-

ing Claude Butler, Dawes and Holdsworthy) but specialize in French cycles. Touring and commuter bikes (three-, five- and ten-speed and folding) are their speciality but they occasionally get secondhand and children's cycles. They also stock a range of touring accessories. Repairs are undertaken, but priority is given to those who've bought from them.
41 Shorts Gdns, WC2 (01-836 1752). Open 10.00–19.00 Mon to Fri; 10.00–14.30 Wed; 10.00–18.00 Sat.

Cousin Jack's Cornish Shop
Modern café with a few tables for light meals. They sell authentic Cornish pasties, fruit pies, saffron cake, Martin's ice-cream, sausage rolls, smoked mackerel, hogs pudding and Cornish cream to take away. Also a selection of crafts by Cornishmen and women.
14 Drury Lane, WC2. Open 10.00–18.00 Mon to Sat.

Anello and Davide
Anello and Davide are a long-established theatrical shoemakers who have several branches throughout the West End. They make shoes and boots from any period to order, stock one-bar Minnie Mouse style shoes in nearly every colour in suede or leather (or will make them up to order), ballet and tap shoes and a range of 'fashion' shoes. Next door they have a permanent sale shop where they import men and women's sandals and shoes from Italy and supplement the stock with lines (uncollected orders, etc.) from Anello and Davide stocks.
30 Drury Lane, WC2 (01-836 1983). Open 10.00–17.30 Mon to Fri.
Also at 33–35 Oxford St, W1 (see page 3).

Philip Poole and Co
A giant pen hangs over Mr Poole's pretty window display of old pen nibs. Inside the shop are ranges of fountain pens, quill pens, quill cutters, pen wipers, inkwells, blotters and the only 18 varieties of nibs made today. Mr Poole has over 5000 nibs long out of production but mostly not for sale.
182 Drury Lane, WC2 (01-405 7097). Open 9.00–17.30 Mon to Fri.

RUSSELL SQ

Smiths
Established in 1830 with the original elaborate sign still intact, Smiths is *the* place for umbrellas, walking sticks and shooting sticks. Sadly, they no longer make or repair umbrellas.
53 New Oxford St, WC1 (01-836 4731). Open 09.00–17.30 Mon to Fri.

Zeno
Books on every aspect of Greece, the Greek islands and Cyprus can be found at this specialist bookshop. Literature in Greek, history, art and architecture in English, dictionaries, guidebooks, travel, etc.
6 Denmark St, WC2 (01-836 2522). Open 09.30–18.30 Mon to Fri; 09.30–17.30 Sat.

Forbidden Planet
The eventual aim of this science fiction and comic bookshop is to stock every new publication from this country and the States. They also stock posters and cards. A fascinating place to browse and because it's well laid out everything is easy to find.
23 Denmark St, WC2 (01-836 4179). Open 10.00–18.00 Mon to Sat; 10.00–19.00 Thurs.

Cinema Bookshop
For the past 15 years, the Cinema Bookshop has been selling everything in print (books, posters, stills, ephemera, magazines, etc.) related to the cinema since its inception to the present day.
13 Great Russell St, WC1 (01-637 0206). Open 10.30–17.30 Mon to Sat.

Collet's Chinese Bookshop
As well as being a bookshop specializing in books about China in English and Chinese, Collet's also keep a small range of beautifully coloured paper kites, counting beads, silk animals and many other small decorative items from China. They also stock Mao's Red Book in many languages.
40 Great Russell St, WC2 (01-580 7538). Open 09.45–17.45 Mon to Fri; closed Sat.

Davenports
A huge painted metal sign of a rabbit being pulled out of a top hat marks Davenports, the magic shop. The window displays a fraction of the stock of jokes, tricks, funny and terrifying face masks and smoke bombs. This is where conjurers and magicians buy the tricks of their trade. Excellent for cheap quirky presents and stocking-fillers, also fireworks all the year round.
51 Great Russell St, WC2 (01-405 8524). Open 09.00–17.00 Mon to Fri.

Westaway and Westaway
Always crowded because they sell very cheap, good quality Scottish knitwear, particularly cashmere and Shetlands (made on a hand-frame), blankets, wool shirts, kilts, gloves, ties and scarves. As most of their customers are foreign, staff in the chaotic old-fashioned shop speak French, Italian and Spanish.
65 Great Russell St, WC1 (01-405 4479). Open 09.00–17.30 Mon to Fri; 09.00–13.00 Sat; also at 29 Bloomsbury Way,

WC1 (01-405 2128). Open 09.00-17.00 Mon to Fri; 09.00-12.45 Sat.

Clover Press
An old-established commercial stationers who proudly told me that all their staff are past the age of retirement. They don't go in for 'fancy stuff for the tourists' but supply stationery of all kinds mainly to local university students, academics, hotels and offices.
66 Great Russell St, WC1 (01-405 9091). Open 08.30-17.30 Mon to Fri.

Theosophical Bookshop
Books related to Eastern and Western religions, the occult, metaphysics, astrology, yoga and Western mysticism.
68 Great Russell St, WC1 (01-405 2309). Open 9.30-17.00 Mon to Sat.

Sharuna
This Indian delicatessen and grocery is part of the Indian-run hotel and excellent vegetarian restaurant next door. Delicious hot and cold snacks to take away; pickles, spices, popadoms, Indian groceries, health foods and general groceries. Limited dairy produce but no eggs.
107 Great Russell St, WC1 (01-636 5922, restaurant only). Open 11.00-22.00 Mon to Sat; 13.00-21.00 Sun.

Tibet Shop
Quite unconnected with the similarly named Chelsea shop, this small, well-stocked shop imports goods made by Tibetan refugees living in Nepal and Northern India. Mostly clothes, all highly coloured and woven with wool or cotton, including woollen jackets, a range of shirts, felt embroidered boots, waistcoats, shoulder bags, some jewellery, rugs, books about Tibet, posters and incense.
10 Coptic St, WC2 (01-636 5529). Open 10.00-18.00 Mon to Sat; closed 12.00-13.00 for lunch.

M. Ayres
Mr Ayres is an antiquarian book dealer who stocks some of the very earliest titles and specializes in incunabula (books produced pre-16th century), and 16th-, 17th- and 18th-century illustrated books. Also art reference and classical titles.
31a Museum St, WC1 (01-636 2344). Open 10.00-18.00 Mon to Sat.

Atlantis
New, secondhand and out of print books on all aspects of the occult. From astrology to Zen, including alchemy and magic.
49a Museum St, WC1 (01-405 2120). Open 11.00-17.30 Mon to Fri; 11.00-17.00 Sat.

Louis Bondy
Miniature books all under 90mm (3½in) high and as tiny as 38mm

(½in) are the speciality at Mr Bondy's rare book shop. Most were produced at the turn of the century and some are still sold with their original magnifying glasses. Mr Bondy also keeps a good range of old children's books, 16th- and 17th-century emblem, art and caricature titles.
16 Little Russell St, WC1 (01-405 2733). Open 10.00–17.00 Sat (otherwise ring).

Dillons
London University's bookshop with large sections on most subjects both academic and general.
1 Malet St, WC1 (01-636 1577). Open 09.00–17.30 Mon, Thurs and Fri; 10.00–17.30 Tues; 09.00–19.00 Wed; 09.30–13.00 Sat.

BLOOMSBURY

Westaway and Westaway
Chaotic, old-fashioned Scottish knitwear shop where goods are piled high on open shelves, and reserve stocks kept in large drawers below. There are several other rooms hidden downstairs for rugs, children's knits, cashmeres and kilts. This is the smallest branch of Westaway and Westaway but it has a large selection of kilts and cloth as well as Scottish woollens, with the emphasis on cashmere and shetlands. The best quality and cheapest Scottish knitwear in London. It gets very busy with (mostly) Italian and German tourists – wise to go early; avoid lunchtime.
29 Bloomsbury Way, WC1 (01-405 2128). Open 09.00–17.00 Mon to Fri; 09.00–12.45 Sat.

Rolandos Pâtisserie
Delicious French loaves and rolls can be bought hot from the oven at this Swiss pâtisserie. They specialize in florentines and fresh cream gateaux, and are expert at decorating their cakes with flaked and piped chocolate. They also do hot snacks.
33 Tavistock Place, WC1 (01-387 3876). Open 08.00–18.00 Mon to Fri; 08.00–15.00 Sat.

Continental Stores
Continental Stores is my idea of an ideal local grocers. It specializes in continental delicacies both tinned and frozen. Nuts, spices and dried herbs are sold loose from large jars; there are Belgian pâtés and ham on the bone, a range of French and Italian salamis and sausages and a selection of French and Italian cheeses. Also three blends of whole coffee beans.
54 Tavistock St, WC1 (01-837 6616). Open 09.00–17.45 Mon to Sat; 09.00–14.00 Thurs.

Samuel Gordon
Parts of Bloomsbury are blessed with good food shops. Samuel Gordon the fishmonger displays the day's fresh fish on a central

slab, will get any fish (within reason and season) to order, and always has a varied selection of smoked fish and live eels.
76 Marchmont St, WC1 (01-387 2271). Open 08.00–17.30 Tues to Sat; 08.00–17.00 Thurs; 08.00–1800 Fri; 08.00–16.00 Sat.

Discount Shop
Previously called Copperfields and part of a chain of discount women's fashion clothes, the Discount Shop is really a factory outlet. By buying ends of lines, cutting down profit margins, and being dead-on, as opposed to ahead of, fashions, they sell many leading fashion names at half the normal price. Allow plenty of time to search through the packed rails.
68 Lambs Conduit St, WC1 (01-405 6016). Open 10.00–18.00 Mon to Sat.

Gallery 57
This pretty, canopied shop sells a well chosen mix of fine art reproductions, wrapping papers, cards, children's books and novelty items, basketware, T-shirts and gift items. Also provides a framing and block-mounting service.
70 Lambs Conduit St, WC1 (01-405 1408). Open 09.00–18.30 Mon to Sat.

Workshop
Cartoonist Mel Calman sells his own and other leading cartoonists' original artwork together with prints, lithographs and the odd 'Heath Robinson' type collector's item. Regular exhibitions, too.
83 Lambs Conduit St, WC1 (01-242 5335). Open 10.30–17.30 Mon to Fri; 11.00–12.30 Sat.

Holborn Village Craft Shop
Andee Cromarty opened this craft shop which specializes in cheap custom-made knitwear several years ago. She designs most of the cardigans and jerseys on sale (always 150 on display) and takes a limited number of commissions a week which she and outworkers knit up. They keep an extensive number of patterns in the shop which can be worked through and adapted if necessary. Other specialities are hand-painted badges, hand-made toys and stationery.
17 Rugby St, WC1 (01-405 4281). Open 11.00–18.00 Mon to Fri; 11.00–15.30 Sat.

Wheelers
This small delicatessen in a row of food shops specializes in cheeses. It also sells cold meats, a ham on the bone, quiches, ready-made sandwiches, good bacon and general groceries. Friendly, cheerful service.
59 Red Lion Sq, WC1 (01-405 4204). Open 08.00–16.00 Mon to Fri; 08.00–13.00 Sat.

HOLBORN

Condor Cycles
Mr Young has built a world-wide reputation for this specialist bike shop which he opened just after the war. Condor's are best known for their custom-built bikes and their stock of parts for DIY bike enthusiasts. They also keep cycle accessories, spare parts, an extensive range of clothing and a wide range of three-, five- and ten-speed cycles for touring and racing.
90 Grays Inn Rd, WC1 (01-837 7641). Open 09.30-18.00 Mon to Fri; closed 14.30-15.30 for lunch; open 09.30-15.00 Sat.

John Charlick Foods
John Charlick's recently opened delicatessen and take-away food shop attractively displays its wares in the window – home-cooked ham, pies, quiches, various pâtés, tarts, cakes and cheesecake. A 'menu' is available; also cheeses, bread and fresh orange juice. Useful in an area totally devoid of this kind of shop.
142 Grays Inn Rd, WC1 (01-278 9187). Open 09.00-18.30 Mon to Fri.

Hubbards Office Furniture Ltd
Hubbards is the largest of a cluster of shops in this part of Grays Inn Rd which sell new and secondhand office furniture – filing cabinets, desks, tables, chairs, etc., in all states and at all prices.
199 Grays Inn Rd, WC1 (01-837 4366). Open 09.00-17.00 Mon to Fri.

Thornfields
There are up to 50% reductions on Sanderson's wallpapers at Thornfields. Most papers are in stock but those that aren't can be ordered within 48 hours. All their paints (from leading manufacturers) are at discount prices; special offers are regularly advertized in the *Evening Standard.*
321 Grays Inn Rd, WC1 (01-837 2996). Open 08.00-17.00 Mon to Fri; 08.00-16.30 Sat.

Knobs and Knockers
Knobs and Knockers use original moulds to make their reproduction Georgian, Victorian, early Elizabethan and modern door furniture. Everything is displayed and priced to make choosing easier. Next door, at their Louvre Centre, they specialize in external, louvre and wardrobe doors.
61-65 Judd St, WC1 (01-387 0091). Open 09.00-17.30 Mon to Fri; 09.00-16.00/16.30 Sat.

Athena
Athena manufacture everything they sell and provide good quality art reproductions at a price everyone can afford. A choice of cards, posters and

prints either block-mounted, aluminium-framed, wooden-framed or frameless.
76 Southampton Row, WC1 (01-405 2742). Open 09.30-18.00 Mon to Fri; 10.00-17.00 Sat.

Unitex
Unitex has been selling cut-price women's clothes for ten years. They buy out of season from designers and wholesalers end of ranges, sample collections and seconds, and supplement the stock with cheap non-seconds lines. The selection of styles is extensive and covers all seasons.
82 Southampton Row, WC1 (01-405 6565). Open 09.30-22.00 Mon to Fri; 09.30-18.00 Sat and Sun (during summer). Open 09.30-18.00 Mon to Sat (during winter).

J. I. Horwit
A very fine selection of antique jewellery can be viewed at Mr Faber's old-fashioned jewellers. They specialize in jewels and silver and undertake fine repairs.
94 Southampton Row, WC1 (01-405 0749). Open 11.00-18.00 Mon to Fri.

Morgans Stationery
A large stationers set out in supermarket style. They buy in bulk and always have special offers on commercial stationery. Also souvenirs and gift items.
102 Southampton Row, WC1 (01-405 0027). Open 09.00-21.00 Mon to Fri; 09.00-18.00 Sat.

Carwardines
Carwardines roast 15 different blends of coffee on the premises. They grind to order and sell appliances for all the various methods of coffee making.
5 Victoria House, Southampton Row, WC1 (01-405 4115). Open 09.00-17.30 Mon to Fri.

Dennis Groves
Dennis is one of the original partners of Adeptus, the foam furniture people. At this, formerly Adeptus's first West End showroom, Dennis has diversified into Persian kilims, cheap neon lighting, and scaffolding framed furniture. Everything on sale is very reasonably priced and the furniture (chairs, beds, sofas etc.) is exclusive to the shop.
9 Sicilian Ave, WC2 (01-405 5603). Open 09.00-18.00 Mon to Sat.

EHW & Co
EHW have been established for over 40 years as one of the best stamp and coin dealers in the world. They deal in the entire British Colonial range from Victorian days to the present. They buy and sell fine used and mint condition stock.
12 Sicilian Ave, WC1 (01-405 5509). Open 09.00-17.30 Mon to Fri.

E. H. Rann

For over 40 years Rann's have been tie and heraldic shield specialists. They keep over 1000 ties in stock – public schools, university, regimental and services, medical and professional, and will make up ties to people's specifications. Their main business, though, is hand-working heraldic shields.

21 Sicilian Ave, WC1 (01–405 4759). Open 09.00–17.30 Mon to Fri; closed Sat.

John Keep

Paint specialists John Keep enjoy a high reputation and reckon to stock all paints available under one roof. Also manufacture their own gloss, eggshell and emulsion paints and provide a matching service, even for small orders. Also sell transluscent glass paints. Friendly and competent advice given.

15 Theobalds Rd, WC1 (01–242 0313). Open 08.00–17.30 Mon to Fri; 08.00–13.00 Sat.

Stanley Gibbons

Stanley Gibbons, leading philatelists with a world-wide reputation, have been selling stamps since 1850. They are a general stamp shop selling mint condition and old stamps from all over the world, albums and all the necessary accessories. At the main Southampton St premises they also run a map shop where they sell antique maps for the collector and prints. At 399 Strand they hold monthly exhibitions and have a rare stamp department and a bonds and share certificates section. The Coin Shop (known as Collectors' Corner) stocks coins of all ages, bank notes, war medals, playing cards and related antiquarian first editions.

Stanley Gibbons, 399 Strand, WC2 (01–836 8444); Stanley Gibbons Mapseller, 37 Southampton St, WC2. Open 09.00–17.00 Mon to Fri; Coin Shop, 395 Strand, WC2. Open 09.00–17.30 Mon to Fri; 09.30–12.30 Sat.

Australian Gift Shop

Foodstuffs, postcards, maps, wall hangings, T-shirts, badges and stick-ons, stuffed koalas, and a whole gamut of souvenirs of Australia can be bought here.

115 Strand, WC2 (01–836 2292). Open 09.00–17.30 Mon to Fri; 09.00–13.00 Sat.

The City Bag Store

This is the cheaper branch of the virtually comprehensive (fashion) bag shop in South Molton St, W1. Here at this vast shop they offer a complete range of handbags, holdalls, grips and belts.

Unit 2, 2–434 Strand, WC2 (01–379 7762). Open 09.00–18.00 Mon to Fri; 09.00–18.30 Thurs and Sat.

Badges and Equipment
A stalwart in government/army surplus circles, Badges and Equipment regularly stocks services shirts, socks, boots, seamen's jerseys, coats and jackets and a wide range of service badges. Also a range of grips, anoraks and sleeping bags.
421 Strand, WC2 (01-836 6237). Open 09.00-18.00 Mon to Fri; 09.00-17.00 Sat.

HMSO
Besides stocking copies of all parliamentary papers, Acts, Regulations and Hansard, HMSO stocks pamphlets and books on a surprising number of subjects. The entire range of Ordnance Survey maps, *The Highway Code, Post Office Guide* and other useful handbooks rub shoulders with superb reprints of First World War postcards and posters.
Mail Ordering Service: PO Box 569, SE1. 49 High Holborn, WC1 (01-928 6977). Open 08.30-17.15 Mon to Fri.

Beatties
Beatties is one of England's biggest model shops. Formerly known as Bassett-Lowke, they were founded in the early 1900s. They sell model railways of all gauges, plastic construction components of all types, die-cast toys and collectors' items, Meccano and wooden boat kits. They operate a flourishing secondhand die-cast and model railway section.
112 High Holborn, WC1 (01-405 6285). Open 09.00-18.00 Tues to Sat; 10.00-18.00 Mon.

Brunnings (Holborn) Ltd
Brunnings are the people for secondhand (some new) scientific apparatus. They specialize in cameras, telescopes and microscopes; and not only sell complete instruments but also keep extensive stocks of parts, particularly lenses and lens caps. The majority of their old instruments have special features no longer incorporated into modern cameras and microscopes, and Brunnings are one of the few sources of replacement parts.
133 High Holborn, WC1 (01-405 0312). Open 09.30-17.30 Mon to Fri; 09.00-11.45 Sat.

John Brumfit
Established in 1864 and with an olde worlde wooden frontage, Brumfit's are high-class tobacconists selling a wide range of English and imported cigarettes, cigars from all over the world, Smith's snuffs, pipes and pipe tobacco and lighters.
337 High Holborn, WC1 (01-405 2929). Open 08.00-18.00 Mon to Fri.

3
FINSBURY AND CITY

Hatton Garden, Finsbury, City

Don't expect to go shopping in this area on Saturdays; at the weekend the City and its surroundings are like a desert. Shops, anyway, are few and far between. Like the East End, parts of Finsbury are wastelands where industry has moved on. In the City itself shops centre around the markets; Leadenhall, Smithfield and Billingsgate with occasional relics from Victorian days like Mitchell, Inman and Co, in Cloth Fair.

Streets around the jewellery centre, Hatton Garden, house long established instrument maker/supplier shops associated with the silver, jewellery and clock trades. Near by is Leather Lane, a flourishing street market and the area's food centre.

See also Islington, Camden and Hampstead.

TRANSPORT

Hatton Garden
Tube stations: Farringdon, Barbican, Moorgate, Temple, Chancery Lane.
Buses: 8, 11, 22, 25, 133.

Finsbury
Tube stations: Angel, Old St, King's Cross.
Buses: 30, 73, 214.

City
Tube stations: St Paul's, Mansion Hse, Bank.
Buses: 11, 25, 133.

LOCAL OPENING HOURS

Very few shops are open in this area on Saturdays, nearly all work weekdays only.

REFRESHMENTS

East West Natural Foods
196 Old St, E1. *Open 11.30–21.00 Mon to Fri.* Snack bar for soft drinks, also tea and home-made cakes.

HATTON GARDEN

Pindisports
This two-floor sports shop splits

itself between camping, including back-packing, and climbing and skiing. There is always a stock of all the necessary equipment for both activities but during Sept to March skiing predominates while during March until Sept, camping takes over.
14–18 Holborn, EC1 (01-242 3278). Open 09.00–17.30 Mon to Sat; 10.00–19.00 Thurs.

Jodies Drapery Store
Small shop specializing in well-chosen fabrics, mostly for dress-making. Its sources include shops closing down, remnant and foreign shops, and prices are always very low. Stock varies, but they regularly have linings, jersey, cotton, corduroys and silks.
143–144 Holborn, EC1 (01-242 2649). Open 10.00–18.00 Mon to Fri.

Warehouse Utility Clothing Co
Cut price women's fashion clothes. (See page 138–9 for full details.)
143 Holborn, EC1 (01-405 1753) Open 10.00–18.00 Mon to Fri. Also at 99a Cheapside EC2.

Blacks Camping and Leisure
Part of the enormous and long-established group, Black and Edgington, which is known world-wide for its camping equipment. This self-service style store specializes in equipment for climbing, potholing and walking. Accessories are sold on the ground floor.
146 Holborn, EC1 (01-405 4426). Open 09.15–19.00 Thurs; 09.15–17.30 Mon to Sat.

Feltons
Old-established company selling first-class quality cut flowers and plants.
15 Holborn Viaduct, EC1 (01-236 6308). Open 08.30–17.30 Mon to Fri. Also at 5 Cheapside EC2.

J. A. L. Franks Ltd
A general stamp dealer selling and buying stamps from all over the world.
140 Fetter Lane, EC4 (01-405 2170). Open 10.15–17.30 Mon to Fri; 10.15–19.00 Thurs.

Felt and Hessian Shop
This small, insignificant looking shop with a window display of rather soppy soft toys, manufactures and stocks over 100 different coloured felts in two widths or cut in large squares, and a similar number of different coloured backed and unbacked hessians. The felts are kept in the shop and the hessians are cut to order in their vast warehouse next door. Also stock felt-covered soft toys.
34 Greville St, EC1 (01-405 6215). Open 09.00–17.00 Mon to Fri; closed Sat.

A. R. Ullman Ltd
This large shop in the heart of the jewellery trade displays all its wares in glass counters. Be prepared to haggle over prices of all the secondhand and antique jewellery including a fine display of Georgian and Victorian silver pieces, silver chain bags, objets d'art, scent bottles, brooches, rings, watches and pendants.
10 Hatton Garden, EC1 (01-405 1877). Open 09.30-17.00 Mon to Fri.

C. B. Salvo
In the middle of Hatton Garden, Salvo's is a very functional-looking shop selling tools for the jewellery and allied trades. They are always busy and haven't a lot of time for indecisive unknowledgeable buyers but are happy to serve retail customers who know exactly what they want.
88-90 Hatton Garden, EC1 (01-405 7445). Open 10.00-17.30 Mon to Fri (approx, sometimes later).

Mineral Stones Ltd
In the heart of London's jewellery business world, Mineral Stones Ltd specialize in precious and semi-precious stones, minerals and some tumble stones. They will cut and prepare rough stones, cut stones to fit any findings (clasps, etc.) and sell a range of gold and silver findings.
111 Hatton Garden, EC1 (01-405 0197). Open 09.30-17.30 Mon to Fri.

R. Holt and Co
Hatton Garden is the centre of the jewellery trade and many of the shops sporting fine displays of jewels and old jewellery don't welcome retail trade. Holts is one of the few that do. It's pleasantly decorated in bamboo with long cabinet displays of stocks of every gem listed in the dictionary of gem stones - anything from a diamond to an agate. They obviously have more time for their serious customers. Downstairs there is a mineral display and lapidary workshop that the public is welcome to view.
111 Hatton Garden, EC1 (01-405 5286). Open 09.30-17.30 Mon to Fri.

The Jewel House
One of the first dealers to move into the retail trade. One window display shows over 700 diamond rings and around 200 different types of gold chain; another gentlemen's jewellery; another displays diamond and sapphire and diamond and ruby rings and over 700 bracelets. The remaining window shows over 300 emerald rings, earrings and various precious stones. The price range is from £15-£2000. All their jewellery is new - they will make to order and undertake repairs.
113 Hatton Garden, EC1 (01-

242 4317). Open 10.00–17.00 Mon to Sat.

Langfords
This delightfully chaotic shop specializes in antique and old silver and Sheffield plate; old model ships and scientific instruments. Some of the model ships are made of bone by Napoleonic prisoners of war.
46/47 Chancery Lane, WC2 (01-405 6402). Open 09.30–17.30 Mon to Fri.

Sothebys
This branch specializes in auctions of books dating from 1830 onwards. The emphasis is on illustrated, travel and children's books. Sales are held every two weeks on Thursday and Friday from 13.00; viewing until midday the day of the sale. Ring for a catalogue.
115 Chancery Lane, WC2 (01-405 7238). Open 09.30–17.00 Mon to Fri.

Newmans Chocolates
Newmans run a chain of shops and their hand-made chocolates are made at a central factory. Recipes are both English and Continental and most chocs are sold loose – you choose and Newmans box them for you.
31 Fleet St, EC4 (no phone). Open 09.30–17.30 Mon to Fri.

Merry Paul Sweetshop
Merry Paul looks far more interesting than the average sweet shop. They specialize in regional British sweets: Edinburgh rock, Kendal mint cake and home-made fudge from Minehead. Other more general confectionery includes Italian chocolates and ice-cream. They do special lines at Christmas and Easter.
59 Fleet St EC4 (01–834 6320). Open 09.00–18.30 Mon to Fri.

Geographia
A useful place to remember for maps, globes and atlases.
63 Fleet St, EC4 (01–353 2701). Open 09.00–17.30 Mon to Fri.

Sharaton Pâtisserie
In a street devoid of shops selling nice things to eat, Sharaton is worth a mention. They make up French bread sandwiches but their main trade is their range of breads, tarts, cream cakes and gateaux. They are part of a large chain with branches throughout London.
97 Fleet St, EC4 (01–624 9287). Open 09.00–18.00 Mon to Wed; 09.00–19.00 Thurs and Fri; 09.00–17.00 Sat.

The Right Price
A reliable source of cheap menswear, particularly T-shirts, shirts, jeans, jerseys and socks.
109 Fleet St, EC4 (01–353 5876). Open 09.00–18.00 Mon to Fri.

Cobham Numismatics
Books on numismatics (coins

and banknotes), modern coins, oriental coins, banknotes, bonds and accessories.
147 Fleet St, EC4 (01–353 9447). Open 08.00–20.00 Mon to Sat.

Gordon Grose Sports
Gordon Grose is a sports clothing and equipment shop specializing in weight-training and lifting equipment. The shop also caters for bowls, cricket, golf, tennis, badminton, squash, swimming, rugby, soccer and hockey.
7–9 Ludgate House, Ludgate Circus, EC4 (01–353 0082). Open 09.00–17.45 Mon to Fri.

Leather Lane Market
A flourishing street market that once dealt exclusively in food and is now full of stalls selling jeans, shirts, dresses, shoes, chamois leathers, fabrics, bags, records, toys, haberdashery, plants, hardware and umbrellas. The food side is mainly concerned with fruit and vegetables but also sells eggs. It is lively and noisy, with everyone shouting their wares to compete with the next door stallholder.
Leather Lane, EC1 (from 10.00–14.00 Mon to Fri only).

Health and Beauty Bar
Pop in here out of the Leather Lane bustle for health foods, ginseng and vitamins.
56-58 Leather Lane, EC1 (01–242 9685). Open 08.30–17.30 Mon to Thurs; 09.00–18.00 Fri.

Newgate Gallery
Virtually opposite the Old Bailey this large gallery sells a wide selection of prints of all styles, which range in price from £15 to £200. They frame on the premises and can offer an overnight service.
114 Newgate St, EC3 (01–606 3955). Open 09.30–18.00 Mon to Fri.

FINSBURY

Taylors
Taylors stock an extensive selection of leathercraft tools. If they're not busy they'll pass on advice to novices.
54 Old St, EC1 (01–253 2592). Open 09.00–17.00 Mon to Fri.

H. J. Brooks & Co
Although they deal mostly with the trade, Brooks will sell from their extensive range of small door fittings to the public. Door handles, knobs and locks; many of them Georgian brass.
136 Old St, EC1 (01–253 3887). Open 09.00–16.30 Mon to Fri.

East West Natural Foods
This very specialist health food shop is part of the Community Health Foundation which uses the entire building for lectures and courses on a variety of obscure subjects; runs a wholefoods restaurant (Seven

Sheaves), and a bookshop specializing in subjects to do with health and nutrition. They keep all the familiar wholefoods – rice, pulses, dried fruit etc., but specialize in macrobiotic foods – fermented soya products (misos and shoyu), dried and fresh sea vegetables and fresh organic fruit and veg. Also a minimal range of natural cosmetics, free from animal products and a range of cast iron and stainless steel cookware.
Community Health Foundation, 196 Old St, E1 (01–251 4076 ask for East West). Open 09.00–19.00 Mon to Sat.

Tyzack's Tools
This is one of the most well established and comprehensive tool and machinery shops in this part of London. They have everything from small hand tools to large pieces of electrical machinery for carpenters and engineers. They are most helpful and have years of experience on what is the right tool for the job.
341 Old St, EC1 (01–739 8301). Open 09.00–17.15 Mon to Fri; 09.00–12.30 on alternate Sats.

Whitecross St
A small but popular market in Clerkenwell which serves both local office workers and residents alike. Especially good on cheap jeans and shirts with only a relatively few stalls selling fruit and vegetables. There are also stalls selling bed linen, towels, plants, old magazines, children's clothes and electrical goods. It gets very crowded from 12.30 till 13.30.
Whitecross St, EC1 (weekday lunchtimes only, not Sat).

Fantasy Studios
Fantasy Studios is a surprising find in this neck of the woods. Dazzling disco clothes designed by theatrical costumer Peggy (of *Some Like it Hot* and *Genevieve* fame) are on sale at Fantasy. Catsuits, brocade jackets, blouses, shirts and trousers for men and women, are made in exclusive glittery fabrics. Prices are far more moderate than West End equivalents.
22 Coronet St, N1 (01–739 1948). Open 11.00–20.00 Tues to Fri; 11.00–15.00 Sat.

J. Smith & Sons
Smiths are wholesale suppliers of metal-working tools, brass, aluminium alloys, copper and silver in wires, sheets, rods and flat bars.
St Johns Sq, EC1 (01–253 1277). Open 09.00–17.00 Mon to Fri; closed for lunch 13.00–14.00.

J.Hewitt & Sons Ltd
Hewitt's reckon to be able to supply everything needed for bookbinding. Their trade warehouse has a counter for the public and helpful staff advise on brushes, bookcloths, resin,

mull, tapes, adhesives, knives, bone folders, typeholders, scissors, leather, thread, etc.
9 St John St, EC1 (01-253 1431). Open 09.00-17.00 Mon to Fri; closed for lunch 13.00-14.00.

Gleave and Co
Go here for parts for old and new watches and clocks. Gleave specialize in complete movements including cases and dials, undertake repairs and also sell new watches and clocks.
111 St John St, EC1 (01-253 1345). Open 08.30-17.30 Mon to Fri.

A. Shoot and Sons
Shoot's sell anything and everything to do with old and modern clocks and watches, including books. They deal mainly with the trade but are happy to advise and sell to those of us without a horological bent.
116 St John St, EC1 (01-253 9462). Open 08.30-17.20 Mon to Fri.

Clerkenwell Screws Ltd
Clerkenwell Screws Ltd say they sell anything with a thread on. They sell screws of all sizes in quantity, mostly to model-makers and instrument-makers, and while they're happy to sell to the public, their minimum order is 100 screws!
107-109 Clerkenwell Rd, EC1 (01-405 1215). Open 09.00-17.30 Mon to Fri.

Woodstruck
A brochure is available which shows the hand-made pine, easy-assembly animal book-shelves made by Woodstruck. Choose from dog, horse, cat, frog, penguin or elephant which stand at either end of the shelf unit.
27 Clerkenwell Close, EC1 (01-251 4079). By appointment.

CITY

W. Thurgood
This 60-year-old shop specializes in cigars from all over the world, cigarettes, pipes and pipe tobacco and a few fancy gifts.
161 Salisbury Hse, London Wall, EC2 (01-628 5437). Open 08.45-17.30 Mon to Fri.

Mitchell, Inman and Co
Cloth Fair is a tiny street opposite the Church of St Bartholomew The Great. It is a pocket of peace behind Smithfield Meat Market and is now owned by the Landmark Trust who make sure nothing is modernized. The interior of this long established felt and fabric shop is quite unchanged since it began trading some time in the 1800s. They are really wholesalers but are happy to sell direct to the public who have taken the trouble to seek them out. The cloths are stacked in huge rolls on and in mahogany counters and cupboards. A large clock

ticks peacefully as the scissors snip the cloth. If you're interested, and they aren't too busy you can see their earliest order book.
Cloth Fair, EC1 (01–606 8708). Open 09.00–16.00 Mon to Fri; closed 12.30–13.30 for lunch.

Billingsgate
London's wholesale fish market looks much the same as it did when it was founded in Victorian days. Traders wear special black flat hats for carrying heavy boxes on their heads. Shellfish, smoked fish, freshwater fish and fish from all over the country are sold in large quantities only. They don't appreciate onlookers who aren't buying. The market is scheduled to move to the West India Dock.
Billingsgate, EC1. Open 04.00–08.00 Mon to Fri.

London Architectural Salvage and Supply Co
This huge warehouse is stacked full of items which have been ripped out of old houses and churches to be re-sold to customers who wish to restore their own old houses. Fireplaces, doorcases, panelling shutters, stairs and balustrades are all on sale along with all kinds of wood for flooring. Prices are by no means knock down but are very reasonable.
Mark St Depository, Mark St, EC2 (01–739 0376). Open 09.30–17.30 Mon to Fri; 10.00–12.30 Sat.

Edward Marcus
Edward Marcus specialize in mostly new and some second-hand optical instruments: binoculars, theatre glasses, telescopes, microscopes and barometers.
Moorhouse, 7 Moorfields, Moorgate, EC2 (01–638 0390). Open 09.00–17.00 Mon to Fri.

Exmouth St Market
A small, well-attended market for food; fruit and veg on the stalls, bacon from Higgins (Farringdon Rd end) and meat from Medcalf. At the weekend it's good for clothes. There's a useful shop for home DIY on the corner with Farringdon Rd called Nudecor.
Rosebery Ave, EC1. Open 09.00–17.00 Mon to Sat; half-day Thurs.

Farringdon Rd Market
A small market run by one trader appears most mornings opposite the telephone exchange in Farringdon Rd. Old books, manuscripts and papers are the speciality.
Farringdon Rd, EC1. Open 06.00 until mid-afternoon Mon to Fri (weather permitting).

Fullerscopes
For over 150 years the largest Fullerscope brass telescopes have been made on the prem-

ises. Photos show men at work in the days when their workshop was lit by gaslight, and the shop seems little changed since. There are telescopes from 1" to 24" in diameter and virtually everything to do with astronomy; also optical instruments and binoculars.
63 Farringdon Rd, EC1 (01–405 2156). Open 09.30–17.00 Mon to Fri.

Smithfield Market
There are loads of butchers around Smithfield (notably Harts Corner) who sell in bulk to the general public. The wholesale meat market deals only with traders who are *really* buying in bulk and do so regularly. Row upon row of whole pig and cow carcasses can be seen from the road.
Farringdon Rd, EC1. Open 05.00–10.00 Mon to Fri.

W. A. E. Busby
A tiny, long-established home brewers' emporium where sensible, helpful advice is plentiful. They will make up a kit to order but are more in favour of asking people exactly what equipment they've got and what stage they are at and then selling them the bare essentials. They also stock a wide range of dried fruits and flowers.
96 Farringdon Rd, EC1 (01–837 2273). Open 08.30–17.30 Mon to Fri; 08.30–13.00 Sat.

G. Rushbrooke (Smithfield) Ltd
In the heart of Smithfield, the meat market, Rushbrooke's sell all butchering equipment. Obviously they deal mostly with butchers but are useful to the general public for cutting blocks, knives and large hooks.
67 Charterhouse St, EC1 (01–253 2744/5501). Open 07.00–15.30 Mon to Fri.

Leadenhall Market
This wholesale fruit, vegetable, poultry, game and fish market is centred around an impressive Victorian hall built in 1880. Retail shops/stalls are a boon for City workers and superb fresh and reasonably priced produce is available. An extensive range of shellfish and fish on the slab is sold by Ashdowns; game, meat and their own sausages by Ashby; delicatessen, cheese and eggs from other stalls. Also good garden sundries.
Gracechurch St, EC3. Open 07.00–16.00 Mon to Fri (but slackens after lunch).

Treasure Island
Formerly called Solution, this shop acts as an oasis in the desert of the City, selling china, glass, all kinds of cookware, plus gifts and wrapping paper. Even some jewellery is on sale. Things are not cheap.
Bassishaw Highwalk, Basinghall St, EC2 (01–638 2007). Open 09.00–18.00 Mon to Fri.

4
EAST END

Liverpool St and Whitechapel, Hackney, Shoreditch and Bethnal Green.

Anywhere east of the City of London is known as the East End. Originally the term referred to those neighbourhoods which fringed the Thames where the London Docks flourished till about 10 years ago. In fact dozens of separate areas make up this huge urban sprawl, from Shoreditch to Stratford and beyond.

It's overriding characteristic is inner-city blight. Large scale industry moved out along with the decline of the docks but small businesses pepper the entire area. And while the place is hardly as glamorous as points west, there are many small specialist shops, a range of exciting, vibrant and cheap street markets and a host of ethnic food and clothes shops which have sprung up as new communities have moved into old working class areas. The strong Jewish influence in the East End accounts for the plentiful seafood stalls and rag trade 'cabbage' clothes in all the street markets.

TRANSPORT

Liverpool St/Whitechapel
Tube stations: Liverpool St, Bethnal Green, Wapping, Whitechapel, Mile End.
Buses: 149, 253.

Hackney
Tube stations: London Fields (BR), Old St, Dalston Junction (BR).
Buses: 6, 22, 35, 48, 49, 55, 67, 76, 97, 243, 253.

Shoreditch/Bethnal Green
Buses: 22, 48, 76, 97, 149, 243.

LOCAL OPENING HOURS

All the shops mentioned in this section seem to have varying opening hours. Old established service shops operate Monday to Friday while newer shops close on Monday. General street markets are open on Sunday.

REFRESHMENTS

There are plenty of cafés in the East End but

Centerprise Community Bookshop

136 Kingsland High St, E8 *open 10.00–18.30 Tues to Thurs; 10.00-17.30 Fri and Sat* run a community café serving coffee, tea and snacks.

LIVERPOOL ST AND WHITECHAPEL

Hadley Hobbies

The reason this shop is open on Sundays is its proximity to Petticoat Lane market. The shop is full of all kinds of models from simple Airfix Spitfire kits to expensive model railway systems. And not surprisingly it has become a centre for model enthusiasts, more of whom are grown-up than children.

131 Middlesex St, E1 (01–283 9870). Open 09.30–18.00 Mon to Fri; closed Sat; 09.30–14.00 Sun.

Brick Lane Market

A few minutes' walk from the famous Petticoat Lane is the Sunday market frequented by the local community and Londoners who appreciate its authenticity. It spreads well beyond the confines of Brick Lane. To the west of the Lane are many stalls selling brand new goods at much cheaper prices than you can buy them almost anywhere else: clothes, groceries, china, linen, tools, electrical goods, sports goods, carpets, records, bicycle and car accessories and electrical fittings are just some of the bargains to be found there. To the east of the Lane, the junk or secondhand section begins down Cheshire St. Even though junk has got pricey and many dealers go down the Lane, it's still a treasure trove of bric à brac, old furniture, old clothes and daft things you see and decide you can't possibly do without. Avoid the animals on sale by Bethnal Green Rd part of the market.

Brick Lane, E1 (Sunday mornings).

Columbia Rd Market

Around 25 stalls sell a selection of seasonal cut flowers, house plants, bedding plants, trees, compost and herbs. They hold a good Dutch auction which is particularly good for trays of bedding plants. All the shops lining the road are open.

Bethnal Green Rd, E1. Open 09.00–13.00 Sun.

Petticoat Lane Market

This market is world famous and is all most tourists see of the so-called East End. In fact it happens in an ever extending area around the Lane and Middlesex St and sells mainly cheap clothes, shoes, accessories, jewellery and electrical

goods. It's always crowded and not always as cheap as you might think. But it certainly has a great deal of atmosphere. Recently it has become so much of a tourist attraction that many locals tend to avoid it.
Petticoat Lane, E1 (Sun mornings).

Spitalfields Market
Established in 1682, Spitalfields is one of the five main London wholesale fruit, veg and flower markets. Like all these markets, they don't object to selling to the public as long as you don't hamper their business.
Brushfield St, E1. Open 04.00–10.00 Mon to Sat.

The Great Wapping Wine Co
The bonus of wine buying at Wapping Wine is that you can taste before you buy. The large warehouse, overlooking the river, is full of all kinds of wines from all over Europe. You can only buy by the case but the wines are still cheap. They are all bought cheaply from wine dealers who have a relatively small amount of a particular wine left and will let it go to Wapping at a lower price. Gets crowded on Sunday mornings.
St Helen's Wharf, 60 Wapping High St, E1 (01–488 3988). Open 10.00–18.00 Mon to Sat; 11.00–17.00 Sun.

The Noble Grape
Another discount wine warehouse close to the river; they also sell only by the case. Marginally more expensive than their friendly rivals, Wapping Wine down the road, they seem to be particularly strong on German wines. It gets busy on Sundays.
26 The Highway, E1 (01–488 4788). Open 10.00–18.00 Mon to Sat; 11.00–17.00 Sun.

Rogg
The full range of kosher food and Jewish specialities can be found at this family run, old-fashioned Jewish delicatessen and general food shop. They salt and cook their own beef and tongue on the premises, and the meats can be bought piping hot. Also fresh pickled cucumbers from wooden barrels, chopped liver, gefilte fish balls, chopped and pickled herrings, kippers, smoked salmon and haddock.
137 Cannon Street Rd, E1 (01–488 3386). Open 09.30–18.00 Mon to Fri; 07.00–14.00 Sun; closed Sat.

The Houndsditch Warehouse
This famous four-storey warehouse is really a shop selling all kinds of household merchandise from three-piece suites down to coffee grinders. Not quite as attractive pricewise these days when there are big discount warehouses all over the place, but certainly worth checking if you're looking for anything

in particular and if you're in the Petticoat Lane area on Sunday morning.
Houndsditch, EC3 (01-283 3131). Open 09.00-17.30 Mon to Thurs; 09.00-17.00 Fri; 09.30-13.30 Sun; closed Sats.

Whitechapel Rd Market
A mixed market, with many of the stalls which live during the week in Whitecross St coming down on Fridays and Saturdays. Two or three cheapish jewellery stalls make this market a bit different from its nearest neighbours, Roman Rd and Brick Lane. Once again, new clothes feature strongly here. But the stall-holders seem to be a little more original than many of their colleagues elsewhere. American imported clothes are sometimes to be found, women's formal wear and swimwear, as well as a very popular and fashionable bag stall. Not much fruit and veg but an excellent secondhand record stall plus another one selling cheap rugs keep the market popular and original. Best days Friday and Saturday.
Whitechapel Rd, E1 (Mon to Sat).

Blooms Delicatessen
This world-famous kosher Jewish restaurant has a delicatessen bar at the front of their premises. Salt beef, pickled herrings and chopped liver are among the delicacies which you can buy to take out. Also lots of Blooms own tinned foodstuffs and other Jewish specialities.
90 Whitechapel Rd, E1 (01-247 6835). Open 10.00-22.00 Mon to Thurs; 10.00-15.00 Fri; 10.00-22.00 Sun; closed Sat.

S. Baron Ltd
This company describe themselves as smoked salmon, continental salad and delicatessen merchants. They stock vast ranges of smoked fish and poultry, pâtés, frozen and marinated fish, plus all kinds of sauces like mayonnaise, sea food sauce, horseradish and mustards, as well as pickles and olives. They are basically bulk merchants but sell retail also.
Assembly Passage, Mile End Rd, E1 (01-790 8282). Open 10.15-15.30 Mon to Fri.

Carpet City
There is a chain of these shops which are part of the huge Buffalo Discount Warehouses operation. They specialize in room-length end of roll carpets of all qualities and prices. You might not find exactly the right size, colour and price on your first visit but after a time or two you can usually find a bargain. All their stock is new and unused.
79/89 Mile End Rd, E1 (01-790 2008). Open 09.00-18.00 Mon to Sat.

Tall Trend
This shop, on the borders of

Stepney and Whitechapel, manufactures boots for the retail trade but also sells direct to the public at an average of £10 below West End prices. They specialize in Western-style boots (ready-made), but will make boots to order in most styles. Excellent bargains regularly available.
124 Mile End Rd, E1. (01–790 5532). Open 09.00–17.00 Mon to Fri.

Balls Brothers Cash and Carry
Balls Brothers are wine shippers who also have a chain of off-licences. Their wholesale outlet is a large building near Bethnal Green tube. It acts as an ordinary wine shop where you can buy single bottles of wine at cheaper than their off-licence prices, and you can also order by the case and get further reductions. They have occasional tastings and informative, friendly service. And of course, some excellent wines, not all of which are too expensive.
313 Cambridge Heath Rd, E2 (01–739 6466). Open 10.00–18.00 Mon to Fri; 10.00–14.00 Sat.

HACKNEY

Towards Jupiter
All the shelves of this popular wholefood shop are lined with jars of herbs. Fresh, organically-grown vegetables in season are always on sale along with all the cereals, pulses and nuts we've come to expect from these kinds of shops. This one is run by members of the Rudolf Steiner Society, and one feature that sets it apart from its peers is a range of beautifully made wooden toys, which are not cheap but are still excellent value for money.
191 Mare St, E8 (01–985 5394). Open 09.30–17.30 Mon to Sat.

Paul A. Daniels Ltd
Mr Daniels runs a wholesale and distributing paint service and he regularly sells privately (to the public) amazing paint bargains. They are usually sold in tins with bent or damaged lids, but who cares at his prices? Leading manufacturers, but we can't mention names.
13 Terrace Rd, South Hackney, E9. Open 09.00–16.00 Mon to Fri; 09.00–13.00 Sat.

Benny's Textile Corner
Benny only sells his material by the 3- and 5-yard minimum piece, so this isn't the place to go for the odd remnant to run up a blouse. What you will find is a stunning array of materials geared to the West Indian and Asian market, most fabrics being highly coloured and strongly patterned. It's unusual, good value and a highly decorative shop.
1 Stoke Newington Rd, N16

(01–254 7998). Open 09.30–18.00 Mon to Sat; half-day Thurs; open Sun morning.

Ridley Rd
One of the most colourful and cheap street markets in East London. Dalston is very well served with fresh fruit and vegetables and this market sells a range of foodstuffs to suit the multi-national local community: West Indian, Asian, Jewish and Greek stalls are all there along with the traditional potato and greens variety. Reggae record stalls play music, creating a very relaxed atmosphere, while other stalls sell cheap jeans, hardware, underwear, stationery, haberdashery and much more. The market is much loved by all who shop there; the best days are Fri and Sat.
Ridley Rd, E8 (Mon to Sat; half-day Thurs).

SHOREDITCH AND BETHNAL GREEN

F. H. Brundle
Brundles wholesale all types of nails and wire. They are a specialist company with a trade counter at their offices and are happy to sell their ordinary and not so ordinary wares (old-fashioned cut nails for floors, lath nails, copper boat-building nails, square twisted nails, etc.) to the public.
25 Culford Rd, N1 (01–254 2384). Open 09.00–17.00 Mon to Fri.

Centerprise Community Bookshop
Probably the best general bookshop in east London with special sections on left-wing politics, feminism, local community writing, and a particularly good section on children's books. Next door to the bookshop is a community café which opens at the same time as the shop and some evenings too. It is run by helpful staff who are happy to order titles not in stock.
136 Kingsland High St, E8 (01–254 9632). Open 10.00–18.30 Tues to Thurs; 10.00–17.30 Fri and Sat.

Two Brewers
Fifty different bottled beers from around 40 different breweries makes this off-licence a real ale fanatic's paradise. Draught beer is also on sale in plastic polybins and you can buy up to 72 pints of various different draught ales for a party.
8 Pitfield St, N1 (01–739 3701). Open 11.00–18.30 Mon to Fri; 10.00–15.00 Sat.

N. Jonas & Sons Ltd
Jonas wholesale whole skins of many types of leather. They are happy to sell to one-off retail customers, but point out that they won't cut skins (whole

skins average 20 sq ft) and don't sell off-cuts.
148 Shoreditch High St, E1 (01-739 5450). Open 09.00–17.00 Mon to Fri.

Flip
A vast emporium (20,000 sq ft) of cheap new and used American clothes imported by Alice Pollock and American Paul Wolf. Absurdly cheap baseball, fatigue, tweed and other jackets; tuxedos; jeans; trousers; wool overcoats; numerous types of T-shirt, etc. - all cleaned and pressed. Clothes are from the 40s to 60s period and cheaper than street markets.
96–98 Curtain Rd, EC2 (01-729 4341). Open 10.00–18.30 Mon to Sat; 10.00–15.00 Sun. Also at 191 Kings Rd, SW3 (01-352 4332). Open 10.00–18.30 Mon to Sat.

Roman Rd Market
This market, just north of Bow, sells an amazing range of cheap, new clothes commonly known in the trade as 'cabbage'. They sell at half the price you'd pay in West End shops and represent excellent value. For such a well established and famous street market there are remarkably few fruit and vegetable stalls, and the ones there are usually quite expensive, even if they do still sell high grade produce. Here, as in most East End street markets, you'll find the obligatory seafood stalls, selling herrings, smoked salmon, jellied eels, prawns, whelks, winkles and crabs. Cheap carpet stalls are to be found, too, along with some of the cheapest and most stylish children's clothes. Best days definitely Fri and Sat.
Roman Rd, E3 (Mon to Sat).

Friends' Food
One of the cheapest wholefood shops in London let alone the East End. It is an independent but integral part of the Western Buddhist Order's complex on the site of an old fire station. They have a complete range of wholefoods and have recently opened a bulk store, for large orders, round the corner at 247 Globe Rd, E2.
51 Roman Rd, E2 (01-981 1225). Open 10.00–18.00 Mon to Fri; 09.00–18.00 Sat.

5
ISLINGTON

Pentonville, Highbury and Islington, Holloway.

Much of this area is residential with little of outstanding shopping interest. Holloway's roads are peppered with Greek and continental all-purpose food shops and the very occasional specialist shop.

The bulk of Islington's shopping action is centred around the famous antiques centre, Camden Passage. Antique shops and the open air market sell virtually every type of antique. Small specialist shops like Strike One for old clocks, Clozo for period clothes and fun ceramics and Rau for ethnic clothes and jewellery, proliferate in all the side streets. The nearby Chapel Street Market sells food and junk and is lined with cheap food shops.

Wide, busy, scruffy Holloway Rd has the only department store in Islington, a branch of John Lewis called Jones Brothers. The equally wide, busy and scruffy Upper St and Essex Rd house most of the few interesting shops away from the Passage – war relics at A Call To Arms, old tools at Old Woodworking Tools and superb freshly smoked fish from Steve Hatt. Pentonville, the part of Islington bordering King's Cross, boasts a working farm which sells its produce.

See also City and Bloomsbury.

TRANSPORT

Pentonville
Tube stations: King's Cross, Angel.
Buses: 14, 30, 74.

Highbury and Islington
Tube stations: Highbury and Islington, Essex Rd, Angel.
Buses: 19, 30, 73

Holloway
Tube stations: Holloway Rd, Drayton Park.
Buses: 172, 271

LOCAL OPENING HOURS

Half-day closing in Islington is Wednesday, although many shops ignore it and close early on Saturday. Many antique shops in Camden Passage close all day Monday.

REFRESHMENTS

There are plenty of cafés in Upper St and Islington High St. On market days there is a cheap tea, coffee, buns and sandwich bar upstairs in the Flea Market Arcade, Camden Passage.

SisterWrite
190 Upper St, N1. *Open 11.00–19.00 Tues to Fri; 10.00–18.00 Sat.* This non-profit making feminist bookshop plan opening coffee room by the time this book appears in print.

PENTONVILLE

Jeffries
Jeffries do all their own smoking on the premises (haddocks, cod fillets, mackerel fillets and cods' roe) and boil their own crabs in vinegar. They also sell live crabs, live winkles, whelks and most fresh fish in season. They will get specific fish in specially if given a day's notice.
343 Caledonian Rd, N1 (01–607 2027). Open 08.00–17.30 Tues, Wed and Sat; 08.00–13.00 Thurs and 08.00–18.30 Fri.

Barnsbury Heath Foods
Dave and Pat, the couple that run this pleasant shop, sell a wide range of wholefoods, plus vitamins, minerals and some macrobiotic foods. There is a good selection of herbs both medicinal and culinary, and they also sell vegetarian cheese, yoghurt, bread, natural cosmetics and some books.
285 Caledonian Rd, N1 (01–607 7344). Open 09.30–17.30 Mon to Sat.

Vintage Record Centre
Mike Gordon and Pete Dickerson have been buying and selling old and vintage records at Roman Way for ten years. They import mint condition rhythm and blues and rock 'n' roll golden oldies from all over the world and buy in second-hand chart-oriented records dating from the 1950s up to a few years ago. They cater for collectors and less serious buyers, buying in collections and never touching jazz.
91 Roman Way, N7 (01–607 8586). Open 10.00–17.00 Wed to Fri; 10.00–17.30 Sat.

Freightliners Farm
You may find it hard to believe but there is a working, productive farm in the heart of Islington. It used to be round the corner in York Way and has been operating here as a charity

for the past two years. They sell manure very cheaply (you take your own sack) and have limited supplies of produce which includes eggs, yoghurt, milk and cheese.
Sheringham Rd, N7 (01-609 0467). Open 09.30–18.30.

Autumn 61
Ellen and Robert Devitt have an eye for good quality and interesting old clothes, objects, china, furnishings, and junk/antiques. Everything is appropriately cleaned up and regularly includes Art Deco objects, '30s mirrors, lighting, jewellery, books, lots of china (including entire services) and furniture.
61 Amwell St, EC1 (01-278 1140). Open 11.30–18.00 Mon to Sat; closed Thurs.

HIGHBURY AND ISLINGTON

Ryness
Ryness is a small chain of commercial and domestic electrical accessories. Their speciality is lighting and they keep a wide and varied range at this and all branches.
7 Caledonian Rd, N1 (01-636 8491). Open 09.00–18.00 Mon to Sat. Also at 57 Camden High St, NW1; 326 Edgware Rd, W2; and 54 Fleet St, EC4.

Steve Hatt
In a small parade of shops, way past the fashionable part of Essex Rd, is this excellent fishmonger. It has been run by the Hatt family for three generations and the present proprietor, also called Steve, keeps a surprisingly wide range of superb quality fish and shellfish. Game and turkeys are also available at Christmas, eggs and chickens throughout the year. Locally Hatt's are particularly favoured for their home-cured fish, smoked in the traditional smoke-hole behind the shop, and often on sale while it's still hot.
88 Essex Rd, N1 (01-226 3963). Open 08.00–17.15 Tues to Sat; 08.00–13.00 Thurs.

Jack Hobbs
Previously in Fleet St and then *the* place for cricket equipment, Jack Hobbs is now a more general sports outfitters. They still offer a very wide selection of cricket bats, leg guards, shirts, trousers, socks, bags, boots, etc.
11a Islington High St, N1 (01-837 8611). Open 09.30–17.25 Mon to Sat; half-day Thurs 09.30–12.25.

Rau
Entering Rau is like discovering an Aladdin's cave. It's crammed with things old and antique from Eastern countries including Afghanistan, India, Palestine, and Uzbekistan. Beautiful chunky silver jewellery and boxes; some inlaid with coral

and turquoise are a hefty investment, while many of the clothes are hand-woven and embroidered and seem too fragile to wear. Also superb elaborate wall hangings, tent and animal trappings, and upstairs kelims, rugs and carpet bags in various states of repair.
36 Islington Green, N1 (01-359 5337). Open 11.00–17.00 Mon to Fri; 10.00–17.00 Fri and 10.00–18.00 Sat.

Camden Passage
One of London's most attractive antique centres. (See separate entries.) There is an open-air antiques and bric-à-brac market, together with various covered arcades in the Passage, such as Flea Market Arcade, with two floors of jewellery, brass, militaria, porcelain and furniture; and Georgian Village, with 34 vaults for silver, 50 stalls for antiques, 25 antique shops and galleries.
Off Upper St, N1. Market open Wed mornings and all day Sat.

The Snuff Shop
Over 50 pre-packaged blends of snuff from makers Wilsons and Fribourg and Treyer can be bought at this small, specialist shop. They also sell large spotted snuff handkerchiefs, pipe tobaccos, pipe stands, and some antique pipes. Also a range of speciality teas, gift packaged.
8 Camden Passage, N1 (01-359 9417). Open 09.30–18.00 Mon to Sat.

S. E. Nicholls, Ye Olde Clocke Shop
Mr Nicholls, whose family has run the splendid Ye Olde Clocke Shop since 1869, always displays a fine selection of fob watches in this cramped window. Apart from selling (mainly old) watches, clocks and jewellery, Mr Nicholls' forte is repair work. He's one of the few repairers I know who willingly takes on repairs to old clocks and watches.
25 Camden Passage, N1 (no phone). Open 10.00–18.00 Mon to Wed and Sat; closed Thurs; 14.00–18.00 Fri.

D. S. Levey
The current Mr Levey was born above the shop and has just celebrated 100 years of sewing machine business. The window alone, with its display of reconditioned sewing machines; odd, newish bric-à-brac; old-fashioned sewing machine accessories like hemmers, zip tuckers, rufflers, needles and bobbins, old 78 records; spanners at 5p; mirrors and old books, can keep me occupied for a good 15 minutes. Inside the shelves are crammed with machines for sale (all guaranteed for 12 months), those waiting to be collected after repair and more boxes of bits and pieces. Mr Levey does his repairs behind a counter and

all his spare parts are kept in wooden drawers clearly labelled.
33 Camden Passage, N1 (01–226 3711). Open 08.30–16.00 Tues to Sat.

Anthea Knowles Rare Toys
Anthea Knowles collects and sells old toys: mechanical money boxes, pre-war die-cast toys, early locomotives and British lead soldiers. She also sells old dolls on behalf of a friend. Prices are surprisingly high, even to some dealers.
51 Camden Passage, N1 (01–607 0846). Open 10.00–16.00 Mon to Sat.

Clozo
Clive and Ros Jennings change their stock at Clozo according to the latest fashion trends but they are essentially period clothes dealers specializing in the 1930–60 period. They regularly turn up great finds in old warehouses and stocks move fast. Complementary accessories like coloured plastic sandals, lurex ties and socks, perspex jewellery and brooches are always on sale too.
1 Camden Walk, N1 (01–359 6474). Open 10.00–18.00 Mon to Sat.

Strike One Ltd
Subtitled 'Clocks For Collectors' Strike One has been specializing in 18th-century and early 19th-century English wall clocks for over ten years. All clocks sold are in perfect working order and have one year's international guarantee. All clock and watch repairs undertaken.
1a Camden Walk, Islington Green, N1 (01–226 9709). Open 09.00–17.00 Mon to Sat.

Chapel St Market
Most people know Chapel St as an essentially fruit and veg market, with dairy produce, tinned foods, china, fabrics and a smattering of new clothes stalls. At the weekend it's also a thriving secondhand market (at the junction with Grant St) where an assortment of one person's rubbish and another's bargains is laid out on the pavement and on trestle tables. On Sundays a lot of the shops – butcher, baker and Sainsburys – are open. There is also an excellent baker on the Liverpool Rd end.
Chapel St, N1. Open seven days a week. Best days Fri, Sat and Sun.

Olga Stores Ltd
Hidden in Penton St, Olga Sammarco's Italian grocery and delicatessen is a must for pasta lovers. Olga's are the sole importers of one of the best pastas made in Italy. Called *di cecco*, it's available in 65 different shapes at Olga's along with Parma ham, salamis, and other Italian cooked meats, olives, olive oil, bread, and tinned and

bottled Italian specialities. There is also an off-licence with speciality wines from Siena.
30 Penton St, N1 (01-837 5467). Open 08.00–18.00 Mon to Sat; 09.00–13.00 Sun; half-day Thurs.

Lorna Shoes
Mr Lass stocks bargains in women's Italian shoes; and he specializes in small and large sizes. Styles tend to be on the conservative side.
38 Upper St, N1 (01-226 4565). Open 09.30–17.30 Mon to Sat; closed Thurs.

Call To Arms
Tony Bradley does a roaring trade in war relics at his 16-year-old shop. He specializes in all military clothes, of no particular period, particularly Nazi German uniforms. Also weapons, buttons, flags, etc., but if Tony hasn't got your particular fancy, he'll find it for you. There is also a uniform hire service for fancy dress.
79 Upper St, N1 (01-359 0501). Open 10.30–18.00 Mon to Sat.

Geranium
Bridget Reeves and Maggie McCarthy have a shop full of pine furniture which regularly includes Victorian dressers, tables, chests of drawers and chairs. They make up to order tables, bedheads and shelves using old wood, offer a stripping service for small pieces of furniture; sell Deco lamps and kitsch objects.
121 Upper St, N1 (01-359 4281). Open 10.00–18.00 Mon to Sat.

Brew It Yourself
William Tayleur, a noted authority on the subject of brewing it yourself, and his son run this pleasantly old-fashioned shop. They stock everything for the wine- and beer-maker from a simple kit to all the separate items. There's plenty of advice and often free (empty) wine bottles for the taking.
135/6 Upper St, N1 (01-226 0252). Open 09.00–18.00 Mon to Fri; 09.00–13.00 Sat.

Sister Write
Sister Write is a non-profit-making women's cooperative bookshop. It is pleasantly and informally run with a notice board for feminist events and the promise of a coffee room by the time this book is published. There are lots of posters, sympathetic magazines, non-sexist children's books, imports from America and books on health, politics, poetry and fiction, all with a feminist slant. They operate a mail order catalogue and can get any book to order.
190 Upper St, N1 (01-226 9782). Open 11.00–19.00 Tues to Fri; 10.00–18.00 Sat.

Smokes
This attractive shop seems to stock virtually every brand of cigarette manufactured in most countries. They also sell a limited range of greeting cards and prints, and offer a picture-framing service.
204 Upper St, N1 (01-226 0226). Open 07.00–19.00 Mon to Sat; 07.00–13.00 Sun.

The Market
Despite its very ordinary supermarket layout, this general food shop has a few surprises. It's open late, seven days a week in an otherwise quiet area; has an above average delicatessen counter with a choice of continental cheeses, salamis, cold meats and pâtés; plus a decent range of less familiar fruit and vegetables which can be self-selected and weighed. One way or another (tinned, frozen, fresh, bottled or packeted) The Market can supply virtually any food you require. Also an off-licence.
215/215 Upper St, N1 (01-359 5386). Open 09.00–21.00 seven days a week.

Old Woodworking Tools
Tony Barwick is a mine of information about tools; he has been collecting and selling old tools for years and opened this shop two years ago. Eighty per cent of his tools are in working order. They are between 50 and 300 years old and are for the trades of woodcarving, carpentry, ship building and musical instrument making. Most are far cheaper and better quality than their modern equivalent. Real bargains can be had for a few pence from the dip-in boxes outside the shop.
228 Upper St, N1 (01-359 9313). Open 09.30–18.00 Mon to Fri; 10.30–18.00 Sat.

Fallen Angels
Ann Gunn's shop is a bit like visiting a big one-stall jumble sale; stock varies from day to day but she can be relied upon for velvet curtains and clothes from the Victorian era to the 1950s.
314 Upper St, N1 (01-226 0160). Open 12.00–18.00 Mon to Sat.

HOLLOWAY

The Little Shoebox
Mr Spyrou has been hand-making boots and shoes for the likes of Gary Glitter and Elton John as well as us humbler folk for 17 years. He's a craftsman, very quick when necessary (he's been known to complete orders within 24 hours and sometimes makes a pair of shoes while you wait!) and surprisingly reasonable. All styles/design ideas can be worked out and adapted from a display of footwear in the shop.
89 Holloway Rd, N7 (01-607

1247). Open 08.00–19.00 Mon to Fri; 08.00–18.00 Sat.

Pentonville Rubber Co
This third generation business sells all densities of foam, mostly for mattresses and cushions, foam furniture covered in a vast range of materials, floor cushions, bean bags and foam chips for DIY. Pentonville Rubber is also a specialist rubber manufacturer making mouldings, matting, tubing, sheeting, PVC and plastic vinyls. They are happy to give advice about any aspect of their business.
164 Holloway Rd, N7 (01–609 2700). Open 09.30–17.30 Mon to Fri; and 10.00–16.00 Sat. Also at 52 Pentonville Rd, N1.

Central London Stores
The Myers family run this enormous warehouse overflowing with stocks of surplus bedding, carpets, linen and towels. Prices are ridiculously cheap – they buy in huge quantities from auctions of government surplus and hotel fittings.
100–106 Mackenzie Rd, N7 (01–609 0091). Open 10.00–17.00 Mon, Wed and Fri; 10.00–13.00 Sats.

6
CAMDEN AND HAMPSTEAD

Kentish Town, Camden Town/Chalk Farm, Euston/King's Cross, Hampstead (including Belsize Park).

Euston and King's Cross, like most railway termini, are rather dead areas. British Rail's Collectors' Corner and the army surplus empire Laurence Corner are two of Euston's few interesting shops. Surprisingly, two quality wood craftsmen hide away in a King's Cross backwater. Camden Town is rich in good food, specialist and craft shops and has a flourishing street market in Whitecross St. Parkway, Regents Park Rd, Camden High St and Chalk Farm Rd are the spokes which radiate out from Commercial Place, home of Dingwalls Market and craft workshops. The area thrives on Sundays and is a colourful spot for a weekend shopping spree cum outing. Kentish Town is drab by comparison. The high street houses the inimitable Tempe Davies (home goods) and Chamberlaines (bikes) but is otherwise rather ordinary. Several interesting shops can be found in Belsize Village though the greatest density is in Hampstead itself. Hampstead's food shopping is centred in the high street – a community market and several delicatessens – but many specialist food shops are to be found in back alleys. For the best bread look on either side of the village: at Rumbolds in Southend Rd and Louis in Heath St. Other shops cater for all tastes but particularly for the literary minded and followers of fashion. Flask Walk, one of the many little alleyways in Hampstead, has a concentration of interesting shops.

See also Bloomsbury, City, Marylebone and West End.

TRANSPORT

Kentish Town
Tube stations: Kentish Town, Gospel Oak (BR).
Buses: 27, 134, 214.

Camden Town/Chalk Farm
Tube stations: Camden Town, Chalk Farm, Camden Rd (BR).
Buses: 31, 68, 74.

Euston/King's Cross
Tube stations: Euston, King's Cross.
Buses: 14, 30, 73.

Hampstead
Tube stations: Hampstead, Belsize Park, Hampstead Heath (BR).
Buses: 31, 268.

LOCAL OPENING HOURS

Dingwalls Market, open only on Sat and Sun, has altered the opening hours of many shops in Chalk Farm. The area is a flourishing Sunday shopping centre and most shops re-open on Tuesday. Other shops in Camden Town and Hampstead vary their half-day; some close on Wed afternoon, others Thurs and a few on Sat.

REFRESHMENTS

Dingwalls Market
Chalk Farm Rd, NW1
Semi open-air stall selling hot drinks and delicious wholefood snacks. Also **Sunwheel** wholefood café opposite, for similar, but sit-down.

Louis Pâtisserie
32 Heath St, NW3
Open 09.30–18.30
Very busy Hungarian pâtisserie; queues form for their delicious cakes, croissants, tea and coffee.

Hampstead Community Market
High St, Hampstead, NW3
Open 09.30–18.00 Mon to Sat.
Café in the centre of market, coffee, tea, home-made cakes and light meals.

Hampstead Pâtisserie and Tea Rooms
9 South End Rd, NW3
Open 09.00–21.00 Tues to Sun.
Tearooms serving Austrian and Italian pastries, cakes, croissants, etc.

KENTISH TOWN

Tempe Davies
Tempe Davies takes great pride in her reasonable prices. She chooses all the stock, which encompasses most kitchenware, rugs and other household goods. Everything is practical and attractive, and includes Moroccan blankets; Peruvian, Colombian and Indian rugs and wallhangings; glass, china, pottery, pine furniture (some readily available, some to

order); a variety of quality cooking utensils including the less usually available smokers, chicken bricks and equipment for other cooking techniques. Stock always changing.
107 Kentish Town Rd, NW1 (01–485 1258). Open 10.00–18.00 Mon to Sat.

Kristin Baybars
Tiny and delightful shop run by Heals toy buyer where the speciality is craftsmen-made and small toys at prices to suit all pockets.
3 Mansfield Rd, NW3 (01–267 0934). Open 10.00–17.30 Tues to Sat. Suns at Camden Lock Market.

Honky Tonk Records
The stock covers a broad spectrum of reggae (including 'pre-release' records) soul/disco, rock and new wave, and they attempt to stock all titles from the mushrooming independent 'little labels'.
235 Kentish Town Rd, NW5 (01–267 3995). Open 10.00–18.00 Mon to Sat.

CAMDEN TOWN/ CHALK FARM

Marine Ices
Delicious non-dairy ice-creams made with vegetable fats and fresh fruit. There are 18 different flavours, sold in various sizes of tubs and cornets, also fresh fruit sorbets. At the back of the shop a small licensed restaurant serves pasta, pizzas, coffee (and, of course, ice-creams).
8 Haverstock Hill, NW3 (01–485 8898). Open 11.00–23.00 seven days a week; restaurant closed on Sundays.

Outgroans
Daniele Harris sells all types of children's clothes and equipment like sheets and blankets for new-born babies up to ten-year-olds. Most stock is nearly-new but there is plenty, too, brought from shops closing down. Daniele also acts as a contact for people wishing to sell and exchange large baby hardware – cots, prams, push chairs, etc.
190 Albany St, NW1 (01–387 2018). Open 10.00–17.00 Tues to Fri; 10.00–13.00 Sat.

21 Antiques
21 Antiques may look indistinguishable from its many counterparts in this up and coming antiques centre, but Joen Zinni and her husband have unusual specialities. Joen specializes in old American patchwork quilts while her husband operates a metals workshop in the basement. He restores iron; repairs silver, gold, brass, copper, pewter and spelter; does silver and copper plating; gilding and tinning. He can also handle sand-blasting,

cleaning and metal polishing. In the shop they regularly stock Victorian kitchen curios.
21 Chalk Farm Rd, NW1 (01–485 1239). Open 10.00 to 18.00 Tues to Sat.

Kingsley
High fashion for men at reasonable prices, and civilized opening hours can be found at Kingsley. They design casual, comfortable clothes with well-executed fine details like gathered yokes, unusual pleats and pockets (Brian Gold designs and cuts in an upstairs workshop), and import a range of genuine American clothes (Fruit of the Loom) and smartish, well-cut Italian clothes.
25 Chalk Farm Rd, NW1 (01–267 9403/4). Open 09.30–18.00 Tues to Sat; 10.30–17.00 Sun.

Chalk Farm Nutrition Centre
This large tastefully converted warehouse/self-service shop doesn't specialize in any particular discipline of health foods but is working towards providing the most comprehensive range for anyone interested in nutrition as well as those with particular needs. They sell a range of Ceres breads and cakes, various natural cosmetics and vitamins, a wide range of honeys, preserves and jams, soya protein and textured vegetable protein foods, cooking oils, pastas, mineral waters, teas, soft drinks and de-caffeinated coffee, to name just part of their stocks. On the ground floor there is a separate Dairy Room where English, Dutch and French cheeses are sold. There are Loseley yoghurts in various sizes, tofu (soya bean curd) and cold soft drinks. Grains, stored in large wooden bins, are available in the Grain Room. Upstairs there's a Herb Room selling both growing herbs and pre-packaged dried herbs. In an adjoining room is a large library/bookshop where a wide range of natural cookbooks and books related to food and nutrition are on sale.
41–42 Chalk Farm Rd, NW1 (01–485 0116). Open 09.00–21.00 seven days a week.

Chattels
Attractively laid out shop specializing in domestic and rural antiques. Constant supplies of 19th-century metalware; iron, copper and brass; old cooking utensils and chunky kitchen chairs.
53 Chalk Farm Rd, NW1 (01–267 0877). Open 10.30–18.30 Mon to Sat.

Star Warehouse
Jimmy Broderick used to run a fairground in Ireland, but since 1958 he's been dealing in amusement machines over here. In his huge warehouse, Jimmy has enormous stocks of old

amusement machines in various states of repair. Most are electronic but he regularly finds mechanical ones too. As Jimmy buys the machines in all conditions he has thousands of spare parts for all types of machine.
Camden Goods Depot, Chalk Farm Rd, NW1, (opposite Chalk Farm Garage) (01–435 4308). Open 09.00–18.00 seven days a week. Ring to check.

Camden Lock (Dingwalls Market)
A small lively market centred around Camden Lock which sprawls on to the pavement and across the street. Mainly young people man the 200 stalls selling period clothes, old buttons, home-knitted clothes, clothes imported from China, Mexico and Guatemala, as well as flowers and plants, antiques and bric-à-brac, leatherware and musical instruments, and home-cooked breads, pastries and jams. Behind the market and open all week is a series of workshops where craftsmen can be watched at work. Specialists include Blind Alley for silk-screened and individually commissioned window blinds (see separate entry); five jewellers, three potters; Marc Gerstein, who has a stained glass workshop; and the useful Pine Beds who make DIY beds, cushions and sagbags, and The Sandal Maker who hand-makes sandals to order.
Delicious wholemeal hot and cold snacks can be bought just inside the entrance to the market.
Camden High St, NW1. Open 10.00–17.30 Sat and Sun.

The Stove Shop
All the original cast iron 1890–1940 stoves on sale at the Stove Shop are in perfect working order and can burn any fuel. They are imported from Denmark, Sweden and occasionally France and then totally renovated, given new fire bricks and the cast iron thoroughly cleaned.
Above 'Dingwalls', Camden Lock, Commercial Pl, Camden High St, NW1 (01–624 3055). Open 10.00–18.00 Sat and Sun; Mon to Fri evenings only.

Lead and Light
Marc Gerstein is one of a handful of craftsmen who've revived the old craft of stained glass. His particular specialities include lampshades (Tiffany and other styles), round hangings for windows and whole windows. He keeps stocks in his workshop, undertakes commissions and sells the materials for others to have a go. The other side of his trade is cast metal figures and light trees, which are free-standing lamps complete with globe, and finished with a

choice of antique copper, silver or pewter.
Camden Lock, Commercial Pl, Chalk Farm Rd, NW1 (01–485 4568). Open 09.30–17.30 Mon to Fri; 11.30–17.00 Sat and Sun.

Blind Alley
To quote from Blind Alley's brochure: 'Blind Alley transform roller blinds into functional works of art to enhance any environment'. They hand-decorate the blinds. They keep stocks of their own design range which can be exactly matched to individual interiors; work to one-off commissions and print fabrics which incorporate blinds into the design.
Camden Lock, Commercial Pl, Chalk Farm Rd, NW1 (01–485 8030). Open 10.00–17.30 Mon to Sat; 11.00–17.00 Sun.

The Lock Shop
Despite being in the centre of a craft revival area with numerous workshops, The Lock Shop draws from British craftsmen elsewhere. Everything is handmade and the changing variety of crafts includes jewellery, stained glass, ceramics and pottery, glass, toys, wood working. There are regular exhibitions.
Commercial Pl, Chalk Farm Rd, NW1. Open 10.30–17.30 Tues to Fri; 10.30–18.00 Sat and Sun.

Casa Catalan
Several floors of colourful hand-painted and undecorated terra cotta pottery from Spain. Jugs, pots, plates, plant containers, umbrella stands plus lots of wicker shelving and furniture, macramé hanging pots and green plants.
15 Chalk Farm Rd, NW1 (01–485 3975). Open 10.00–18.00 Mon to Fri; 09.30–18.00 Sat and Sun. Also at 56 Grays Inn Rd, WC1.

After Dark
Sells wired and unwired 1850–1930s light fittings and some accessories.
20 Chalk Farm Rd, NW1 (01–267 3300). Open 11.00–17.00 Tues to Sun.

Hermitage Wine Cellars
This friendly local off-licence sells wine 'loose' by the jug and also in 5-gallon drums. Its Italian carafe table wine is ideal for parties, and very cheap.
67 Regents Park Rd, NW1 (01–722 8576). Open 09.00–21.00 Mon to Sat.

September
Pretty, feminine and unusual clothes incorporating old lace and exclusive to September can be found here. Prices are pretty exclusive too.
75 Regents Park Rd, NW3 (01–722 8523). Open 10.30–17.30 Mon to Fri.

Bookshop
There's a strong local commit-

ment at this bookshop. They make sure to stock books by local authors and operate a really fast ordering system. They keep a wide selection of paperback fiction, reference, cookery, politics and, particularly, poetry titles. Also left-wing and literary magazines.
85 Regents Park Rd, NW1 (01–586 0512). Open 10.00–18.30 Mon to Fri; 10.00–18.00 Sat.

Richard Dare
Quality kitchen utensils can be found at this owner-run shop. A wide range of copper saucepans, glass storage jars, French dinner services (sold separately), including the delightful Quimper pottery, Sabatier (and other) knives, chunky baskets of all sizes, cooking crocks and iron-ware, glass etc., all tastefully chosen by Richard Dare.
93 Regents Park Rd, NW1 (01–729 9428). Open 09.30–18.00 Mon to Sat.

Living Daylights
Gillian Keighley and Ian Harris design and paint roller blinds to order. They keep plain blinds and a range of standard designs in stock but their speciality is working on one-off projects. Also murals.
115 Regents Park Rd, NW1 (01–586 3911). (Or factory 01–267 6055.)

Sesame
Sesame was one of the first wholefood shops. It's a tiny shop full of delicious smells. Home-baked cakes, pastries, savouries and breads; organically grown fruit and veg; pulses, grain and nuts; vegetarian cheeses; vitamins; and a range of natural cosmetics, books, drinks, etc. Specialities are Sesame's unpasteurised Brie and Camembert.
128 Regents Park Rd, NW1 (01–586 3779). Open 09.00–19.00 Mon to Sat.

Primrose Hill Books
Robert Frew and Julian McKenzie have two rooms and a basement crammed with antiquarian books, prints, paintings, engravings and silk prints. Prices range from a few pence to several hundred pounds for collectors' items.
134 Regents Park Rd, NW1 (01–586 2022). Open 10.00–18.00 Mon to Sat.

Atmosphere
Well respected two-floor gallery specializing in British craft (jewellery, pottery, fabric work, etc.) and graphics featuring monthly exhibitions. Browsing and purchasing welcomed.
148 Regents Park Rd, NW1 (01–722 6058). Open 10.00–18.00 Mon to Sat.

Trotters
Ann Dickins and Lynn Button

both describe themselves as shoe fetishists. Their stock of women's shoes reflect their tastes which are both sensible – brogues, well-constructed walking shoes, etc. – and zany. They import largely from Italy.
168 Regents Park Rd, NW3 (01–722 2124). Open 10.00–17.30 Mon to Fri; 10.00–17.00 Sat.

Partymad
As its name suggests; everything for children's parties – balloons, loads of toys, decorations, and colourful trimmings for children of all ages. They specialize in cake decorations and a range of unusually-shaped cake tins. Price list on request with s.a.e.
67 Gloucester Ave, NW1 (01–586 0169). Open 09.00–17.30 Tues to Sat.

Keys Galore
Keys Galore claim they have Britain's largest selection of keys, so it's worth trying here if you have difficulty getting a special key cut elsewhere. There is a huge range of car keys from Maserati to Volkswagen, also motor-bike and scooter keys. Keys cut while you wait include cylinder keys, mortice and Chubb.
96 Gloucester Ave, NW1 (01–722 2731). Open 09.00–13.00 and 14.30–18.00 Mon to Fri; 09.00–13.00 Sat.

Palmers
Mr Palmer's family has been running this pet shop, noted for its wide variety of livestock, since 1918. The puppies and kittens in the window give little indication of Palmers' other stock; snakes and reptiles, monkeys, tropical fish and a veritable zoo of birds including macaws, cockatoos and budgies. Mr Palmer has been known to sell tarantulas, scorpions, iguanas and alligators and will honour specific requests if rabies and quarantine laws permit. Palmers' also sell food and accessories for every kind of animal they keep.
33–39 Parkway, NW1 (01–485 5163). Open 09.00–18.00 Mon to Sat; 09.00–13.00 Thurs.

Klong
Tiny shop crammed to capacity with an assortment of clothes, objects, bags, jewellery, artefacts, crafts and textiles from the hill tribes of Thailand and South East Asia. A source of colourful and unusual gifts. One of the owners, who makes frequent visits to South East Asia, has a superb collection of batiks on the premises, which can be seen on request.
44 Parkway, NW1 (01–485 6846). Open 10.00–18.00 Mon to Sat.

Ironsware
Seconds and new kitchen equipment from many leading names,

cheap and ornamental tins, casseroles, tea towels, linens, aprons and oven gloves, basket-ware and masses of stocking fillers, and plants which spread on to the pavement during the summer.
46 Parkway, NW1 (01–485 7248). Open 10.00–18.00 Mon to Sat.

Candle Shop
One of London's first specialist candle shops. Candles of all shapes and sizes from small simple ones to elaborate hamburger and other shapes, candlemaking equipment, scented candles, candle holders and a range of incense, cards and small novelties.
89 Parkway, NW1 (01–485 3232). Open 10.00–18.00 Mon. to Sat.

Dudu Boutique
Mary Ove's choice of women's clothes and accessories is always more imaginative, interesting and cheaper than many other small boutiques. She always has a lot of French Connection (sometimes marvellous sales of discontinued lines), clogs and a variety of casual, colourful jeans / dungarees / T-shirts / dresses / scarves / bikinis / tights/socks/stockings and hats. Also extraordinarily cheap Indian patchwork quilts in block-printed fabrics.
95 Parkway, NW1 (01–267 1097). Open 10.00–18.00 Mon to Sat. Also at 219d Finchley Rd, NW3.

Three Star Products
Three Star Products roast, grind and sell the following coffee beans in small and bulk quantities: Santos, Kenya, Mocha, Brazilian blend, Kenya blend and their own Delancey blend. There are price reductions on quantities over 15 lbs.
11 Delancey St, NW1 (01–387 4080). Open 09.30–18.30 Mon to Sat; 09.30–18.00 Sun; 09.30–13.00 Thurs.

Camden Antique Market
This two-year-old open market catches the overflow of the very popular and much older Dingwalls market. Like Dingwalls, it happens at the weekend only and stallholders vary from week to week. Bargains in ethnic clothes, new shoes from leading manufacturers, hand-dyed wools, antiques, records, jewellery and junk. Potential stall holders should contact John on site.
Corner Brick St, Camden High St, NW1. Open 10.00–17.00 (approx) Sat and Sun.

Alfred Kemp
An enormous Aladdin's cave of good quality, new and nearly new men's clothing.
20 Camden High St, NW1 (01–387 1744). Open 09.00–17.00 Tues to Fri; 09.00–15.30 Sat.

Frank Romany Ltd
One of the best respected tool shops in North London, Romany's stock virtually every tool imaginable for all trades except plumbing, both hand- and electrically-operated types. There is also a full range of ironmongery, including door and window fittings.
52 Camden High St, NW1 (01–387 2579). Open 09.00–17.30 Mon to Sat; 09.00–13.00 Thurs.

Camden Wine and Cheese
Mrs Martin's delicatessen and wine shop is particularly good for cheese. She keeps large chunks of English, French, German, Swiss, Norwegian and Italian cheeses and an extensive range of biscuits and crisp-breads. Salads, quiches, pâtés, pizzas and sandwiches are made fresh daily and there is always fresh pasta. Coffee beans are ground to order (discounts are available on their own blend, on whole cheeses and crates of wine) and they sell French ice-cream.
214–216 Camden High St, NW1 (01–267 9981). Open 10.00–19.30 Tues to Fri; 10.00–16.00 Sat; 11.00–16.00 Sun.

Compendium
Leading 'alternative' bookshop with good sections on fiction, psychology, Eastern philosophy, alternative technology and feminism.
234 Camden High St, NW1 (01–485 8944). Open 10.15–18.30 Mon to Sat.

Oriental Food and Wines
The shelves of this self-service grocery are laden with foods from India, Pakistan, China, West India, the Orient and the Middle East. There are also some English grocery goods, and wines from Greece, France, Germany and Cyprus.
241 Camden High St, NW1 (01–485 2533). Open 08.00–19.00 Mon to Sat; 10.00–18.30 Sun.

Gohils
Gohils have been producing leather made-to-measure boots for years; customers choose from the display of designs or discuss their own ideas which can usually be executed. Rolls of leather are kept in the shop and the window sports a variety of Gohils ready-made leather sandals.
246 Camden High St, NW1 (01–485 9195). Open 09.00–18.00 Mon to Fri; 09.00–13.00 Thurs; 12.00–1300 closed for lunch; 09.00–17.00 Sat.

Talbys
Talbys specialize in fish from the south coast of England but stock a decent range of fresh seasonal fish and shellfish and their own highly praised smoked fish.
263 Camden High St, NW1

(01–485 5000). Open 08.00–17.30 Tues to Thurs; 08.00–18.00 Fri; 08.00–17.00 Sat.

Galerie 1900
Galerie 1900 is stuffed full of Art Nouveau and Art Deco decorative objects, furniture, lights, mirrors and glass.
267 Camden High St, NW1 (01–485 1001). Open 10.00–18.00 Mon to Sat.

Acquisitions
Acquisitions buy and sell anything old and interesting but their speciality is Victorian and Edwardian fireplaces which they restore to their former glory. They also make reproduction cast iron fireplaces from the same period, and sell original cast iron and reproduction fireside accessories including fire irons, fenders, trivets, coal buckets, tongs and bellows.
269 Camden High St, NW1 (01–485 4955). Open 10.00–18.00 Mon to Sat.

Inverness St Market
Small flourishing market which blossoms on Saturdays. Mainly fruit and veg; some junk.
Off Camden High St, NW1. Open 09.00–17.00 Mon to Sat. Half-day Thurs.

Greek Food Centre
Many of the delicious foods you enjoyed on a Greek holiday can be found here. Imported yoghurt, fetta and other Greek cheeses, olives and olive oils, nuts, filo pastry and spicy chorizo sausages. The small, family-run shop also specializes in Middle Eastern herbs and spices, oriental and continental foods; also off-licence.
12 Inverness St, NW1 (01–485 6544). Open 08.30–18.00 Mon to Sat. Half-day Thurs.

Montague Saxby
Established in 1903 and retaining its original character, Montague Saxby sells an unbeatable collection of suitcases, trunks, travel cases and holdalls.
24 Camden Rd, NW1 (01–485 1302). Open 08.30–17.30 Mon to Sat; half-day Thurs.

Swanky Modes
On the corner of Royal College St in dismal Camden Town, the flashy, colourful window display of Swanky Modes is a real eye-catcher. Three ex-dress design students make up a rail of witty, crazy, extravagant, fun clothes for women and men which are sold from stock or made to customers' size, colour choice etc. Swanky Modes have been new wave for about eight years. Skin-tight jeans, slinky sexy dresses, leather outfits and see-through macs. Also 50s jewellery and funky accessories.
106 Camden Rd, NW1 (01–485 3569). Open 10.00–18.00 Mon to Sat.

Sally Lawford's Country Kitchen
Old country-style furniture (stripped pine dressers, tables and chairs) and anything connected with a country kitchen; old carbon steel carving knives, cutlery, china jelly moulds, baskets, rag rugs etc. Also home-made jams and preserves (prepared by Sally in the shop's back room) and Candy Reiter's pretty little fabric bags and cushions.
241 Royal College St, NW1 (01-267 1483). Open 10.30–18.30 Tues to Sat. Also alternative Sundays at Camden Lock Market. See separate entry.

EUSTON/ KING'S CROSS

Mike Flyn
Mike Flyn and his wife live and breathe juke boxes. Mike repairs and renovates them, sells them, hires them and keeps spare parts. The number in stock at his electrical shop varies as do the machines' ages.
90 Chalton St, NW1 (01-388 1512). Open 09.00–18.00 Mon to Sat; 08.00–13.30 Wed.

Jock's Tattoo Studio
Big Jock has been tattooing for 33 years and has photographic and illustrative examples of his work all round his small studio. He will tattoo anything or anyone, anywhere, as long as they are over 18; the age Jock reckons safe for making unwavering decisions. He sterilizes all implements and has a good reputation in the business.
297 Pentonville Rd, N1 (01-837 0805). Open 11.00–18.30/19.00 seven days a week.

Woodstock Ltd
Woodstock import, plane, glue under high pressure, and oil high quality Canadian maple. They make it into chopping blocks, variously sized and shaped tables, and sell it by the foot for kitchen work surfaces. The wood has fine qualities – it does not stain, warp or give off rancid smells and is extremely durable. It is expensive but should never need replacement – butchers and bakers use maple for their blocks because of its durability. Catalogue on request.
Albion Yard, Balfe St, N1 (01-837 1818). Open 10.00–17.00 Mon to Sat.

Stokecroft Arts Ltd
Stokecroft Arts are pioneers of the return to hand-made furniture. They specialize in beds and make every item entirely by hand, with joints dowelled and glued under pressure without the use of screws. They use fine quality solid pine timber and their designs are simple, solid and durable. Aside from their range of beds (with or without

mattresses) they have a range of solid tables, shutters, settees, foam orthopaedic and sprung mattresses.
94 Caledonian Rd, N1 (01-278 6874). Open 09.30-17.30 Mon to Fri; 10.00-17.30 Sat.

Collectors' Corner
This is where British Rail sell off all their unwanted signs, station clocks, bits of trains, lights, crockery, and junk no longer wanted. A delight for railway fanatics and occasionally a real bargain for ordinary folk. Also BR buttons and delightful coloured enamel train badges.
Cardington St, NW1 (01-387 9400 ext 2537). Open 09.00-17.00 Tues to Sat.

Laurence Corner
Laurence Corner is a pillar of the army surplus world. They keep enormous stocks of army surplus clothing - hats of all types including berets, straw hats, caps, woolly hats - and all kinds of helmets; jackets, trousers and knitwear in various states of repair. Also camping equipment, bags, grips and a load of equipment like old medical kits, glasses, etc. Their catalogue is worth its price.
62 Hampstead Rd, NW1 (01-387 6134). Open 09.00-17.30 Mon to Sat.

HAMPSTEAD (including BELSIZE PARK)

Cucina
(See page 127 for full details.)
8 England's Lane, NW3 (01-722 7093). Open 10.00-18.00 Tues to Sat.

Castaways
Catherine Horwood sells nearly new clothes and small pieces of equipment for the under-sixes from her home. Everything is cleaned and pressed and in good order; prices average half the normal retail price, or less depending on quality. Catherine has a sufficiently large turnover to be able to totally equip a prospective new mum. She doesn't have the space to store large pieces of equipment but somehow finds the energy to act as an agent and charges 10% of the price. If you wish to sell through Catherine, she sells on a sale or return basis, keeps items up to three months and keeps ⅓ of the selling price. She pays out every two weeks. If selling, ring first for an appointment.
133 Haverstock Hill, NW3 (01-586 0908). Open 10.00-12.00 and 13.00-15.00 Fri; and 10.00-12.00 Sat.

Cane and Table
Annie Taylor stocks a wide range of cane and bamboo

furniture, particularly tables, framed mirrors, shelving units, chairs, mats, trays, hampers and basketware. Stock is supplemented by home paraphernalia including tastefully chosen kitchenware, glassware, pottery and imported knick-nacks. A good place for presents.
36 Rosslyn Hill, NW3 (01–435 2431). Open 10.00–18.00 Mon to Sat.

Rosslyn Hill Delicatessen
This Italian delicatessen keeps a wide selection of salamis and smoked meats, continental cheeses and numerous prepackaged pastas.
55 Rosslyn Hill, NW3. Open 09.30–18.30 Tues to Sat; 09.30–14.00 Sun.

Delicatessen Shop
A delicious range of home-made salads, taramasalata and homous, quiches, and meat and fish pâtés can be seen at the counter of this streamlined and efficient delicatessen/grocery. The real forte of the shop is its cheese. The proprietor, John Cavaciuti, is one of the few independent British shopkeepers to belong to the Guilde des Fromages. He sells (at least) 150 varieties of cheese both hard and soft, most of which are displayed on the counter or stacked in the window, on the floor and up the walls. He also sells 12 blends of coffee beans, loose herbs, French, Greek and wholemeal breads, and a range of groceries at the end of the shop.
23 South End Rd, NW3 (01–435 7315). Open 09.30–19.00 Mon to Sat.

Mexique
Mexique import a range of pretty, pastel-coloured, lacy, muslin, fine cotton and ribbon-decorated dresses, skirts and blouses from Mexico. Ideal for unusual wedding dresses.
11 Kingswell, Heath St, NW3 (01–435 9407). Open 10.00–18.00 Mon to Sat.

Village Games
Tucked away in Kingswell, Village Games sell games for children and adults. They have over 300 board games, 100 war and fantasy games plus all the traditional games like backgammon, chess, mah jong, go and jigsaws. They also stock twenty different types of Tarot cards.
15 Kingswell, Heath St, NW3 (01–435 3101). Open 10.00–18.00 Mon to Sat.

Paper Moon
This is the wholesale office of the Paper Moon wallpaper and fabric company. Here they keep samples of their entire range of complementary and matching wallpapers and fabrics plus an extensive range from other companies. They are friendly

people who are happy to give design advice.
Upper Kingswell, Heath St, NW3 (01–794 1019). Open 09.30–17.30 Mon to Fri; 10.00–17.00 Sat.

Monsoon
Delightful range of Indian clothes. See page 11–12 for full details.
1 Hampstead High St, NW3 (01–435 1726). Open 10.00–18.00 Mon to Sat.

High Hill Bookshop
Enormous bookshop covering virtually every subject in paperback and hardback; staff are friendly and will find and/or order anything you want.
6 Hampstead High St, NW3 (01–435 2218). Open 09.30–18.30 Mon to Sat.

Peace and Quiet
Peace and Quiet is one of many women's fashion shops in Hampstead. Unlike many similar shops, they have no heavy sales pitch. Clothes are casual and cover a variety of 'looks'. They are good on accessories – shoulder bags, sunglasses, belts and fake jewellery – and have recently opened a shoe annexe at the back of the shop for espadrilles.
15 Hampstead High St, NW3 (01–435 6969). Open 10.00–18.00 Mon to Sat.

H. Knowles Brown Ltd
Established in 1891, this old-fashioned jeweller, silversmith and clock repairer and seller displays its wares in glass cabinets. Bargains don't abound but it's an interesting shop to visit. They also buy, sell and price secondhand and antique jewellery.
27 Hampstead High St, NW3 (01–435 4775). Open 09.00–17.30 Tues to Fri; 09.00–13.00 Sat.

Formula
Sister shop to Peace and Quiet (see separate entry) where they sell a range of fashionable track suits and sporty casual wear.
70 Hampstead High St, NW3 (01–435 6969). Open 10.00–18.00 Mon to Sat.

Hampstead Community Market and Saturday Market
In a narrow alley beside the old village hall is the Community Market selling vegetables and fruit, wet fish, pet food and dairy products. The Saturday market has various stalls including bric-à-brac and pottery plant holders. Not to be missed is Rumuche which sells hand-made babies' bootees, clothes, dungarees, quilts and quilted jackets; all exquisitely made by hand in 'Mabel Lucy Attwell' colours. Clothes can be made to order. Also at the market is a café serving coffee, tea, brown-

ies, flapjacks, quiches, pasties, etc.
78 Hampstead High St, NW3. Open 09.30–18.00.

Keith Fawkes & Stanley Smith Antiquarian Books
Enter through a small door and step down into a quiet room packed with piles and piles of books. Mr Smith has a little office at the back of the shop where the very valuable antiquarian books are stored; they are 'very expensive'. The main stock is secondhand books selling at 25p-£100 which the shop both buys and sells. They will also find secondhand books for customers.
1–3 Flask Walk, NW3 (01–435 0614). Open 10.00–18.00 seven days a week.

Lodders At the Coffee And Tea Warehouse
This used to be a coffee and tea postal/wholesale shop. When Mr Lodder took over, the price of postage became prohibitive and so he opened up a wholefood (as opposed to healthfoods) shop and stocks a wide range of all that is good for you. The small shop is packed to the gunwales with dried nuts and fruit and 110 different types of herbs and spices.
2 Flask Walk, NW3 (01–435 0959). Open 09.30–17.30; closed Thurs.

Culpeper
Herbal delights and remedies. (See page 8 for full details.)
9 Flask Walk, NW3 (01–794 7263). Open 10.00–18.00 Mon to Sat.

That New Shop
Enormous gift shop with varied quality china, glass, pottery, wood, candles, lampshades, stationery, children's and adults' games, linen, kitchenware, rugs, bags, belts, jewellery, kites, scarves and some women's clothes.
14 Heath St, NW3 (01–435 4549). Open 09.30–19.00 Mon to Sat.

Fords
Fords is a superb old-fashioned fruit and veg shop run by Mr Jackman and a staff of six. It is always busy, and service is fast and friendly. They'll get anything to order but always keep a wide range of the less usual fruit and veg, such as four different types of lettuce.
16 Heath St, NW3. Open 09.30–17.30.

Hampstead Antiques Emporium
There are approximately 30 stalls inside this covered antiques market. It's a labyrinth of passages, and stalls sell goods of very mixed quality: antiquarian books, furniture, glass, jewellery, lamps, mirrors, silver,

clocks, Victoriana, bric-à-brac and African crafts.
18 Heath St, NW3. Open 10.00–18.00 Mon to Sat.

Hampstead Bazaar
Hampstead Bazaar always has a colourful window display of their soft, flowery, ethnic clothes. Once inside a lot of time is needed to browse through the rails to mix 'n' match as efficiently as the window display. Clothes range from antique Chinese fringed shawls, hand-stitched peasant blouses from Hungary and Romania, full-skirted and colourful dresses from Afghanistan to matching outfits and dresses from India. Also accessories.
30 Heath St, NW3 (01–794 6862). Open 09.30–17.30 Mon to Sat.

Skin
Skin specialize in a range of up-to-the-minute women's fashions made in leather and suede. They have a basic range in cream and beige but also produce clothes in primary colours. They also stock a very good range of T-shirts and clothes with a nautical look.
42 Heath St, NW3 (01–794 7230). Open 09.30–17.30.

Chic
Chic is where the rich and famous go to buy clothes from the cream of the British collections. There is something for all tastes and the sales team give excellent advice and really do help customers choose. No 74: shoes, boots and sandals; No. 78: lingerie and dressing-gowns; and No 82: day and evening wear, smart separates and coats, elegant knitwear and leather accessories.
74/78/82 Heath St, NW3 (01–435 5454/5). Open 09.30–17.30 Mon to Sat.

Elena
Done out like a small Dickensian cottage, Elena sell a superb range of 40 different fresh cream chocolates. All are imported from Belgium and are prettily gift-wrapped in little pink boxes in the shop. Noted for its truffles and pralines.
87 Heath St, NW3 (01–794 0798). Open 10.00–17.30 Mon to Sat.

A Button Shop
Hand-painted buttons, Victorian and mother of pearl buttons; ducks, cats, flowers, ships, faces and fruit-shaped buttons; wooden toggles and glass buttons from a few pence up to pounds.
91a Heath St, NW3 (01–653 1844). Open 09.00–17.30 Mon to Sat; 09.00–13.00 Wed.

Future Tense
Barbara Dearsley runs this colourful shop which sells commercial signs as works of art. Coloured rainbows, exclama-

tion marks, lifesize motorbikes, stilettos; in fact, anything to order. Prices average £100 per piece.
105 Heath St, NW3 (01-794 7688). Open 10.00–18.00 Mon to Sat.

Fairfax Kitchen Shop
A large corner shop sporting a wide selection of English, French, German and Italian kitchen equipment. Unusual specialities include a pasta machine, asparagus cooker and fish kettle.
1 Regency Parade, Finchley Rd, NW3 (01-722 7476). Open 09.00–17.30 Mon to Fri; 09.00–17.00 Sat.

Cash 'n' Carry
Everything photographic including 40 different makes of camera, 12 types of projector, lighting stands, films, paper, etc., both new and secondhand is on sale at Cash 'n' Carry. The 10-year-old shop, hard by the Odeon Cinema, keeps prices very competitive by quick turnover.
8 Regency Parade, Finchley Rd, NW3 (01-722 1031). Open 09.00–17.30 Mon to Fri; 09.00–16.00 Thurs and Sat.

D. E. Fisher
You can help yourself to used car spares at Fisher's Dump.
269a Finchley Rd, NW3 (01-435 9294). Open 08.00–17.30 Mon to Fri; 08.00–14.00 Sat.

7
KILBURN

Kilburn/West Hampstead, Maida Vale, St Johns Wood.

Amongst many Irish pubs and Irish and Arab banks, the shops in Kilburn's High Road are pretty down to earth. There is a Woolworth, several freezer centres, a Mothercare, a Marks and Spencers, a Halfords and numerous cheap clothes shops. John Brown's motorbike gear and the Camping Centre are two notable exceptions.

There are a few specialist shops in West End Lane including Harum Records, The Pine Shop and Beta Bikes, but most of the area is residential and littered with corner shops.

Nearby Maida Vale and St Johns Wood are residential areas with limited shopping opportunities.

However, Maida Vale has a good garden centre, Clifton Nurseries, and Clifton Road has a good Jewish delicatessen, Pribik and Sterman, as well as a fishmonger, Vandersluis.

See also Bayswater and Notting Hill.

TRANSPORT

Kilburn/West Hampstead
Tube stations: West Hampstead, Kilburn Park, Royal Oak.
Buses 8, 16, 32.

Maida Vale
Tube stations: Maida Vale, Warwick Ave.
Buses: 6, 18

St Johns Wood
Tube stations: St Johns Wood.
Buses: 13, 15.

LOCAL OPENING HOURS

The few shops mentioned in this section (mostly food) work long hours and don't honour a local half-day.

REFRESHMENTS

There are no 'special' tea and coffee places: only cafés in Kilburn and Maida Vale.

KILBURN/WEST HAMPSTEAD

Ackerman's Chocolates
Ackerman's hand-make all their chocolates on the premises. They wrap up various gift boxes but the majority of chocolates are displayed loose. Specialities include truffles and stem ginger in sugar syrup. There is a gift-wrapping service for special orders.
9 Goldhurst Terrace, NW6 (01-624 2742). Open 09.00–18.00 Mon to Fri; 09.00–13.30 Sat.

Osaka
A colleague who lives in Goldhurst Terrace tipped me off about this wholesale food shop. They operate a trade counter and sell foods unpackaged, preferably in large quantities, at very good prices, especially grains, beans and specialities from India (including confectionery, savouries and henna), the West Indies, China and Japan.
17/17a Goldhurst Terrace, NW6 (01-624 4983). Open 08.00–20.00 Mon to Sat; 11.00–19.00 Sun.

John Brown Wheels
At John Brown Wheels you can choose from a wide selection of all kinds of accessories that are put on a motorbike, or worn when riding it. They boast the largest range of helmets in London and offer 10% discount on Yamaha and Laverda helmets.
288 Kilburn High Rd, NW6 (01-328 4619). Open 09.00–17.30 Mon to Sat.

Design Point
From his studio at the rear of this bright red and yellow corner shop, Clinton Smith designs a range of greetings cards and wrapping papers. These and other young designers' work (other cards, brooches, wrapping paper and modern bric-à-brac) are on sale at Design Point.
122 West End Lane, NW6 (01-624 2275). Open 11.00–18.30 Mon to Sat.

The Pine Shop
Over the five years that The Pine Shop has been trading they've built up an extensive range of pine furniture; in fact they claim to have the widest range in London. Prices are reasonable, everything on sale is new, and stock includes tables, chairs, mirrors, Welsh dressers, wall units and wall clocks. It's a friendly, helpful and informal place and they operate a fast delivery service.
176/178 West End Lane, NW6 (01-435 1044/4462). Open 09.00–18.30 Mon to Sat; 10.00–13.30 Sun.

Studio Design
Wally Allanswick and Arnold

Ray design and make up a range of sofas, sofa beds and upholstered seating. They are new to the business and offer lots of perks: free delivery in London; credit facilities; and they don't make an additional charge to upholster in fabrics supplied by the customer.
223 West End Lane, NW6 (01–794 5166). Open 09.30–18.00 Mon to Sat.

Harum Records
Joe Palmer and John Ellison run this very friendly and well stocked independent record shop, with discounts on all new albums and tapes and quite a good selection of secondhand records at varying prices depending on popularity. Various accessories are also available.
250 West End Lane, NW6 (01–794 8000). Open 09.30–18.30 Mon to Fri; 09.00–18.00 Sat.

Alexis
The Mark family have run this pâtisserie and continental bakery for over 20 years and are known locally for their strudel, petits fours, cheesecakes and fresh cream gateaux as well as plainer pastries. They also sell fresh yeast.
272 West End Lane, NW6 (01–794 2617). Open 09.00–18.00 Mon to Sat; 09.00–13.00 Sun.

Beta Bikes
Beta Bikes stock most leading manufacturers' lightweight and general purpose cycles, cycling accessories and clothing. They undertake repairs and offer a hire service on three-speed folding bikes and ten-speed tourers. Their most unusual feature is that they stock tandems.
275 West End Lane, NW6 (01–794 4133). Open 09.00–18.00 Mon to Sat; closed Thurs; 11.00–13.00 Sun.

Rent-A-Scooter
Hire out automatic mopeds, 70cc Honda bikes and large bikes too. A hefty deposit is required; insurance is extra.
5–7 Broadwell Parade, Broadhurst Gdns, NW6 (01–624 8491).

B. and G. (Leathercloth) Ltd
After 27 years in the West End, B. and G. moved here seven years ago. Although they specialize in leathercloth, they also sell all types of plastic, PVC, suede, lurex and other glittery fabrics, which are ideal for displays, theatre backdrops, curtains, costumes, car upholstery etc. They are a good source of fabrics for fancy dress costumes.
71 Fairfax Rd, NW6 (01–624 8100). Open 09.00–17.30 Mon to Fri; 09.00–11.00 Sat.

Camping Centre London
Claiming to be London's largest

camping equipment showroom (900 sq m), Camping Centre London and its sister showroom, South London Leisure Centre, SE1 (750 sq m), stock a very comprehensive range of tents and camping equipment.
20–24 Lonsdale Rd, Queens Park, NW6 (01–328 2166). Open 10.00–18.00 Mon to Sat.

Bliss Chemist
This chemist is open 24 hours.
Bliss Chemist, 54 Willesden Lane, NW6 (01–624 8000).

MAIDA VALE

Clifton Nurseries
One of inner London's few well-respected nurseries. They stock all types of bedding plants, trees, herbs and house plants – displayed in two vast greenhouses with prices ranging from 50p to £200 for the more exotic varieties – as well as a range of gardening accessories including compost and terracotta pots. Advice on any type of plant is given on request.
5a Clifton Villas, Warwick Ave, W9 (01–286 9888). Open 09.00–18.00 Mon to Sat; 10.30–13.00 Sun.

Pribik and Sterman
This Jewish delicatessen and grocer keeps a wide range of Jewish specialities including rye bread, smatana, cold kosher meats, salamis and cheeses. It also sells fresh coffee and international groceries.
21–23 Clifton Rd, W9 (01–286 1668). Open 07.00–19.00 Mon to Sat; 07.00–13.00 Sun.

Popular Book Centre
In this shopping wasteland between Paddington and Kensal Green, the Popular Book Centre cannot be missed. It's a book and comic exchange centre with a difference: here you can buy comics one week and return the following week for half back on your next purchase. All the books and comics are displayed on huge tables and decorate the walls. Collectors' items like pre-1946 copies of *Marvel* and first editions can also be found.
453 Harrow Rd, W10 (no phone). Open 10.00–18.15 Mon to Fri; 10.00–17.30 Sat.

R. Rowe & Son Ltd
This is the head office of a small chain of excellent fishmongers. Wonderfully fresh fish are displayed on sloping chunks of ice. A wide range is always available, and includes the less popular varieties like octopus, snappers, conger eel, cuttlefish, sea bream and shark, as well as boiled crabs, jellied eels and smoked fish.
554 Harrow Rd, W9 (01–969 1512/2545). Open 08.00–17.30 Tues to Sat.

Treadwell's
This traditional London fishmonger dating back to 1924 specializes in home-cooked crabs, lobsters and eels, and cooked and jellied eels (done on the premises). It also stocks other seasonal shellfish, smoked fish and a range of fish traditionally popular with the English.
97 Chippenham Rd, W9 (01-286 9267). Open 08.00–17.30 Tues to Sat; 09.00–13.30 Sun.

ST JOHN'S WOOD

Five Star Foods
Late shopping is a non-event in St John's Wood so Five Star's two shops selling above-average general provisions, delicatessen, continental cheeses, fresh fruit and vegetables, are invaluable. They also sell cooked chicken, pizzas, etc; fresh coffee, and have an off-licence.
5 St John's Wood High St, NW8 (01-722 1248). Open 09.00 to 23.00 7 days a week. Also at 1A St John's Wood High St; open 09.00 to 21.00 7 days.

Hellenic Stores
Previously a cornerstone of Charlotte St, the Hellenic Stores continues to be one of London's best Middle Eastern food shops at its new address. Go here for Greek cheeses, fruit and vegetables, houmos, taramasalata, olives and olive oils, honey, halva, rice and pulses. There is a limited range of Middle Eastern cooking utensils such as little coffee makers .
53 St Johns Wood High St, NW8 (01-586 3400). Open 09.00–19.00 Mon to Sat.

8
MARYLEBONE

Edgware Rd, Baker St, Wigmore St, Marylebone.

Marylebone is an exclusive little patch of London housing some exclusive little shops. David Shilling's dotty, extravagant hats and Crispins high-fashion shoes for big-footed ladies give you a taste of what to expect. Interesting specialist shops flourish in Marylebone High St and Marylebone Lane, Crawford St, Chiltern St and Wigmore St, while more worldly shops like Afia Carpets, Fine Dress Fabrics and Chalfont Cleaners – one of the few cleaners who will dye for you – can be found in Baker St.

Edgware Rd is a hi-fi centre with two colourful street markets running off it to the east. Bell St, the smaller market, is a mini antiquarian and secondhand book centre, while Church St is the centre of the area. This lively market street is lined with interesting junk shops at the Lisson Grove end and overshadowed by the giant Alfie's Antique Market.

See also West End and Camden and Hampstead.

TRANSPORT

Edgware Rd
Tube stations: Edgware Rd, Marble Arch.
Buses: 6, 8, 16.

Baker St
Tube stations: Baker St, Great Portland St.
Buses: 2, 30, 74, 159.

Wigmore St
Tube stations: Marble Arch, Bond St, Regents Park.

Marylebone
Tube stations: Marylebone.
Buses: 27.

LOCAL OPENING HOURS

Food shops in this area tend to

close at half-day on Sat while other shops stay open late on Thurs. Some closing mid-afternoon on Sat; some are closed all day Sat.

REFRESHMENTS

Maison Sagne
105 Marylebone High St, W1. *Open 09.00–16.40 Mon to Fri; 09.00–13.00 Sat.*
Swiss pâtisserie and bakery. Tea/coffee and delicious croissants, cakes and pastries in adjoining tea-rooms.

Bonne Bouche
2 Thayer St, W1 (01-*935 3502). Open 08.30–18.00*
Ideal for breakfast – they serve brioches and croissants – or a sumptuous tea with a selection of delicious pastries, tarts, fresh cream gateaux and petits fours. Small selection of breads. Also at Bute St and Fulham Rd, Chelsea.

EDGWARE RD

Garroulds
For over 100 years Garroulds have been supplying hospitals and the catering trade with uniforms and overalls. Their enormous retail shop stocks maids' and reception uniforms as well as nursing and catering uniforms for men and women. They will make up designs to customers' specifications. Good for authentic (i.e. strong) butchers' striped aprons and cotton jackets.
104 Edgware Rd, W2 (01-723 1001). Open 09.00–17.30 Mon to Sat.

Direct Photographic Supplies
Direct Photographic cater for amateur and professional photographers. They keep a limited range of cameras; specializing in a few brands at competitive prices (Kodak, Polaroid, Canon, Olympus and Nikon). They are very strong on chemicals and papers and stock a fair range of colour and black and white enlargers. They have recently installed a fast Japanese processing plant in their four-storey building and offer a two-hour developing service on black and white and colour film. The staff are very helpful and willing to explain the advantages and disadvantages of particular types of cameras.
224 Edgware Rd, W2 (01-262 4427). Open 09.00–18.00 Mon to Sat.

Henry's Radio
There are 8,500 different electronic components and spare parts for radios, TVs and tape recorders on sale at Henry's. For 40-odd years the shop has been a mecca for all electronic hobbyists. There's a specialist department for micro-computers, and all the necessary test

equipment for their stock, plus a range of accessories like headphones and microphones. Their sister shop Audio Electronics at 301 (01-724 3564) specializes in test equipment, calculators and watches.
303 Edgware Rd, W2 (01-723 1008). Open 09.00-18.00 Mon to Sat.

Budget Herald
This branch of Herald, which sells a wide range of curtain fabrics and provides a free curtain-making service, is where ends of lines, soiled stock, etc. is sold at 50% off. Regular reductions on linen, duvets and fabrics.
384-386 Edgware Rd, W2 (01-723 9574). Open 09.00-18.00 Mon to Sat.

Cooker Centre
The Cooker Centre is a reliable source of secondhand cookers which they take in part exchange for new models. They deal with all leading brands (Mains, Parkinson, Lec, New Realm, Bellings, Bosch, Hotpoint, Creda, Indesit) at competitive prices and operate a delivery service. They also sell most domestic electrical appliances and new fridges.
420 Edgware Rd, W2 (01-723 2975). Open 09.00-17.00 Mon to Sat; half-day Thurs.

Church St Market
On Saturday the entire length of Church St becomes one of London's liveliest general markets. There are over 200 licenced stalls selling fruit and veg, dairy produce, fish, shellfish, hot snacks, tinned food and a wide variety of clothes, shoes, sports gear, tools, toys, china, towels, fabric and sheets. It's particularly known for jeans (often with labels cut out) and 'cabbage' clothes. Toward Lisson Grove it changes into a junk market.
Off Edgware Rd, Church St/Lisson Grove, W2. Open 09.00-17.00 Mon to Sat.

Alfie's Antique Market
There are approximately 150 stalls, workshops and showrooms of various size within the four buildings which interlink to make up this antique market run by Bennie Gray. Most stallholders are young and it's a bit chaotic because of the different staircases leading up and down between the four floors. Period clothes, old bathroom and kitchen fittings, country-style furniture, old dolls and toys, jewellery, paintings from many periods, china, glass, stained glass, old tiles, lace and books.
13-25 Church St, NW8 (01-723 6066). Open 10.00-18.00 Tues to Sat.

Ol' Texas Sells The Past
After 35 years on the road as a medicine man, 80-year-old Victor Webb (usually wearing a tartan hat) 'buys and sells the

past – it will last after you're gone, you will not get it again' in a ramshackle four-storey shop. The building is bursting at the seams with crockery, glass, hooks and handles, irons, candlesticks, pictures, furniture, cutlery, mirrors, lamps, keys and numerous bits of junk. It could be a source of something you've never known where to find.
36 Church St, NW8 (01–723 0285). Open 09.00–17.00 Mon to Sat.

Marylebone Auction Rooms/Phillips Son & Neale
Sales of secondhand furnishings and bric-à-brac are held every Friday at 10.00 with viewing the previous Thursday from 09.00–17.00. Every second week they hold 'the least known picture sale in London'. The periods covered are mainly Victorian and modern for both sales; specialist sales of dolls, toys, lead soldiers, etc., are held on Wednesdays. Phillips are a well-known source of bargains.
Hayes Place, Lisson Grove, NW1 (01–723 2647).

The Dolls' House
Wide range of wooden dolls' houses ranging from Georgian designs to modern-day. Also houses made to order and a range of exquisitely made dolls' furnishings.
116 Lisson Grove, NW1 (01–723 1418). Open 10.00–17.00 Mon to Sat.

Bell St Market
Although it's been going far longer, Bell St Market has been somewhat superseded by nearby Church St. It's small, concentrates on fruit and veg and is less of a hassle than Church St.
Off Edgware Rd, NW1. Open 09.00–17.00 Mon to Sat.

Bell Street Bikes
Bell Street Bikes sell new and secondhand bikes of all styles for children and adults. They stock a complete range of accessories for all the bikes they sell, do repairs and hire out cycles at very competitive rates.
73 Bell St, NW1 (01–724 0456). Open 10.00–18.00 Mon to Sat; closed Thurs.

BAKER ST

Karo-Step Bedding Centre
Karo-Step, a German company, are continental quilt (duvet) specialists. They sell them with a variety of fillings from the very luxurious and expensive pure eider duck down to the cheapest natural filling, feather and down. They operate a cleaning service run on traditional lines which cleans by tossing the feathers and re-covering the quilt. They also sell white and coloured sheets, pillow cases and valances.
138 Marylebone Rd, NW1 (01–

935 0196). Open 09.30–16.30 Mon to Fri; 09.00–13.00 Sat.

Gandolfi
Established in 1920, Gandolfi are theatrical and ballet costumiers selling ballet shoes, leotards, footless tights, leg warmers, etc., in several colours.
150 Marylebone Rd, NW1 (01-935 6049). Open 09.00–17.30 Mon to Fri; 09.00–13.00 Sat.

Afia Carpets
Afia cater for all pockets. They hold rollover (ends of rolls used to supply larger orders) sales twice a year in the spring and autumn when carpet is sold at below half price, and have a 'rollover board' in the shop which daily advertises one-off rollover bargains. Afia keep over 200 different coirs and sisals – very hardwearing carpeting made from the fibre of coconut husks and from the leaves of a pineapple-type plant. The colour range is enormous and they stock geometric designs as well as plain colours. Their Afia cord range is very competitively priced (they sell 1000 yards a week) as is the more luxurious Afia Wilton. There's also plenty of choice at the luxury end, including a range of designer carpets.
81 Baker St, W1 (01–935 0414). Open 09.00–17.30 Mon to Fri and 09.00–13.00 Sat.

Fine Dress Fabrics
It's somewhat chaotic at this small fabric shop and plenty of time is needed for a good browse. All their fabrics are intended for dressmaking and they import an exclusive range of silks, cottons and cotton jersey from Switzerland and Italy.
87 Baker St, W1 (01–935 5876). Open 09.00–17.30 Mon to Fri; 09.30–13.00 Sat.

Arts and Crafts of China
All things Chinese can be found here. Reasonably priced wickerware, basketware, ceramics, decorative items and clothes plus a pricier range of jade, ivory, enamels, furniture and jewellery.
89 Baker St, W1 (01–935 4576). Open 09.00–17.00 Mon to Fri; 09.00–13.00 Sat.

Wholefood
Everything sold at Wholefood is organically grown – grains, carrots, potatoes and other seasonal vegetables. They bake their own bread and sell a full range of health foods, yoghurt, cheeses, etc. One particular speciality is French wines and sherries made from organically grown grapes. The shop incorporates a butcher, round the corner at 24 Paddington St, which sells pâtés, pies, free-range eggs and guaranteed free-range meat, i.e. naturally reared.
112 Baker St, W1 (01–935

3924). Open 09.00–18.00 Mon; 09.00–18.30 Tues to Fri; 09.00–13.00 Sat.

Jaws
Originally a small, one-room delicatessen, Jaws has expanded next door and now keeps an extensive range of English and continental cheeses, cold meats, salamis and pâté. They make up a range of salads daily, stock bread and cakes, a limited choice of condiments, groceries and hot take-away sausage rolls.
220 Baker St, NW1 (01–486 3367). Open 09.00–18.30 Mon to Fri; 10.00–17.00 (approx) Sat and Sun.

Chalfont Cleaners and Dyers
A big sign in their window says that Chalfont Cleaners and Dyers are willing to dye for you; now a rare service. They will dye almost anything (Mr Cohen, the manager, draws the line at living beings) in guaranteed fast dyes. Their range of colours is good (industrial dyes not available to the public) but colours cannot be guaranteed. They've been dye specialists for four years and also provide a general cleaning and repair service.
222 Baker St, NW1 (01–935 7316). Open 08.30–18.00 Mon to Fri; 09.00–13.00 Sat.

Clare's Chocolates
Parking near this small, canopied shop which sells over 70 different kinds of hand-made chocolates, is impossible. But their superb liqueur chocolates, truffles and Easter eggs (specials to order), are worth the inconvenience.
3 Park Rd, Baker St, NW1 (adjacent to the park) (01–262 1906). Open 09.00–19.00 seven days a week.

Le Trousseau
Where brides-to-be can go to be kitted out for the Great Day and the honeymoon. Brides' and bridesmaids' dresses; floaty, flouncy lingerie – negligées, petticoats, etc.
Accurist Hse, 64 Blandford St, W1 (01–935 9776). Open 09.30–17.30 Mon to Fri; 10.00–13.00 Sat.

Crispins
Dawne Gutteridge sells quality fashion shoes for big-footed ladies: 7–10 English sizes. Fittings are average and narrow.
5 Chiltern St, W1 (01–935 7984). Open 10.00–18.00 Mon to Fri; until 19.00 Thurs; 10.00–16.00 Sat.

Grey Flannel
Grey Flannel provide the elegant English look in men's fashions. They use classic fabrics, up-to-the-minute styling, and offer fully co-ordinated colour tones for everything except underwear.
7 Chiltern St, W1 (01–935

4067). Open 09.30–18.00 Mon to Fri; 10.00–17.30 Sat.

Beauty Without Cruelty
An extensive range of cosmetics, creams, lotions and potions made from products entirely free of animal extracts.
16 Chiltern St, W1 (01–486 2845). Open 10.00–17.00 (promptly) Mon to Fri; 10.30–15.30 Sat.

Wardrobe
Wardrobe is unique in giving young, unknown designers a chance to sell their collections. Their often weird and unrepeatable clothes sell along with top designer collections from France and Italy; also fashion shoes, bags and other accessories.
17 Chiltern St, W1 (01–935 4086). Open 09.30–17.00 Mon to Wed; 09.30–19.00 Thurs; 09.30–17.30 Fri; 09.30–17.00 Sat. Also Bond St, W1.

Long Tall Sally
Everything except underwear, footwear and swimwear for the tall woman. Clothes tend to be of classic design.
40 Chiltern St, W1 (01–487 3370). Open 10.00–18.00 Mon to Fri; 10.00–19.00 Thurs; 10.00–16.00 Sat.

Early Music Shop
Wide range of pre-1800 reproduction musical instruments including a lot of keyboard instruments. The shop also sells kits for making various instruments.
47 Chiltern St, W1 (01–935 1242). Open 10.00–17.30 Mon to Fri; 10.00–12.30, 13.30–16.00 Sat.

The Small and Tall Shoe Shop
Ladies' casual, walking and fashion shoes for small feet – 13 to 2½ – and large – 8½ to 11. Most are hand-made, and they will get some of their designs made in any colour. Also made-to-measure boots.
71 York St, W1 (01–723 5321. Open 10.00–17.30 Tues, Wed and Fri; 10.00–19.00 Thurs; 10.00–19.00 Thurs; 10.00–17.00 Sat.

Blagdens
This fishmongers has been on the premises for 100 years and Mr Blagden has been running it for over 25. Much of their fish comes daily from Aberdeen: Scotch salmon, lobster (kept alive in tanks) and dressed crab are particular specialities; also expensive fish like halibut; a range of the cheaper seasonal fish; smoked haddock, trout, mackerel, cods' roe and Arbroath smokies.
64 Paddington St, W1 (01–935 8321). Open 08.00–17.00 Mon; 08.00–17.30 Tues to Fri; 08.00–13.00 Sat.

Briglin Studio

Briglin specialize in functional earthenware pottery which is made in their downstairs studio. Tea, coffee and wine sets, plant pots, mugs and plates all with brushwork finish. They also sell hand-made craft of all types.
23 Crawford St, W1 (01–935 0605). Open 09.00–17.30 Mon to Sat.

David Shilling

David Shilling's mum does a lot to advertise his hat-making talents every time she goes to Ascot. Aside from his extraordinary and fabulous occasion hats, David makes simple hats (to measure) in a few hours. Should you buy one of his creations, you get a free DS hat pin.
36 Marylebone High St, W1 (01–487 3179). Open 09.00–18.00 Mon to Fri.

Hirsh Jacobson Merchandising Co Ltd

Suppliers of all lapidary tools and equipment, Jacobson's are helpful to both amateurs and specialists. They operate a mail order service – catalogue available on request.
91 Marylebone High St, W1 (01–935 4709). Open 09.45–17.00 Mon to Fri.

WIGMORE ST

The Button Queen

Mrs Toni Frith had been running The Button Queen in St Christopher's Place for nine years before she moved here to much larger premises three years ago. She specializes in old, rare and antique buttons, cuff links and silver buckles. Also some modern horn, leather and blazer buttons.
19 Marylebone Lane, W1 (01–935 1505). Open 10.00–17.30 Mon to Fri; 10.00–13.30 Sat.

Divertimenti

A specialist kitchen shop which imports practical, well-made utensils and tableware largely from France. Stock is sensibly laid out for easy self-service and includes the full range of Sabatier and Victorinox knives, cutlery and specialist cooking utensils, food processors, sieves, scales and measures, a wide range of baking moulds, copperware pots and pans, English and French porcelain, earthenware and specialist cooking equipment. Colour catalogue available; check price.
68–72 Marylebone Lane, W1 (01–935 0689). Open 09.30–18.00 Mon to Fri; 10.00–14.00 Sat.

Wedgwood

The showroom/shop for the

entire classic Wedgwood range of fine china.
34 Wigmore St, W1 (01–486 5181). Open 09.00–17.15 Mon to Fri.

John Bell and Croyden
Surprisingly few people know that this enormous 100-year-old chemists operates a dispensing service until 21.00 on weekdays and until 20.00 on Sundays. The chemist has several departments and is particularly respected for its invalid aids and appliances, health aids and instruments. It has a vast dispensary, and pharmacy, perfumery and photographic departments.
54 Wigmore St, W1 (01–935 5555). Open 09.00–18.00 Mon to Fri; 09.00–13.00 Sat; dispensary open 08.30–21.00 Mon to Sat; 10.00–20.00 Sun.

Olof Daughters
When Olof Daughters retreated back to Sweden from their South Molton Street shop, there was such an outcry for their clogs (in all colours) and most particularly their leather, crepe-soled lace-up ankle and knee-high boots for men and women, that they began a mail order service. Happily they have returned to this shop and have extended their range.
65 Wigmore St, W1 (01–486 4772). Open 10.00–17.30 Mon to Fri; 10.00–15.00 Sat.

Ideas
Despite having novelty value, all the ceramics on sale at Ideas must have a functional quality. Aside from ceramics (egg cups with feet, doggy toast racks, piano ashtrays, etc.) they sell a range of gift items like soft towelling giant telephones, plastic (working) radios shaped like the word, giant matchstick-shaped lighters, and so on.
69 Wigmore St, (01–486 2752). Open 10.00–18.00 Mon to Fri; 10.00–16.00 Sat. Also South Molton St, W1.

Under Two Flags
Under Two Flags is a small colourful shop selling antique, old and new metal toy soldiers, model soldiers, military books, prints and porcelain. All periods and countries are covered.
4 St Christopher's Place, W1 (01–935 6934). Open 10.00–17.00 Tues to Sat.

Turak
Turak hold regular exhibitions of modern jewellery but the bulk of their finely displayed stock is old and antique handmade jewellery from Afghanistan, Ethiopia, India, Morocco and the Yemen. Many pieces are made of silver, chunky and heavy with amber, coral and turquoise stones.
5 St Christopher's Place, W1 (01–486 5380). Open 10.00–18.00 Mon to Fri; 12.00–16.00 Sat.

Sassa
When Christine Westwood ran the fashion special offers for *The Sunday Times* a large part of her correspondence bemoaned the fact that the offers only came in sizes up to 16. It seems that larger ladies are very badly off for pleasant, well-cut clothes. So Christine opened Sassa; which stands for '16 and several sizes above' and sells non-frumpy clothes for all those ladies who couldn't fit Christine's special offers. Sassa has its own label and has commissioned several well-known designers to contribute to their collection. Emphasis is on classic styles, adaptability – clothes which can be dressed up or down and made to look quite different – using natural fibres.
10 Gees Court, alley off Oxford St, W1 (01–408 1596). Open 09.30–17.30 Mon to Fri; 09.30–17.00 Sat.

See also West End, particularly Bond Street.

MARYLEBONE

London Transport Posters
A lavish, full-colour catalogue of London Transport's current posters, postcards, reproductions of old underground posters, T-shirts, maps, books and related souvenirs can be had from the address below. Choose from stock at their modern shop and at St James' Park and Charing Cross stations, or buy by mail order.
280 Old Marylebone Rd, NW1 (01–262 3444). Open 09.00–16.00 Mon to Fri.

Chess Centre
Everything connected with chess and chess-playing can be found here including an enormous variety of sets, old and modern, plus clocks, boards, score sheets and books.
3 Harcourt St, W1 (01–402 5393). Open 09.30–17.30 Mon to Fri; 09.30–16.00 Sat.

Paddington and Friends
A specialist shop for Paddington Bear where Paddingtons (in all sizes) and a variety of Paddington-decorated games, puzzles, cards, stationery, badges, purses, books, rubbish bins, suitcases, rulers, oven-gloves, socks and even a ring-making set are on sale. The small shop even sports a Paddington carpet.
22 Crawford Place, W1 (01–262 1866). Open 10.00–17.00 Mon to Fri; closed 13.00–14.00 and Sat.

9
BAYSWATER

Paddington, Bayswater.

Queensway, the heart of Bayswater, is alive from dawn to dusk seven days a week. Between the many cheapo clothes shops, newsagents selling the world's print and bureaux de change, there are some superb ethnic food shops, such as the pâtisserie at Pierre Pechon and various Chinese minisupermarkets; while nearby Moscow Rd sports an Athenian grocery and French pâtisserie Maison Bouquillon.

Whiteleys, Bayswater's department store, brings a little sobriety to the area, with a smattering of everything except food. Round the corner Westbourne Grove (known locally as The Grave) has London's only 24-hour food shop, the famous late-night jean shop, Dickie Dirts, and several good ethnic food shops.

Paddington is a total contrast. Around the station Paddington's shops consist mainly of poor quality food shops, souvenir shops and fast-order restaurants. The exclusive part of Bayswater/Paddington centres around Connaught and Kendal Streets. Here a small cluster of high quality food shops are the area's only shopping attraction.

See also Kilburn.

TRANSPORT

Paddington
Tube stations: Lancaster Gate, Paddington, Edgware Rd, Marble Arch.
Buses: 15, 27, 88.

Bayswater
Tube stations: Bayswater, Queensway.
Buses: 18, 88, 15, 27.

LOCAL OPENING HOURS

Little happens before 10.30 in Bayswater but it stays happening until late at night and on Sun. Paddington tends to operate a full six days, Mon to Sat.

REFRESHMENTS

Pâtisserie Française Maison Pechon
127 Queensway, W2.
Open 08.00–17.00 Mon to Sat.
Large tearoom serving French pâtisserie.

Maison Bouquillon
41 Moscow Rd, W2
Open 08.00–22.00 Mon to Sat; closes earlier on Sun.
Top quality French pâtisserie in small, busy tearoom.

Le Relais Basque
28 Westbourne Grove, W11.
Open 09.00–23.00 Tues to Sat.
A branch of Maison Bouquillon with a larger upstairs tearoom.

PADDINGTON

Barry Bros
Locksmiths providing most services, including safe opening and repairs. The shop has a huge range of locking devices and security fitments – from door handles to safes, and they have a wide selection of keys, cut on the premises, including cylinder, mortise and car keys. Their emergency service only operates up to 9 p.m.
123 Praed St, W2 (01–262 2450, emergency service (01–734 1001). Open 09.30 to 19.00 Mon to Sat.

Sandell, Perkins and Broads
Sandell, Perkins and Broads have been timber merchants for many years with several timber yards dotted throughout North and East London. Comparatively recently they moved into the builders' merchants' business and at this vast self-service shop with a trade counter, they split the two businesses equally. If they haven't got the timber required, customers are referred to their nearest stockist. Full range of ironmongery, paints (Dulux and Crown), brushes, tools, door knobs, etc.
2–4 South Wharf Rd and 22 Praed St, W2 (01–723 7061 and 01–723 8808). Open 08.30–17.00 Mon to Fri; 08.30–12.00 Sat.

Crispins
In an affluent area, Crispins supply the very best in groceries and delicatessen. They keep 35 different French, English and other continental cheeses; an excellent selection of cold meats, and meat pies which are specially made for them. They employ several small companies to make up pâtés (also imported from France), cheesecakes and a selection of made-up salads. They are known for their fresh

bagels, a wide range of frozen, tinned and bottled gourmet foods, fresh coffee, Loseley ice-creams, and many international specialities.
24 Kendal St, W2 (01-262 9122). Open 09.00–18.00 Mon to Sat; 10.00–18.00 Sun.

Markus
Friendly and efficient Eva Markus runs this small coffee shop, which has been in her family for 20-odd years. The delicious aroma of the beans (roasted on the premises) wafts into the street. Aside from selling 32 different types of bean, they stock a wide range of coffee-making products and accessories, a range of quality biscuits, chocolates, honey and a limited range of teas. There is a mail order service.
13 Connaught St, W2 (01-723 4020 and 01-262 4630). Open 08.30–17.30 Mon to Sat.

John Gow
This large, old-fashioned fishmonger and game dealer has been trading for over 100 years. They will get anything to order, stock a wide selection of seasonal fish, shellfish (live crabs or cooked to order) and game, and a range of smoked fish including salmon, eels, trout, haddock, mackerel. They also sell quails' eggs.
55 Connaught St, W2 (01-723 1612). Open 07.30–16.30 Mon to Fri; 07.30–11.00 Sat.

Boobs
This basement shop provides an outlet for newish secondhand clothes for women. Because it is positioned in such a classy area, clothes tend to be smart and often include hardly worn leading designer garments. Everything on sale is in tip-top condition. Appointments aren't necessary if you wish to sell through Boobs but they don't take in clothes on Sats.
33 Sussex Place, W2 (01-723 2413). Open 10-30–17.30 Mon to Sat.

BAYSWATER

Athenian Grocery
John Joannides and his large family run this Greek/Arabic/Middle Eastern food shop. There is an excellent range of spices for Arab cooking; olive oil in large tins; Greek wines; a wide range of Greek and Arabic breads (fresh daily); honey from Greece; feta cheese from Cyprus and Bulgaria; delicious fat olives; their own houmous and taramasalata, tinned groceries and a range of vegetables.
16a Moscow Rd, W2 (01-229 6280). Open 09.00–19.00 Mon to Sat; 10.00–13.00 Sun.

Maison Bouquillon
Since a recent re-organization, delicatessen, charcuterie, French cheeses and loaves predominate in one shop, while the almost

adjoining premises serve their own cream cakes, pastries, tarts, brioches and croissants. Both delicatessen foods and cakes can be eaten on the premises or taken away. Excellent quality but small premises; it's often necessary to queue for a table.
41 and 45 Moscow Rd, W2 (01–727 4897). Open 08.00–22.00 Mon to Sat; early closing Sun.

Whiteleys
Established in 1863, Whiteleys has recently survived an enormous re-vamp. The vast premises are now almost entirely open-plan, and you can wander from department to department. They sell everything you would expect from a department store and put emphasis on value for money.
Queensway, W2 (01–727 6636). Open 09.30–17.30 Mon to Thurs; 09.30–18.00 Fri and Sat.

Words and Music
Words and Music are a small chain of bookshops known for remaindered and cut-price books. At this branch, manager Tenebris Light is tightening up stock, with less cheap and light reading, and concentrating on building up sections on art, non-sexist children's books, English feminist literature, paper- and hardback quality English fiction, and new, unestablished authors. Remaindered books are loosely ordered by subject and piled on the floor while other books are author-indexed. They also stock maps and guidebooks.
21 Queensway, W2 (01–229 0500). Open 10.00–20.00 seven days a week.

Pâtisserie Française, Maison Pechon
Pierre George Pechon and family maintain a high standard of bread and pâtisserie baking which was set by his grandfather when the shop/bakery/tearooms opened in 1925. A rotation of over 116 types of cakes and pastries is baked on the premises in a coke-fired oven, and 29 kinds of French and English loaves and croissants are baked round the corner. They buy in nothing except crumpets in the winter. The back of this large shop is a café serving breakfast, lunch and teas.
127 Queensway, W2 (01–229 0746). Open 08.00–19.00 Mon to Sat. Restaurant closes 17.00.

Lodge Enterprises
As an enthusiastic amateur weaver, Angela Lodge was struck by the difficulty of finding and buying natural yarns. Apart from Handweavers in Walthamstow (see Worth a Trip section), yarns are largely available only by mail order. In her small shop tucked inside her husband's sound recording studios, Angela has on display a superb selection of natural yarns ranging from cottons for

macramé to worsted, silks, linens and cashmeres, from Yorkshire, Greece, Belgium, Iceland and Aran. Everything is selected for texture and sold by the hank. Prices are very good indeed. Some yarns are suitable for knitting. A mail order catalogue is available on request, but ring for current prices.
23 Redan Place, off Queensway, London W2 (01–229 0101). Open 10.00–17.00 Mon to Sat.

Dickie Dirts
Ever since Dickie Dirts opened some three years ago it has been very busy – understandably, as they sell what are probably the cheapest jeans and men's shirts in London. Nigel Wright, who runs Dickie Dirts (rhyming slang for shirts), operates on a low profit margin, extreme optimism, careful buying and a large turnover. Labelling is meticulously honest – if a shirt/pair of jeans is going to shrink a size or two in the first wash, the label will say so. Unfortunately, the narrow, cramped shop where clothes are laid out for customers' easy selection can't cope with the increasing numbers who flock to the shop at all hours. It is best to go at the most uncivilized hour.
58a Westbourne Grove, W2 (01–229 1466). Open 09.00 to 23.00 seven days a week.

African Trading Centre
On my latest visit to this curiously mixed shop, the staff were busy cleaning out the resident monkey's cage! The large cavernous shop sells carvings, pictures, hats, bags, clothing, pieces of cloth, hides and jewellery from various parts of Africa. Mixed in with this is a load of cheap fashion clothes and macramé hanging plant holders. Worthy of a good long browse.
59 Westbourne Grove, W2 (01–229 8835). Open 09.00–22.00 Mon to Sat; 13.00–20.00 Sun.

French Kitchenware and Tableware Supply Co
The trade showroom for the retailer Divertimenti, where they don't exactly encourage retail trade, but don't turn it away either. The long narrow room with a counter at the end is piled to the ceiling with French cooking utensils, porcelain, earthenware, glass and cutlery.
60 Westbourne Grove, W2 (01–229 5530). Open 09.00-18.00 Mon to Fri; 10.00–18.00 Sat.

24-Hour Supermarket
If you pine for cheese or fags in the middle of the night, need emergency food at uncivilized hours or get the urge to spring-clean at 3 am, remember this shop. For nine years, the 24-Hour Supermarket has been a reliable source of tinned, frozen and packed foods; fresh veget-

ables and fruit; tobacco shampoos, soap and other bathroom gear; needles and cotton; in fact, almost all you'd expect from any supermarket. Prices are marginally higher.
68 Westbourne Grove, W2 (01-727 4927).

Central Bazaar
Until a few months ago the Nyman family had run this china shop for over 80 years. The new owner continues to specialize in English china, particularly the patterned sort, and reckons to be able to match patterns up to 50 years old.
70 Westbourne Grove, W2 (01-229 3388). Open 09.00–18.00 Mon to Sat.

D. Morgan
The Morgan family have run this reliable, old-fashioned fishmonger for 50-odd years. Fish and poultry are displayed on a central marble slab with daily 'specials' chalked on a blackboard. They smoke their own haddock and bloaters on the premises and sell freshwater as well as seawater fish.
80 Westbourne Grove, W2 (01-229 5239). Open 10.00–16.45 Tues to Fri; half days Mon and Sat.

Corfu Trade
A long, glass-covered counter on the left as you enter this delicatessen houses a superb display of named and priced cold meats and salamis, pâtés, various fat olives, taramasalata, Greek, Continental and English cheeses, cakes, cheesecake, Cyprus yoghurt and a range of prepared salads. Behind the counter are spices, tinned and bottled groceries and pastas. On the right of the shop is an off-licence selling wines and beers from many countries.
97 Westbourne Grove, W2 (01-221 5972). Open 10.00–23.00 Mon to Sat; 12.00–22.30 Sun.

DoDo
Liz Farrow runs this interesting shop where she sells, hires and buys old advertising signs, packaging, labels, mirrors, enamel signs, shop and display materials, posters and ephemera including pretty tins, old toys, games and antique clothing from the 1880s to the 1940s.
185 Westbourne Grove, W11 ((01-229 3132). Open 12.00–18.00 Tues, Wed, Fri and Sat, or by appointment.

The Façade
Although Façade deal almost exclusively with the trade they will sell their Art Deco and Art Nouveau lamps to the public. Most are original but they have several popular reproductions sold with original shades. They also stock Edwardian and Victorian gaslight fittings and 1900–1930's decorative items.
196 Westbourne Grove, W11

(01-727 2159). Open 10.00-18.00 Mon to Sat.

E. J. Barnes
Barnes keep a selection of all types of bikes for adults and children from manufacturers Claude Butler, Holdsworth, Carlton, Viscount, Raleigh and Puch. They sell secondhand when they can get them, keep stocks of accessories and do repairs.
285 Westbourne Grove, W11 (01-727 5147). Open 11.00-19.00 Mon to Sat.

10 NOTTING HILL GATE

Notting Hill, High St Kensington, Holland Park, Shepherds Bush/Hammersmith.

Antique shops of all types proliferate in Notting Hill. The grand ones selling ornate objects are to be found in Kensington Church St; the less grand in Westbourne Grove and in and around the famous antique street, Portobello Rd. Portobello's market flourishes on Saturdays, changing progressively into a fruit and veg then a junk market as it hits Golborne Rd. Superb delicatessens pepper the area and on Notting Hill itself. Boots and W. H. Smith have large branches on the Gate and there are numerous food supermarkets. Pembridge Rd, a good lead-in to Portobello Rd, houses many interesting shops. Holland Park is the exclusive bit of Notting Hill; a small cluster of specialist shops can be found at the end of Portland Rd.

In the days of Biba, Kensington High St was the centre of young fashion, eclipsing the King's Rd for variety. There are still plenty of boutiques (Che Guevara, Slick Willies – for skateboard and US sports gear – Crocodile and Derber for shoes) particularly near the High St end of Kensington Church St. Many covered markets sell cheap and often tatty gear, and Kensington Market, in the High St, still outshines them all. The only big store left is Barkers, a good general purpose shop now fully geared to tourists.

Shepherds Bush and Hammersmith are not particularly interesting areas, a bit slow to up and come. But the Bush has a great market, a Jewish delicatessen, a cut-price menswear shop, a US custom car specialist and a few other surprises. Hammersmith, too, has a good, if small, fruit and veg.

market, an excellent architectural fittings shop, a sci-fi games shop and the new King's Mall shopping centre; particularly useful for its branches of Mothercare and Habitat.

See also Knightsbridge and Chelsea.

TRANSPORT

Notting Hill
Tube stations: Notting Hill Gate, Ladbroke Grove.
Buses: 27, 28, 31, 52, 88.

Holland Park
Tube stations: Holland Park.
Buses: 12, 88.

High St Kensington
Tube stations: High St Kensington.
Buses: 9, 27, 28, 49, 73.

Shepherds Bush/ Hammersmith
Tube stations: Kensington Olympia, Hammersmith, Goldhawk Rd, Shepherds Bush.
Buses: 6, 11, 88.

LOCAL OPENING HOURS

Few shops observe a half-day closing in Notting Hill and surrounds; most open 10.00–18.00 Mon to Sat.

REFRESHMENTS

There are several cafés in Notting Hill, Kensington High St, Shepherds Bush and Hammersmith. The only notable place in the area is

Julie's Bar
137 Portland Rd, W11.
Open 16.00–17.30 seven days a week.
Gothic-style wine bar with lush plants, comfy sofas and church pews. Home made cakes and tea.

NOTTING HILL

The Fool
Myrna Shoa and Ruti Cohen design and make a range of clothes based on medieval and Victorian fashions. They are continually doing museum research and dye all their own (natural) fabrics to subtle, muted shades. Designs are mainly for women and they use a lot of lace, cheesecloth, cotton velour and vibrant coloured velvet (their only synthetic fabric). Everything is washable and design detail work is impressive. Their small shop (workshop below) is in a bit of a nowhere land opposite a vast corrugated fenced building site. *14 Shrewsbury Rd, W2 (01–229 4354). Open 10.00–17.00 Mon to Fri; Sat market stall at junction of Portobello Rd and Westbourne Park Rd.*

Mr Christian's
Glynn Christian's imaginatively stocked delicatessen and off licence is highly reputed locally. He is an expert on cheese (author of *Cheese and Cheese-making*) and keeps an excellent range including several farm-house cheeses. His pâtés are sold by Harrods, and together with home-made pies, quiches, Justin de Blank bread and croissants plus a wide range of salamis, cold meats, herbs and spices, teas and fresh coffee make it a popular shop. There is an imaginative and unusual selection of wines, including their own vin ordinaire, plus an outside catering service.
11 Elgin Crescent, W11 (01–229 0501). Open 09.00–19.00 Mon to Fri; 09.00–18.00 Sat; 09.30–14.30 Sun.

Buyers and Sellers
Buyers and Sellers electrical appliance shop used to specialize in 'brown goods' until they diversified by pure chance into fridges and freezers some ten years ago. By buying in bulk, and selling demonstration models and machines with slight external faults, Buyers and Sellers reckon to undercut leading discount houses by 20%. Everything sold is in perfect mechanical condition and comes with the manufacturer's guarantee. Beside fridges and freezers, they also sell washing machines and other electrical equipment, depending on what comes their way. They provide a 48-hour delivery service.
120/122 Ladbroke Grove, W10 (01–229 1947). Open 09.00–17.00 Mon to Sat; 09.00–12.00 Thurs.

Tyre and Wheel Co
By buying in bulk, the Tyre and Wheel Co can give up to 50% off new, remould and part worn tyres. You can't miss the bright yellow shop with the piles of tyres outside. They reckon to be able to 'suit' most cars, can get anything to order with less of a discount, and will mend punctures, fix batteries and balance wheels.
353 Ladbroke Grove, W11 (01–969 9340). Open 08.30–18.00 Mon to Sat.

Portobello Road Market
The famous road of antique shops, which is smart at the top and becomes progressively more tatty towards Golborne Rd and the motorway overpass. Many of the shops close during the week but the whole street comes alive on Saturdays when an open-air market selling bric-à-brac, old clothes, jewellery, antiques and all sorts of oddities takes place. There is a real feeling of vitality to the market but these days bargains are few and far between. Further down the road is another market under the Westway motorway

arches. It is more craft and home industry oriented, with fewer real dealers, and is held on Friday morning and Saturdays.
Portobello Rd, W11. Sat all day.

Stout's
Mr Stout's old-fashioned English grocery (established 1921) specializes in English cheeses, all of which they cut to order. It also sells good bacon and coffee ground to order, as well as all the usual grocery items.
144 Portobello Rd, W11 (01-727 7066). Open 08.30-13.30, 14.30-17.30 Mon to Fri; 08.30-17.30 Sat; closed Thurs.

Tigermoth
Nine years ago when Tigermoth was founded, the choice of clothes for babies and children was limited to mass-produced Mothercare and pricey French numbers from Harrods with nothing in between. So Tigermoth set about finding reasonably priced 'different' children's clothes, with the emphasis on the sporty rather than the pretty look. They began by dyeing babygrows and coveralls themselves, sought out foreign clothes, and eventually did some designing themselves. Now they are known as one of the leading shops for unusual, functional and attractive clothes and underwear for the up to 14-year-olds. They still sell Petit Bateau underwear and T-shirts but import largely from Scandinavia. Their Shetland knitwear with rainbow stripes is very popular. Although they admit to being more up-market (it's impossible to find individual things at reasonable prices) they always have a sale rail or a bargain basket. They publish a mail order catalogue every March and September and regular customers get 10% off in the months (January and July) preceding the sale.
166 Portobello Rd, W11 (01-727 7564). Open 09.30-17.30 Mon to Sat. Also 425 Richmond Rd, East Twickenham (01-891 1971). Open 09.30-17.30 Mon to Sat.

Martins and Smiths
Specialize in foreign and less familiar fish like cuttlefish, regularly selling 40 different varieties, and everything in season. There are also live and cooked crabs and smoked fish.
202 Portobello Rd, W11 (01-727 9843). Also run by the same management, **Martins** *202 Portobello Rd, W11 (01-727 9843),* **Smiths** *208 Portobello Rd, W11 (01-727 6223). Both open 08.00-17.30 Tues to Sat; 08.00-13.00 Thurs.*

Ceres Bakery and Wholefoods
Wholefood's pioneer Craig Sams runs this highly reputed and now ten-year-old natural food shop and bakery. They mill

their own flour (using a mixture of wholemeals milled from different grains) and bake a range of breads, pastries and cakes round the corner in Preston Rd. They bake pies in the shop, which accounts for the delicious smell, and sell an extensive range of grains, beans, seeds, herbs, teas, organically grown vegetables, dairy products and juices. They also sell related books, run a mail order service for the sale of instruments and machines for a healthy life (hand-mills, etc.) and sell in bulk as well as in small quantities.
269A Portobello Rd, W11 (01-229 5571). Open 10.00–18.00 Mon to Sat.

London Bicycle Auctions
Stocks bicycles in various states of age and repair, which it sells every Saturday from 14.00; viewing from noon. Bicycles are accepted for sale up to 11.00, there is a 10% commission charge.
Bay 49, Westway Flyover, Portobello Rd, W11 (01–221 7272). From noon, Sats only.

London Postcard Centre
Although it looks like one shop, the five-year-old London Postcard Centre is really a market with a series of dealers, all specializing in different periods/subjects of old postcards. The postcards are categorized under subject for easy reference.
21 Kensington Park Rd, W11 (01–229 1888). Open 11.00–18.00 Mon to Fri; 09.30–18.30 Sat.

Rough Trade
Rough Trade specialize in singles from every small independent record label with particular emphasis on new wave. They keep stocks of all new wave singles and albums from all groups except The Stranglers. They also have a strong, pre-release reggae singles Jamaican import section and a limited selection of British release 7" reggae singles. There are limited second-hand stocks, and a choice of release and pre-release rock, soul, disco, reggae, blues and country 12" singles and albums. The shop also sells music papers and a limited selection of badges.
202 Kensington Park Rd, W11 (01–727 4312). Open 10.00–19.00 Mon to Sat.

Warwick
Warwick keep samples of their entire international collection of fabrics and matching or complementary wallcoverings in the shop. Customers then choose and order – delivery, from the wide and varied selection, depends on accessibility; it may be within 24 hours for some English designs and up to six weeks for Swiss and American

fabrics. They make up blinds to order and keep a standard range ready made, as well as providing a curtain making, loose cover and upholstery service. They stock a limited selection of original graphics, etchings, lithographs and screenprints by local artists.
5 Ladbroke Rd, W11 (01–229 1637). Open 09.30–17.30 Mon to Sat.

Retro
Period clothes. (See page 168 for full details.)
21 Pembridge Rd, W11 (01–229 0616). Open 10.30–18.00 Mon to Sat.

Yak
Clothes, kelims, antiques and jewellery from Afghanistan. (See page 135 for full details.)
41 Pembridge Rd, W11 (01–727 9193). Open 10.00–18.00 Mon to Sat. Sometimes closed 1.30–2.30 for lunch.

Plum
Plum is a small and highly individual shoe shop run by the owners of 'Yak' and 'The Natural Shoe Store'. Like all their shops 'Plum' resulted because Rachel Floater and Robert Lusk saw a gap in the market, this time for a 'nice' but special shoe shop. At Plum they concentrate on extravagent, fun shoes and boots, that are well made and finished at prices that aren't totally unrealistic. Decor is plum, furniture is comfortable and virtually all stock is on display. For women there are ankle strap sandals, bejewelled evening sandals and tiger print courts. For men there are two-tone saddle shoes, co-respondents, jazz shoes, lace ups and brogues.
51 Pembridge Rd, W11 (01–727 0418). Open 10.00–18.00 Mon to Sat.

The Brass Shop
Although they allow a bit of haggling the owners of this shop are far too clued up to let any real bargains slip through their fingers. They specialize in antique pewter, brass and copper, and also sell steel pokers, forks, firesets, bed-warmers, candlesticks, kettles, scuttles, plates, door furniture and a limited range of reproduction stuff, mainly door furniture and hunting horns.
23 Pembridge Rd, W11 (01–727 8643). Open 10.00–17.00 Mon to Sat; other times by appointment.

Carrie's
Carrie's always attracts a lot of window-shoppers who marvel at its fine window display of Victoriana, dolls' houses and furniture. Inside the small shop is crammed to capacity with mugs, china dogs, pictures, china figures, cup and saucers; as well as the Victorian dolls, dolls' houses, dolls' furniture and toys; stuffed birds and

animals and curiosity pieces. It is a specialist shop, as the prices reflect.
32 Pembridge Rd, W11 (01–727 4805). Open 11.00–17.00 Mon to Fri; 10.30–18.00 Sat.

John Oliver
John Oliver is a very useful centre for interior design advice and a wide range of wall coverings, matching and complementary fabrics and paints. Their paints are mixed to order and they are known for good strong colours – they can match anything in emulsion. John Oliver's own hand-printed wallpapers are kept in stock; those from other companies are bought to order.
33 Pembridge Rd, W11 (01–727 3735). Open 10.00–18.00 Mon to Sat.

Momtaz Gallery
Irene Momtaz took over the running of this small specialist gallery from her father 14 years ago. She has a superb collection of 8th- to 14th-century Islamic and Persian pottery, glass, metalwork and more recently, wood. She also sells pre-Islamic bronzes dating from 500B.C. Because of 'unfortunate incidents' Irene keeps the door closed and customers must ring the bell. It if means anything to you, Irene's pottery comes from the following regions: Nishipur 9th- to 11th-century; Gurgan 12th- to 13th-century; Rayy and Mina'i 13th- to 14th-century and the Seljuk period. It makes nice window shopping.
42 Pembridge Rd, W11 (01–229 5579). Open 10.00–17.00 Mon to Sat, or by appointment.

Mandarin Books
Mandarin is a small, packed and busy general bookshop with a particular leaning to the humanitarian subjects. They have been open 18 years and have built up strong politics, history, poetry, drama, philosophy, music, literary criticism and art book sections.
22 Notting Hill Gate, W11 (01–229 0327). Open 10.00–18.30 Mon to Fri; 10.00–18.00 Sat.

N.H.G. Panzer
Panzer run two delicatessens next door to each other; No. 24 is the main one with an extensive range of specialist and exotic foods from countries including France, the Middle East and America. They keep 200 different cheeses, many prepared salads, cold meats, salamis, pâtés, high class confectionery, fresh coffee, wines and beers. Next door at 24A is self-service and they sell croissants, cream cakes, tarts and pastries. Panzer also run a fruit and vegetable shop at No. 20 and a pasta and pizza restaurant at No. 14.
24 and 24A Notting Hill Gate, W11 (01–229 0822). Open

08.30–19.00 Mon to Sat; 09.30–13.00 Sun.

Bland and Son
Blands sports one of my favourite shop signs: a cut out metal umbrella. The 100-year-old shop still sells a wide range of umbrellas, but recently they've stopped making their own. They also sell leather goods, notably handbags, luggage and other travel accessories. Stock is conservative, but they are notable for their umbrella repair service. They also do handbag, suitcase and shoe repairs.
24B Notting Hill Gate, W11 (01–229 6711). Open 09.00–18.00 Mon to Sat.

Dress Pound
Rosalind Hanneman used to manage the Frock Exchange (see Earls Court) and four years ago opened her own shop to take on sale or return men's, women's and children's nearly new clothes. Clothes taken for resale must be in good condition (though the shop does do simple repairs like split seams, missing button, zips etc) and not dated. Because of their location (close to Campden Hill) they're heavily patronized by wealthy smart young ladies and a lot of their stuff is pretty up market. They reckon to sell at ⅓ or ½ the original price and give the 'seller' 25% of the original price. They also sell a lot of new end of lines at half price. All clothes and accessories, mostly for women. Appointment not necessary to show clothes. Children and women at Chelsea branch.
125 Notting Hill, W11 (01–229 3311). Open 10.00–19.00 Mon to Fri; 10.00–18.00 Sat.

Virgin Records
(See page 3 for full details.)
130 Notting Hill Gate, W11 (01–221 6177). Open 10.00–19.00 Mon to Sat.

Variety Trading Centre
For the past two years Ali Dina and his family have run this well-stocked mixed bag shop. He reckons to be 50–60% cheaper than street markets. Stock changes, depending on what he can buy in job lots. He regularly carries hardware, china, glass, suitcases, tools, gift lines (tourist style, also watches and lighters) gaudy children's toys, knives and radios. He candidly says, 'Some things are so cheap people think they are not worth buying.' Definitely worth checking regularly when in Notting Hill.
129–131 Notting Hill Gate, W11 (01–727 9044). Open 09.00–18.00 Mon to Sat.

Quality Delicatessen
Small and dark it may be, but Mr Salik's delicatessen enjoys a high reputation with Notting Hill locals. His leading speciality is cheeses, which he imports

from France, Italy, Austria, Denmark and Holland, then matures them himself and tends them with loving care. Brie is a particular speciality which can be bought at various different stages, and many English cheeses are also on sale. Mr Salik is known locally for his Polish sausages and frankfurters, delivered daily and made by a small local Polish firm. Other cooked meats include various salamis and pâtés imported from France and Belgium. Rye, French, plaited and pumpernickel breads, tinned and bottled groceries and seven different types of coffee beans ground to order are also available. Mr Salik has seen many delicatessens in the area come and go. He succeeds because he maintains a high respect for the food he sells.
133A Notting Hill Gate, W11 (01–229 3689). Open 09.45–19.00 Mon to Fri; til 18.00 Sat.

House and Bargain
Cut-price kitchenware.
142 Notting Hill Gate, W11 (01–229 9797). Open 09.30–18.00 Mon to Sat.

The Ski Shop
The Ski Shop sells a range of American, French, Italian and Scandinavian skiing equipment, clothes and après ski goods. They cater for amateurs but are much frequented by professionals. Tennis equipment, also to a professional level, windsurfing gear and wetsuits, are also on sale on the same floor. Downstairs they run a separate boutique selling clothing for disco-dancing, roller-skating and skate-boarding. They sell a wide range of clothes, equipment and all the accessories.
158 Notting Hill Gate, W11 (01–221 6042). Open 10.00–18.00 Mon to Sat; until 19.00 Wed.

The Hire Shop
The most central branch of a 20-year-old general hire firm. Full details of hire stock is listed under Worth a Trip section, page 208.
192 Campden Hill Rd, W8 (01–727 0897). Open 08.30–17.30 Mon to Fri; 08.30–13.00 Sat. Also at Ealing.

Zodiac
Peter Bull and Don Busby's astrological emporium is a tiny but fascinating shop. They have purposely geared the shop to the serious astrologer and the casual gift buyer alike. Over the six years they've been open, their stock of books on all aspects of astrology has reached mammoth proportions and takes up a large part of the shop's space. Amazingly, they sell 30 different types of Tarot cards, from the world's tiniest to the elaborate Visconti-Sforza cards. Aside from numerous gift items, Zodiac offer all sorts of personalized services

including pictures, tales, portraits (with or without birthdate details) beautifully painted on stones, and crystal glass engraved to order. Zodiac have a resident clairvoyant / tarot reader who gives readings on Tues, Wed, Fri and Sat by appointment in an upstairs room. Incidentally, Peter Bull sells signed copies of his book *Book of Teddy Bears* for the cover price.
3 Kensington Mall, W8 (01-229 8032). Open 10.00-18.00 Mon to Sat.

HIGH ST KENSINGTON

Distinctive Trimmings
Opened in 1965, this shop sells braids, cord tie-backs for curtains, fringes, borders (some with tassles or bobbles) to enliven home decoration. There is a wide range, both English and imported. If D.T. cannot match your colour scheme from stock, they will make tie-backs to order. Also a postal matching service.
17 Kensington Church St, W8 (01-937 6174). Open 09.30-17.30 Tues to Fri; 09.30-13.00 Sat. Also at 11 Marylebone Lane, W1.

Patisserie Française
Queues form at this popular French patisserie for its delicious English and French breads, croissants, tarts and cakes. All are baked in Queensway at the parent branch.
27A Kensington Church St, W8 (01-937 9574). Open 09.00-18.00 Mon to Sat.

Pom
Pom sell a range of clothes imported from France and Spain for 0-14-year-old boys and girls. Styles for all occasions include an exclusive range of heavy knitwear and a range of pretty print dresses. They also sell accessories.
47 Kensington Church St, W11 (01-937 8641). Open 10.15-18.00 Mon to Sat.

The Lacquer Chest
This unpretentious antique shop has been a favourite of mine for years. The owners always provide both value for money and a novelty element in their choice of stock. They concentrate on Victoriana, and like things to be functional.
75 Kensington Church St, W8 (01-937 1366). Open 09.30-17.30 Mon to Sat.

Eila Grahame
Eila Grahame sells all types of 16th-, 17th- and 18th-century continental glass, and always has a stock of superb rummers and other special drinking glasses.
97a Kensington Church St, W8 (01-727 4132). Open 09.30-17.30 Mon to Fri; closed 13.00-14.15 for lunch; open 11.00-16.00 Sat.

Bedlam
Everything to do with beds and going to bed from night-shirts, hats, socks, novelty pyjamas (convict arrows, etc) to sheets, duvets, mattresses and beds. The bedridden model in the window raises a smile.
114 Kensington Church St, W8 (01–229 5341). Open 10.00–18.00 Mon to Sat; until 20.00 on Thurs.

Studio Bookshop
This canopied general bookshop is particularly good for second-hand books and publishers' remainders on all subjects. It also stocks Sothebys' and other auctioneers' catalogues, Japanese books, and prints.
123 Kensington Church St, W8 (01–727 4995). Open 10.00–18.00 Tues to Sat.

Kensington Bookshop
The emphasis is on children's books at this general bookshop stocking both paper- and hard-back titles. They also keep a decent range of greetings cards and wrapping paper.
140 Kensington Church St, W8 (01–727 0544). Open 10.00–18.00 Mon to Fri; 10.00–17.30 Sat.

Patricia Roberts
Here knitwear designer Patricia Roberts sells her range of wools, called Woollybear Yarns, which are in bright primary colours like the shop's decor. There are mohairs, Shetlands, cashmeres, alpacas and thick and thin cotton bouclés. There is a mail order service, and a range of exclusive and expensive, Patricia Roberts' designs on sale. A pattern book is available.
1B Kensington Church Walk, W8 (01–937 0097). Open 10.00–18.00 Mon to Sat.

Barkers
The only remaining Kensington department store, Barkers offers a little of everything. There are fresh flowers and vegetables adjacent to the Food Hall which has a good cheese counter; cosmetics, hosiery, haberdashery, stationery and gifts are all on the ground floor. Furnishing and dress fabrics, domestic electrical equipment, kitchenware, children's clothes and toys, young and not so young fashions, records and sportswear can be found on the other three floors.
Kensington High St, W8 (01–937 5432). Open 09.00–17.30 Mon, Wed and Fri; 09.30–17.30 Tues; 09.00–19.00 Thurs; 09.00–18.00 Sat.

Tree House
This children's toyshop is equally popular with children and adults alike. They sell a wide range of toys, small and large, including lots of those imaginative, novel, pocket-money toys which adults find irresistible. Their bath/water

toy section is very much appreciated by small children.
37 Kensington High St, W8 (01–937 7497). Open 09.30–17.30 Mon to Sat.

Slick Willies
Slick Willies opened and came into its own at the beginning of the skateboard craze. They still stock a wide range of skateboards and accessories but also sell adult leisurewear, largely imported from America, such as American secondhand sporting clothes, lots of baseball gear, T-shirts, jackets, shorts, baseball boots and plimsolls.
47 Kensington High St, W8 (01–937 9547). Open 09.30–18.30 Mon to Sat; 09.30–19.00 Thurs.

Reeves/Dryad
A large two-floor craft shop with Dryad down-stairs and Reeves up-stairs. Downstairs stocks craft DIY equipment and custom-made supplies for weaving, bookbinding, chair-making, raffia work, enamelling and jewellery making. Upstairs there is a wide range of beads, artist's materials and equipment for silkscreening, batik and dyes. They provide a picture framing service as well as selling DIY equipment.
178 Kensington High St, W8 (01–937 5370). Open 09.00–17.30 Mon to Fri; 09.00–17.00 Sat.

Tempo Electrical Discount Store
Tempo is an electrical cut-price store. Their prices are worth checking against other similar stores for TVs, fridges, cookers, irons, toasters and accessories like batteries, radios and calculators.
190 Kensington High St, W8 (01–937 5166). Open 10.00–20.00 Mon and Fri; 09.00–18.00 Tues, Wed, Thurs and Sat.

Booksmith
The largest branch of this small chain of bookshops which specializes in remaindered books; subjects are very broadly ordered but you really need plenty of time to look through them. They also stock a wide range of new paperbacks.
201 Kensington High St, W8 (01–937 5002). Open 10.00–20.00 Mon to Sat.

Mitsukiku
One of a chain of shops selling decorative and functional items from Japan. Everything is displayed for easy viewing. There are polyester and cotton mix kimonos of all lengths in a choice of plain fabric with Japanese embroidered word/symbol, or flowered fabric (for men, women and children), jackets and Japanese sandals, toys and traditional games, mobiles, rice bowls, mugs and chopsticks.
209 Kensington High St, W8

(01-937 1440). Open 10.00–18.00 Mon to Fri; 10.00–19.00 Sat. Also at 4 Pembridge Rd, W11; 157 Victoria St, SW1; and 15 Old Brompton Rd, SW7.

Banham Burglary Prevention
The entire Banham range of locks, alarms and safes can be seen and their virtues discussed at this shop. They operate a lock-out service during opening hours and will advise on fitting burglar alarms and changing locks. They also operate a key-cutting service.
233 Kensington High St, W8 (01-937 4311 or 01-584 3568). Open 09.30–17.30 Mon to Fri; 09.30–12.00 Sat.

Boat Showrooms of London
What can be seen in the window belies the vast and varied stock of this 16-year-old company. They market pleasure boats, anything from rubber dinghies to a 20-metre long boats, including sailing boats. They are the largest international agent for AMF, who make Harley Davidsons amongst other things, and manufacture work boats and paramilitary boats.
286-290 Kensington High St, W14 (01-602 0123). Open 09.00–17.30 Mon to Fri; 09.00–19.00 Thurs; 09.00–13.00 Sat. Open 7 days by arrangement.

Tomlinson and Tomlinson
This large and pleasant knitwear shop uniquely displays its wares on wooden poles slipped through the arms of jumpers. Like their parent shop Scottish Merchant (see Bloomsbury), T and T keep an extensive range of Scottish knitwear including Fair Isles, striped and plain Shetlands, Hebridean guernseys, various knitted hats, gloves and shawls, but they specialize in designer knitwear. The variety of styles, shapes, patterns, techniques and yarns used is enormous. The shop is informal and relaxed and there's a 'comfy corner' where friends/children can wait while you look.
8 Hornton St, W8 (01-937 5173). Open 10.00–18.00 Mon to Fri; til 19.00 Thurs and 10.00–17.30 Sat.

Dilemma
All manner of quirky gift items can be found at Dilemma. Their current mail order catalogue (ring for price) features a 45-cm light-up Mr Michelin man; various funny clocks; sunglasses with wipers; a range of odd ceramics (birthday cake teapot, egg cups with feet, etc.); modern tin toys and a range of jokey stocking fillers.
22 Thackeray St, W8 (01-937 9059). Open 10.00–18.00 Mon to Sat.

Animal Fair
Animal Fair specialize in small breed pedigree puppies and kittens. Since the import ban, their other speciality of tame parrots has been curtailed but they regularly keep a few. Also gerbils, rabbits, mice, budgies, etc., and an extensive range of tropical fish. All accessories and food for the pets they sell are also on sale. Animal Fair operate a pet care centre (kennelling) and a grooming service.
17 Abingdon Rd, W8 (01–937 0011). Open 09.30–18.00 Mon to Sat.

Aquinas Locke (London) Ltd
Go here for contemporary and modern cast (hand-made) and spun (machine-made) pewter – goblets, plates, figures, candlesticks, ashtrays, trays, teasets, etc.
Pewter Centre, 87 Abingdon Rd, W8 (01–373 7025 or 01–937 4118). Open 09.30–17.30 Mon to Fri; 09.30–16.00 Sat.

Nannies
Nannies is a small toyshop for children up to five years old. Their preference is for harmless cuddly toys, enormous French teddybears, Snoopys, model cars and toys for the bath.
16 Stratford Rd, W8 (01–937 3299/2333). Open 09.30–17.30 Mon to Fri.

HOLLAND PARK

Cucina
Cucina is a good port of call if you're stuck for a present. This branch (see Englands Lane Hampstead) is small and cluttered and spills on to the pavement whenever weather permits. Hand-painted colourful Spanish pottery is virtually exclusive to this shop, and includes egg cups, mugs, plates and bowls, and, particularly unusual, various sized flower pots with matching saucers. Their range of basketware is varied and their bamboo furniture (bookcases, framed mirrors, plant holders, tables, chairs, screens, bedbacks and sofas) is attractive, plain and reasonably priced. They sell various cooking crocks including a cast iron range. They produce a mail order catalogue every few months which they will send on request.
4 Ladbroke Grove, W11 (01–229 1496). Open 10.00–18.00 Tues to Sat. Also Englands Lane, Belsize Village, NW3.

David Black
David Black and partner Clive Loveless sell old and antique kelims. Their shop is more of a showroom – three, in fact – where rugs are piled high and displayed on the walls. Their key speciality is vegetable-dyed kelims, but they also

stock old and antique tribal and village rugs from the Caucasus, Persia, Turkey, Russia and Turkestan. Sadly, because of the high prices these beautiful rugs fetch, 60% of the stock goes abroad. Current prices range from £100 up to thousands, but they have many in the £200 price range. If that is way out of your league, they are happy for people to just look and are probably the most informal shop of their type. They do occasionally get hold of small pieces which make attractive wall-hangings or cushion covers. The shop offers a hand-cleaning service for rugs, and restoration is undertaken, as is valuation for insurance.
96 Portland Rd, W11 (01–727 2566). Open 14.00–18.00 Mon to Sat.

Virginia
This small shop is literally brimming over with period clothes, lace, bric-à-brac and French enamel stoves. Over the seven years that the shop has been open it has built a reputation for the unusual, if not for bargains. They regularly stock Edwardian and Victorian christening dresses, stained glass windows, lamps, enamel stoves and old basins, though the speciality is clothes. There is a rail of cheaper clothes downstairs while the rest – up to £80 for a real beauty – beaded, heavily laced or panne velvet, are upstairs. They tend to favour evening dresses, many of which are very beautiful.
98 Portland Rd, W11 (01–727 9908). Open 14.00–18.00 Mon to Sat; often open from 11.00.

Myriad
This is an interior designer's paradise which sells old brass light switches, door knobs and bath taps, wicker, bamboo and other decorative junk with the emphasis on bathroom and kitchen things. It's a small shop which has become almost too popular, and is a wonderful find if you favour old kitchen and bathroom paraphernalia. They do a lot of hiring out for film sets which helps to keep prices down.
133 Portland Rd, W11 (01–229 1709). Open 11.00–18.00 Mon to Sat.

Scoffs
This attractive and colourful high class grocery and delicatessen was a welcome arrival to this mini-village. It's a corner shop with groceries, pastas, condiments, etc. displayed for self-service, and a counter with a delicious and freshly prepared array of home-cooked meats (casseroles, pasta dishes) and salads, pâtés, ham and cheeses. They sell Ceres breads and a range of wines.
141 Portland Rd, W11 (01–727 4831). Open 09.00–19.00 Mon to Sat.

Elon Tile (UK) Ltd
From a small and pleasant showroom Elon display a fraction of their range of superb handmade plain and patterned Mexican terracotta tiles, basins and complementary fittings. The painted and glazed tiles all follow traditional designs using subtle shades, while the plain glazed tiles come in vibrant colours. The tiles are dried in the sun and tend to be rather irregular which adds to their charm but can make laying them a bit tricky. A catalogue of the entire range is available (ring for current price) but be warned, these delightful round basins and tiles don't come cheap.
8 Clarendon Cross, W11 (01–727 0884). Open 10.00–17.30 Mon to Fri; 10.00–13.00 Sat.

Peter Eaton Ltd
Peter Eaton's shop was the first custom-built antiquarian bookshop to open in London. The floor to ceiling plate glass window caused a stir 20 years ago and still turns heads now. There is a large secondhand section in the basement, but the bulk of books are collectors' items on all subjects.
80 Holland Park Ave, W11 (01–727 5211). Open 10.00–17.00 Mon to Sat.

Intervision Video Ltd
Intervision is the oldest manufacturer of video cassettes and currently has around 300 titles available for sale and hire. An illustrated catalogue is available (ring for details of charge) and their range includes serious/art films, a selection of Hollywood classics; horror movies; several programmes of short chess masterpeices; and extensive pop music coverage including several rare footages of Hendrix, Otis Redding and The Byrds. Cassettes are available on daily rental.
102 Holland Park Ave, W11 (01–221 5081). Open 09.00–17.45 Mon to Fri; 09.00–17.00 Sat.

SHEPHERDS BUSH/ HAMMERSMITH

Olympic Sewing Machines
For over ten years Olympic have sold and repaired all types of new, secondhand and very old domestic and industrial sewing machines. They keep an extensive range of spare parts, can service virtually any machine made, and give a 48-hour repair service.
1C, 1D Shepherds Bush Rd, W6 (01–743 6683). Open 09.30–18.00 Mon to Sat.

Brook Green Essences
Brook Green Essences is linked somewhere along the line with the original Chelsea branch but while they stock similar gear they don't work together. They

stock clothes for women from the 1920s to the 1940s with a preference for floaty, very feminine styles. Also fur coats, shawls, silk scarves and camiknickers.
107 Shepherds Bush Rd, W6 (01–603 2326). Open 15.00–18.30 Mon to Fri.

Shepherd's Bush Market
The site of this market is called Railway Approach; it is free of cars and runs between Uxbridge Rd and Goldhawk Rd. It is lined with cosmopolitan food shops (Pak International and Hawkins are good for cheap bulk rice, etc.), record shops and cheap and cheerful fashions. There are places selling Afro hair gear, hand and electrical tools at W.G. Stores, wood from R.W. Dunn & Sons, fish from W.H. Roe, pets and pet food from Ellis's and remnants and ribbons from Rhoda's. Behind the shops and market is a large fashion/luggage/boot and shoe arcade. The market itself is largely fruit and veg with a smattering of gaudy fabric stalls, hats, plastic flowers, outsize bras and girdles, mixed and broken biscuits, cut price chemist gear at Gino's and The Cut Price Stall, foam chips and plants. The best days are Fridays and Saturdays.
Goldhawk Rd, W12. Open approx. 09.00–17.00 Mon to Sat; half day Thurs.

Ashkens
Ashkens is an enormous Jewish grocery with a large delicatessen counter. They keep all the usual groceries and Jewish specialities as well as Polish, Greek and Turkish favourites.
15/19 Goldhawk Rd, W12 (01–743 3554/6491). Open 08.00–18.30 Mon to Thurs; 08.00–19.30 Fri; 08.00–18.30 Sat; 08.00–13.00 Sun.

Cromwell's Bazaar
Cromwell's Bazaar claims to have London's lowest prices on certain lines in jeans, shirts, jackets and other items of men's clothing. Their enormous window regularly sports changing bargains from most leading manufacturers.
20 Goldhawk Rd, W12 (01–749 6909). Open 09.00–18.00 Mon to Sat.

West London Hairdressing Sundries
This cluttered self-service style shop presided over by George boasts all those hair requisites which are normally expensively packaged, in large plain containers at cash and carry prices. Here you can buy shampoo, conditioner, hair spray, dyes and rinses, cream rinses and rollers from all the leading manufacturers in trade containers at trade prices. Bona fide hairdressers get a further 10% discount.
56 Goldhawk Rd, W12 (01–743

1632). Open 09.00–18.00 Mon to Sat.

Andy's

Andy's narrow shopfront displays a variety of men's and women's boots and shoes, both stylish and flamboyant. Andy will make up from drawings, ideas and the most obscure designs. All boots are leather lined, heeled and soled, and there is a choice of all the basic leather colours, plus snakeskin and a range of printed leathers. Andy has been making made-to-measure boots for nearly 20 years and enjoys a high reputation.

61B Goldhawk Rd, W12 (01–734 4978). Open 09.00–17.30 Mon to Sat.

A.R. Roberts

This small narrow shop, on the premises for over 60 years, keeps an extensive range of (mainly Swiss) spare parts and tools for repairing clocks and watches. The two gentlemen who search through numerous drawers behind the trade counter for the particular bit you require are patient and helpful. They do not do repairs however.

61A Goldhawk Rd, W12 (01–743 1411). Open 09.00–17.30 Mon to Sat; closed 13.00–14.00 and Thurs.

V.W. Humphries

The Humphries family have run this small sewing machine shop and adjoining repair workshop for the past 25 years. They specialize in Bernina, Pfaff and Frister and Rossman (main dealers) machines of all ages and keep a full complement of spare parts. They average 15–20% off recommended prices and offer HP terms through a finance company. They service and repair all machines, give demonstrations on all machines sold and keep a small selection of industrial machines. They also sell some haberdashery.

78 Goldhawk Rd, W12 (01–743 3834). Open 09.00–17.00 Mon to Sat; closed Thurs.

Prop House

Peter Rutherford spends a lot of time turning away people who want to buy from his fine collection of domestic dressings from most periods. He specializes in 1920's, 1930's and 1950's, things all of which are carefully displayed in his numerous showrooms. Everything is available for hire and Peter's clients include all the TV companies, advertising agencies and film companies. He can do a complete Victorian grocery, period windows, doors, butcher sets, juke boxes (he's particularly proud of a beautifully preserved Wurlitzer), old radios, tea services from all periods, brassware, lamps, stained glass and a

fantastic battery of bric-à-brac and period incidentals.
142 and 154 Goldhawk Rd, W12 (01–743 0835). Open 09.00–17.30 Mon to Sat.

Cliff Davis Cars Ltd
Cliff Davis had been in the car business for years before he gave in to his passion for American cars and opened this garage/shop in 1931. His son and son-in-law are now involved and they sell secondhand, and occasionally new, US cars, spares, bolt-on goodies and custom equipment, and do servicing and repairs. They are quite a landmark in the area – as if the masses of huge limos parked outside wasn't enough, they've mounted a giant green frog from the film set of *Queen Kong* on the roof. Details of American car races in this country are available from this shop.
247/251 Goldhawk Rd, W12 (01–748 5689/9595/9449) spares 01–748 2817. Open 09.30–18.30/19.00 Mon to Sat.

Boules
Boules are wholesalers of reasonably priced, informal and mainly cotton clothes for women. Their own designs are made up for them in India in plain and printed Indian cottons, and they also import a range of leather and other belts, bags, jewellery and split bamboo blinds. Boules use their retail shop for regular sales of discontinued lines, damaged stock samples and clothes which haven't moved as expected. There is always a superb, colourful window display.
146 King St, W6 (01–748 5379). Open 10.00–18.00 Mon to Sat.

Sewcraft
Sewcraft are the largest independent sewing and knitting machine dealers in the country. They keep all leading names and sell all their machines at between 15% and 40% discount. They have a secondhand department, take in part-exchange, and do repairs.
150 King St, Hammersmith, W6 (01–748 0808/5511). Open 09.00–17.30 Mon to Sat; 09.00–13.00 Thurs.

Hammersmith Market
There are only a dozen stalls at this market, selling mostly fruit and veg, with reliable, good quality produce. In addition, the Tydeman family run two fish stalls; smoked and fresh fish, and shell fish. The best day is Saturday.
Hammersmith Grove/King St, W6. Open 09.00–17.00 Mon to Sat; half day Thurs.

Sellar Bros (Fastenings) Ltd
A family-run architectural ironmonger specializing in fittings and tools. The tool side is largely restricted to woodworking but they have some electrical tools too, notably the Black and

Decker range of drills and accessozies.
5 Beadan Rd, W6 (01-748 7162). Open 09.00-18.00 Mon to Sat; 09.00-13.00 Thurs.

Surplus Military Clothing Co
Andrew Sparsis sells flying suits, gas masks and a whole range of surplus military clothing.
77 Glenthorne Rd, W6 (01-748 1456). Open 09.30-17.30 Mon to Sat.

Games Workshop
Somewhat off the beaten track, this small shop run by enthusiasts is a real find for games buffs. There are computer games, video and war games, as well as over a thousand fantasy and science fiction miniature figures, posters, cards and jigsaws.
1 Dalling Rd, W6 (01-741 3445). Open 10.30-18.00 Mon to Fri; 10.00-17.30 Sat.

Hammersmith Home Brewing Centre
A small but well-stocked shop keeping everything for the novice and expert home brewer alike. Advice is happily given, particularly to beginners, whom they steer away from kits. Many dried fruits and flowers are available as well as tinned juices.
210 Talgarth Rd, W12 (01-741 0833). Open 10.00-18.00 Tues to Sat.

11
FULHAM AND EARLS COURT

West Kensington, Earls Court, Fulham, Parsons Green.

Close to Gloucester Rd air terminal, Earls Court and its surroundings are traditionally bedsit land, particularly popular with students and young overseas visitors to London. The shops reflect this transient and disordered lifestyle and many of the shops (particularly in the Earls Court Rd) stay open late. Shoddy clothes shops and multi-racial food shops form the basic shopping.

Fulham proper is very different. Its 'real' character is that of a working class residential area with corner shops to serve the community's needs. But, located close to Chelsea, pockets of Fulham – Parsons Green, the Chelsea ends of Fulham Rd and Kings Rd, and, less so, around Fulham Broadway – have become fashionable residential areas. To match the new character of the area, antique shops and new specialist shops now rub shoulders with the old-fashioned and down to earth variety. Some of Fulham's back streets, like Munster Rd and Lillie Rd, are still a junk hoarder's (and dealer's) paradise with their many bric-à-brac and house-clearance shops.

See also Knightsbridge and South of the River.

TRANSPORT

West Kensington
Tube stations: West Kensington, Kensington Olympia.
Buses: 14.

Earls Court
Tube stations: Earls Court.
Buses: 31, 74

Fulham
Tube stations: West Brompton,

Fulham Broadway, West Kensington, Barons Court, Parsons Green, Putney Bridge.
Buses: 11, 28, 30, 73, 295.

Parsons Green
Tube stations: Parsons Green, Putney Bridge.
Buses: 14, 22, 28, 30.

LOCAL OPENING HOURS

The many delicatessen/general food shops in Earls Court Rd stay open up to midnight. Other shops in Fulham either observe the traditional Thurs half-day or close early on Sat. Newer shops in the area either close all day Thurs or Mon or open six days a week.

REFRESHMENTS

There are plenty of 'plastic' snack bars in Earls Court and Gloucester Rd. The rest of the area is peppered with cheap cafés.

WEST KENSINGTON

Candle Makers Supplies
CMS were pioneers of the craze for candle illumination some 14 years ago. They used to sell their own hand-made candles but for years have concentrated on supplying candle makers with all their materials, from a beginner's kit to the most obscure accessory. They now also specialize in the related craft of batik-dyeing and sell all the necessary equipment.
28 Blythe Rd, W14 (01-602 4031). Open 10.30-18.00 Mon to Sat; 10.30-13.00 Thurs; closed 13.00-14.00 for lunch.

Upholstery Workshop
The Upholstery Workshop is a member of the Master Upholsters Association. They re-upholster and cover armchairs, chaise-longues and chesterfields. They keep samples of over 10,000 different fabrics and reckon to take between four and six weeks.
13-15 North End Rd, W14 (01-603 9009). Open 08.30-17.30 Mon to Fri.

Yak
Owners Robert Lusk and Rachel Floater, originally used the basement of this shop to make leather sandals. After a trip to Afghanistan to study and make bags they began importing Afghani antiques and clothes. They expanded upstairs and launched Yak, a specialist shop for old and new clothes, rugs, jewellery, bags, objects and antiques from Afghanistan, together with their own leather work. They sell ethnic knitwear in the winter, espadrilles and other comfortable sandals, Turkish kelims and rugs, American satin clothes (bomber jackets, T-shirts, waistcoats and blouses), kelim and leather bags,

a wide range of cheap old and antique jewellery (much is silver), and textiles suitable for cushion covers and mini wall hangings.
20 North End Rd, W14 (01–603 6017). Open 10.00–18.00 Mon to Sat. Also Pembridge Rd, W11.

Natural Shoe Store
It was thanks to the popularity of the backward-sloping shoe at Yak (next door) that the owners opened the Natural Shoe Store. For some time they sold only this type of shoe then gradually they expanded into other types of footwear with the emphasis on comfort and high quality workmanship. Now they sell various Western-style boots including the entire Frye (all-leather American cowboy-style boots for men and women) range, clogs, soft leather hikers (low - heeled, hard - wearing shoes), various brogues and attractive 'sensible' shoes and espadrilles. They keep a range of hide food and boot/shoe cleaning gear, leg warmers and socks. Quality and price are high.
21 North End Rd, W14 (01–602 2866). Open 10.00–18.00 Mon to Sat. Also Neal St, WC2 and Beaufort St, off Kings Rd, SW3.

Maison Desirée
French and Continental bakers with a range of pâtisserie and boulangerie baked on the premises. Highly praised (if somewhat chaotically served) by locals.
27 North End Rd, W14 (01–603 0385). Open 09.30–18.00 Mon to Sat.

Barnum's Carnival Novelties Ltd
Barnum's sell everything to make a party go with a swing – streamers, balloons, carnival heads for hire, etc. Their colourful window display shows only a fraction of their stock of the trimmings for fêtes, carnivals, parties and Christmas. They sell Christmas decorations all the year round and hire out Father Christmas costumes.
67 Hammersmith Rd, W14 (01–602 1211). Open 09.00–17.00 Mon to Fri.

The Carnival Store
Mr Stephanides makes all his theatrical costumes on the premises and he specializes in animals for pantomimes. Clothes can be made to order and he runs a fancy dress hire service.
95 Hammersmith Rd, W14 (01–603 7824). Open 10.00–13.00; 14.00–18.00 Mon to Fri; 10.00–13.00 Sat.

Buy Late Foods
Its late opening hours are the reason for Buy Late's entry. Self-service style foods until 22.00, seven days a week.
99 Hammersmith Rd, W14 (01–603 2300). Open 09.00–22.00 seven days a week.

Any Amount of Books

This general bookshop has several special features. They operate a bargain basement (magazines and novels), run a stall of free books for the over 60s, and have strong children's, feminist and serious modern literature sections.

103 Hammersmith Rd, W14 (01-603 9232). Open 11.00-19.00 Tues to Sat.

Stokecroft Arts

Hand-worked solid pine beds, tables, shutters, settees and foam, orthopaedic and sprung mattresses (see pages 85-6 for full details.)

107-109 Hammersmith Rd, W14 (01-603 8138). Open 10.00-17.30 Mon, Tues, Fri and Sat.

EARLS COURT

C. Rassell Ltd

The Rassell family have run their pretty nursery and gardening shop from these premises since 1904. It remains a family business with staff who care about plants, and though it's often very busy with Kensingtonites noisily stocking up on house and bedding plants, there is always someone available to give advice. In the shop they sell cut flowers in season, seeds and houseplants, while the extensive back open nursery (the entire square) keeps a wide range of bedding and herbaceous plants, shrubs, herbs, vegetables and gardening equipment. They specialize in the less usual plants and sell Italian terracotta containers/pots of all sizes. Pricey but good quality.

80 Earls Court Rd, W8 (01-937 0481). Open 09.00-17.30 Mon to Sat; 09.00-18.30 Thurs.

Nimbus

Keen camper Les Bryan is all set to equip would-be back-packers from head to toe with everything they will need for a self-sufficient camping holiday. Les operates a hire service, sells secondhand gear, takes in part exchange and offers very competitive prices on new equipment. The L-shaped shop displays everything in supermarket, help-yourself style with new equipment upstairs and second-hand downstairs. Les and the shop's owner, Mr Williams, aren't interested in equipping families with frame tents and luxury equipment - only in lightweight essential or useful gear for solo campers. They will buy everything back when it's finished with and offer discounts to almost any group or organization. Nimbus keeps a particularly good range of packs (rucksacks) and sleeping-bags.

121 Earls Court Rd, SW5 (01-373 8343). Open 09.30-18.00 Mon to Thurs; 09.30-19.30 Fri; 09.30-18.30 Sat.

Fotofast
Fotofast is a functionally-designed shop done out in black and bright yellow. Behind the counter they stock Kodak b/w and colour film and Ilford b/w film. Aside from photographic film sales, they offer a full developing and printing service and specialize in a 6-hour Mon-Fri colour developing service. They have many shops throughout London and film is developed at a central laboratory in Kings Cross. The idea is that customers drop in their film on their way to work and pick it up on the way home, or drop it in at the end of the day and pick it up the next morning. Prices are very competitive.
147 Earls Court Rd, SW5 (01–370 5979). Open 08.30–18.00 Mon to Fri; 09.30–17.00 Sat.

Robert Troop Master Baker
Robert Troop bakes all kinds of white and brown bread and rolls, sticky buns, scones, doughnuts and other confectionery. Noted for their hot sausage rolls (all day) and above average Cornish pasties.
151 Earls Court Rd, SW5 (01–370 1020). Open 08.30–18.00 Mon to Sat.

J. W. Carpenter
This 80-year-old double-fronted ironmongers is part of a 105-year-old chain. Half of their stock is household hardware and the rest is hand and electrical tools for all trades; electrical fittings; paints and decorating gear; plumbing equipment; gardening equipment and lawn-mowers; general ironmongery and some camping gear.
188–190 Earls Court Rd, SW5 (01–370 3077). Open 08.30–17.30 Mon to Sat.

The Warehouse Utility Clothing Company
Eleven years ago Maurice Bennett opened the first Warehouse shop just across the road from this new branch. They set out to sell high fashion from leading manufacturers at cut prices. They achieved this by buying late from over-production; buying designs which didn't go into the designer's collection, and by buying end-of-range fabric and getting it speedily made up into their own designer's interpretation of the current and forthcoming season's designs. They now have 10 shops all over London and all have a high reputation for well made, pretty and very fashionable seasonal clothes; mainly separates. Today their sources have changed marginally. You will find British and European designed garments at half the normal prices (usually with the label cut out) and a far larger percentage of their own designs. Warehouse are particularly good for trousers, shirts, blouses, day and smartish

dresses, suits and some accessories. New stock arrives frequently as turnover is fast and they reckon on 40 different styles each season (they count two seasons only – winter and summer) and around 300 garments in each run.
202 Earls Court Rd, SW5 (01–373 2346). Open 09.30–19.00 Mon to Sat. Branches throughout London, including Queensway, W2; Duke St, W1; Cheapside, EC2; Holborn, EC1.

ABC Motor Cycle Clothing Centre
ABC is the place for the latest fashions in motorbike gear. They import from the States, Holland and France as well as stocking British designs. They take commissions for George Hostler's knitwear; lurex names and symbols to order and keep an extensive range of helmets, boots, gloves, scarves and other accessories.
231 Earls Court Rd, SW5 (01–373 4737). Open 10.00–18.00 Mon to Fri; 10.00–17.30 Sat.

Beggar's Banquet
For five years this small, well stocked and busy record and cassette shop has built a reputation for buying and selling good condition, second-hand records and keeping a wide range of classical, jazz, punk, rock and reggae records and tapes. Downstairs they run a quadrophonic centre; stock, they say, is hard to come by as quadrophonic sound hasn't really taken off. B.B. has its own record label. They let people listen to records – within reason – and aside from buying secondhand records for cash they'll take 'almost anything' says manager, Mike Stone, in part exchange. They have branches in Richmond and North End Rd.
8 Hogarth Rd, SW5 (01–370 6175). Open 10.00–21.30 Mon to Fri; 10.00–19.00 Sat. Also at North End Rd, SW6.

Living Art
Solicitor John Harrap and his potter wife Izzy started their craft shop five years ago because they liked the idea of working together. They live above the square, light, corner shop and much of their stock comes from friends; one engraves glass, another illustrates children's books and another paints on china which she makes in the shop's kiln. The stock is continually changing and they welcome visits from craftsmen. They hold regular exhibitions of work and supplement stocks with Briglin pottery (see Marylebone) for details); Culpeper herbs, soaps, pot-pourris and shampoos; basketware; prettily covered notebooks; picture frames and novelty items. They always sell cushion covers, aprons and scarves made from

hand-dyed fabrics; soft toys; pressed flowers pictures; work from Yateley Disabled Industries, and a selection of bags.
35 Kenway Rd, SW5 (01–370 2766). Open 11.00–19.00 Tues to Fri; closed 13.15–14.00; 10.00–16.00 Sat.

Orbis
Thirty-odd years ago during the war, a lorry stocked with Polish books used to tour the various camps. Several shops later, the place for Polish books has come to rest here. It's a cluttered, old-fashioned sort of book shop, staffed by dedicated ladies who know the stock inside out. They stock everything published outside Poland in Polish, books on Poland and Eastern Europe in English, and a selection of books published in Poland. They are also a well-known source of books by oppressed Russian writers and the outlet for the entire range of coffee table books published by Orbis. The shop is decorated with Polish knick-knacks like ornamental pottery dolls, wooden plates and white porcelain animals made by Mrs Wilkinson who has supplied them for 20 years. Four times a year they publish a list of all newly published books which is sent to their many regular customers who buy by mail, and sold for 50p to casual callers to the shop. Orbis sell a limited selection of Polish folk music.
66 Kenway Rd, SW5 (01–370 5900). Open 09.30–17.30 Mon to Fri; 09.30–16.30 Sat.

David Bagott Design
David Bagott's shop is always a bit chaotic; he designs much of the range of pine furniture which includes beds, settees and coffee tables, and imports reasonably priced bamboo furniture, (including very pretty cots) and basketware. Other home-related knick-knacks include pottery, lamps and macramé pot holders.
266 Old Brompton Rd, SW5 (01–370 2267). Open 10.00–18.00 Mon to Sat.

269 Boutique
American Margie Albert runs this pleasant 'mixed bag' shop. The window is always colourfully decorated with whatever she has – usually a mixture of cheap new clothes; secondhand women's and some children's clothes; Polish hunting bags (for which she boasts a good price); other leather belts and bags; highly coloured, wool-fringed Polish woollen shawls; cheap T-shirts of varying quality; pottery and bric-à-brac. Margie sits behind the big oak table and lets customers ponder over her curious selection of wares.
269 Old Brompton Rd, SW5 (01–373 1756). Open 11.00–19.00 Mon to Fri; 11.00–18.00 Sat.

Originelle
In the West End or Kings Road you'd hardly notice Originelle but in this bit of Gloucester Rd it's in a class of its own. It sells well-cut French and Italian women's fashions; silk shirts, trousers, a range of pretty dresses and co-ordinates.
107 Gloucester Rd, SW7 (01-373 4833). Open 09.30-18.30 Mon to Fri; 10.00-17.00 Sat.

FULHAM

Hansen's Equipment
Hansen's sell catering equipment to the trade. This covers anything from large gas ranges (ideal for big families, they say) to crockery, cutlery, kitchen machinery and heavy duty equipment. They are happy to sell to the public.
306 Fulham Rd, SW10 (01-352 7788). Open 09.00-18.00 Mon to Fri.

Farmers
Tools for the woodworker and the engineering trades: Black and Decker, the AEG electrical range, plus Stanley, Record and OK hand tools.
319 Fulham Rd, SW10 (01-351 1024). Open 08.30-17.00 Mon to Fri; closed for lunch; 09.00-13.00 Sat.

A. Clarke & Sons (Marine Stores) Ltd
While its surrounding neighbours have turned into boutiques and smart antique shops, Clarke's remains exactly as it has been for years – a superb junk shop. It's a reliable source of old cutlery, brass taps and hooks, door knobs, magazines, small pieces of furniture and jumble sale quality clothes.
340 Fulham Rd, SW10 (01-352 0615). Open 08.30-16.50 Mon to Fri; 08.30-12.30 Sat.

Frock Exchange
Gabrielle Crawford opened this shop in 1971. Her idea was that many people in public life buy fashion clothes to wear a few times which then just sit in the wardrobe. Stock is not restricted, though, to the cast-offs of the rich and famous; the shop will also sell female clothing and accessories in a good state of repair if not too dated. They take items on a sale or return basis, decide on a realistic price (for them and the seller) and keep the garments for eight weeks. They will see clothes any day except Saturday when they are at their busiest. The standard of clothing has remained consistently high since the shop opened and it's a good place to browse through regularly.
450 Fulham Rd, SW6 (01-381 2937). Open 10.00-17.30 Mon to Sat; closed when there's a home match.

Chelsea Football Souvenir Shop
Despite its name and close proximity to Chelsea's ground the shop is a general football clothing shop. They sell rosettes and scarves for most of the popular teams.
468A Fulham Rd, SW6 (01-385 4915). Open 09.30–17.30 Mon to Sat; 09.30–13.30 Thurs.

Windmill Wholefood
Noel McDonald and Nadine Tesio run this pleasant, low-key wholefoods shop. Their speciality is dried herbs, both medicinal and culinary, but they stock cereals, beans and seeds in large open bins and most things can be bought in bulk by the sackful. Also oils, wholemeal breads, organically grown muesli base and dried fruit.
486 Fulham Rd, SW6 (01-381 1281). Open 09.30–18.00 Mon to Sat.

Tookes
Mr Jones manages this 50-year-old specialist fishing tackle shop. He reckons to supply 99½% of everything required for coarse, sea and fly fishing. Tookes are particularly known for their own manufactured rods, called the London Series. They repair rods.
614 Fulham Rd, SW6 (01-736 1484). Open 09.00–18.00 Mon to Sat.

Sugar Cane
The cane furniture designed by Anita Gopal and made in India is designed to last, with extra support incorporated into the designs. The chairs and sofas are sprung, and cushions are filled with high density aerofoam and covered in calico ready to be upholstered to the customer's specification. Partner John Wilson runs the shop and keeps a range of leading fabric books (including Sandersons and Sekers) and has a limited range of ready-covered furniture in the shop. Catalogue and price list are available on request.
731 Fulham Rd, SW6 (01-731 5550). Open 10.30–18.00 Mon to Sat.

Pollyanna
Pollyanna sell sturdy, practical yet pretty, attractive clothes for the three to twelve age range. They specialize in a co-ordinating mix and match range and are complete outfitters, selling underwear, socks, dresses, T-shirts, shirts and blouses, shorts, trousers, rainwear and coats. During the winter they sell boots and French Kicker shoes; in the summer clogs. A mail order catalogue is available on request.
811 Fulham Rd, SW6 (01-731 0674). Open 09.30–17.30 Mon to Sat; mail order Mon to Fri.

The Leisurecrafts Centre
This large, self-service style

craft equipment suppliers sells everything needed for enamelling (kilns, powders, copper blanks in a wide range of shapes, tools); candle making (kits and individual equipment); casting (various chess sets, a wide range of moulds); modelling; beading and macramé, plus leather and leather-working tools.
2–10 Jerdan Place, SW6 (01-381 2019). Open 09.00–18.00 Tues to Fri; 10.00–17.00 Sat.

F. Richards and Son
Richards can cut a Yale key in 60 seconds, most mortise keys in one to two hours, and can cut keys to locks without patterns. Everything except Ingersoll and Banham keys undertaken, along with scissor- and knife-sharpening.
17 Jerdan Place, SW6 (01–385 2354). Open 09.00–17.00 Mon to Fri; 09.00–13.00 Thurs and Sat.

Wood and Wirecraft Supplies Ltd
Mrs Kreeger runs this old-established shop and now only concentrates on the wirecraft side. She sells a wide range of lampshade frames, natural parchment (white and cream), raffia, chair cane, wicker, seagrass and macramé cord. There is a range of made-up lampshades and basketware.
19a Jerdan Place, SW6 (01–385 2910). Open 10.00–17.00 Mon to Sat; closed Thurs.

Wools and Jools
Jeweller Julie Palmer and knitter Carol Cockayne run their studio/workshop as a retail outlet. Both supply many London shops but can offer far better prices on direct sales. Carol works almost exclusively in mohair and hand-knits everything. Her designs are always in tune with the latest look in knitwear and past looks have included voluminous baggy jerseys and box twinsets. Julie works mostly in silver and titanium – an extremely heat-resistant metal which when charged with an electric current turns one of several shades of blue, green or beige. She specializes in tiny 'pictures' with titanium, framed in silver and worn as a pendant. Both girls are keen for individual commissions.
81 Moore Park Rd, SW6 (01–731 3617). Ring to check opening hours.

Couture Club
A small group of friends with rag trade connections and experience run Couture Club as a club where women can buy top name clothes at an average of 50% off normal prices. Their two-room showrooms, complete with video equipment to give buyers a real all-round view of potential purchases, is informally run, and members can wander in, check through the rails of clothes and try anything

they fancy. Members pay £12 a year; first-year members pay 55% of the normal price. Styles tend to be smartish – classic and well cut designs in natural fibres – and feature clothes for all occasions; jeans and T-shirts, day and evening dresses, suits and blouses. Their collecton changes regularly and features many leading names (labels have to be cut out in most cases). They also run a custom-made, tailored-finish service. Records are kept of all members' sizes, which helps Couture Club buy in the correct numbers of sizes. The new members' extra 5% charge is purely to cover the cost of each season's unsold clothes.
7 Margravine Rd, W6 (01–385 7813/4). Open 09.30–18.00 Mon to Fri; 09.30–16.00 Sat. Ring for details of changing rota of one late evening per week.

Thames Water Sports
Everything required for sub-aqua diving including underwater photography is on sale at this shop. That means a full range of wet- and dry-suits from all leading manufacturers; goggles; breathing equipment; a cylinder compressor service operated on the premises; a servicing department; life jackets; and instrumentation, which includes watches, knives and other accessories. The underwater photography department sells all necessary equipment from still and movie cameras to lighting units. They also sell good quality inflatable boats and operate a hire service for equipment.
179–183 Fulham Palace Rd, SW6 (01–381 0558/9). Open 09.00–18.00 Mon to Sat.

Repli Guns Ltd
Sandwiched between the two sub-aqua shops is this small gun shop. Very little is on display as a large part of their business is reproduction guns which are sold mainly by mail order. These guns are alarmingly authentic looking, and are sold with blanks which sound exactly like gun shots. They're increasingly popular for protection purposes and a full price list is available on request. A licence is required for all other guns except some air rifles (see Index for details). Repli Guns also sell de-activated bullets; rifle pellets; shotgun cartridges to over 18s; sportsmen knives, collectors' knives and a range of NATO knives, one with a wire cutter.
183 Fulham Palace Rd, SW6 (01–381 2929). Open 09.00–18.00 Mon to Sat.

Sportsways Inter Discount
Sportsways is a small, recently reorganized shop specializing in diving equipment and underwater photographic equipment for serious working divers. They've been here for 12 years and the staff are very know-

ledgeable divers who run a branch of the Sub Aqua Club from the premises. They provide a hire service for all commercial equipment for working divers; an air compressor testing and filling service for diving cylinders; and sell some equipment secondhand. They reckon to offer very competitive prices in a trade rife with discount wars.
185 Fulham Palace Rd, SW6 (01-385 4874). Open 09.00-18.00 Mon to Sat.

Peter Topp Wallcoverings Ltd
Peter offers a specialist wall-covering service; he stocks over 80 English and foreign firms in books and on display panels. Familiar names include Sandersons, John Oliver, Osborne & Little and Coles. Everything, save adhesives and lining paper, is bought to order and Peter reckons on a 48-hour delivery service, except on some American papers which can take three to four months. There's a special effects section which includes some spectacular wallpapers; flocks, vinyls, real leaves on coloured backgrounds, a seashore collection, simulated fur and suede, foil, grass cloths, hessians and murals. The minimum quantity sold is a metre, occasionally two on some papers. They keep a range of co-ordinated fabrics and can get Spectrum paints mixed to order from a choice of 1,350 different shades. As many foreign papers are sold with an edge that has to be cut off, the shop offers a trimming service (half price if the paper is bought from the shop).
343 Fulham Palace Rd, SW6 (01-736 4821). Open 09.30-17.00 Mon to Fri; 12.30-13.30 closed for lunch; 09.30-13.00 Sat.

Ian Brockleys Trade Unlimited
Ian Brockley takes great pride in selling his old and antique pine furniture in tip-top condition. Everything is restored and finished by a team of carpenters, and the choice of stock is restricted to the less usual items. It regularly includes bookcases, dressers (Welsh dressers only at 41 Fulham High St), chests of drawers and boxes.
51 Fulham High St, SW6 (01-736 7887). Open 10.00-18.30 Mon to Sat.

The Doll's Hospital
It's a bit of a disappointment to find that the evocatively named Doll's Hospital is actually a very ordinary toy shop. It has been established over 100 years and behind the scenes they repair Victorian and Edwardian dolls. They have some spare parts (wigs, eyes, arms and legs) for modern dolls but point out that

repair is often impossible. Advice is given with an s.a.e.
16 Dawes Rd, SW6 (01-385 2081). Open 09.30-17.30 Mon to Sat, closed Thurs.

Sitting Pretty
When James Williams and Edward Willis-Fleming got 250 replies to an ad in *The Times* for hand-made wooden lavatory seats, they set up Sitting Pretty. Now they farm out the making of the seats to a mill in Lancashire and offer a choice of whitewood (which can be stained), mahogany and pine. James and Edward concentrate on the business of hand-painting coats of arms, crests, monograms and wallpaper designs on to the finished seats. They also make thunder boxes, do 'boxing in' and undertake complicated commissions. At the shop they specialize in antique bathroom equipment, plants and good loo reading. Stocks of old patterned loos, tiles, loo roll holders, baths, taps and basins change frequently.
131 Dawes Rd, SW6 (01-381 0049). Open 09.00-17.30 Mon to Fri; usually open Sat; sometimes closed for lunch 13.00-14.00.

I. Grizarde Ltd
Grizarde keep an extensive range of hand, power and precision tools for virtually every job. They'll advise on the right tool for the job.
84a/b Lillie Rd, SW6 (01-385 5109). Open 09.00-18.00 Mon to Sat; 09.00-13.00 Thurs.

Cornucopia
Situated in a shopping nowhere land, this tiny shop is good for last minute presents. They keep limited stocks of English and Portuguese glass, china and pottery, basketware, candles, cards and a few plants.
93 Lillie Rd, SW6 (01-385 4591). Open 10.00-18.00 Mon to Sat.

Patricks
The splendid model railway display in the window of Patrick's gives a hint of their speciality. Upstairs at this general toyshop they keep over 8,000 items concerned with model railways, gauges N and OO. They keep all the leading names (Mainline, Hornby, Airfix, Fleischmans and Scalectrix) and an enormous range of trimmings and accessories including flock and scatter. Downstairs there is a wide range of kits and toys and their other speciality, Airfix models.
107-111 Lillie Rd, SW6 (01-385 9864). Open 09.00-17.30 Mon to Sat; closed 13.00 Suns.

Hitchcock & Co
Hitchcocks, the plate glass and timber merchants, is a well-known landmark in Fulham, but they deliver all over London. The timber side of the business specializes in pine and

sells some ramin mouldings but does not cut to size. The plate glass people do.
glass: 234 & 248 Lillie Rd, SW6 (01–385 4596). Open 08.30–17.30 Mon to Fri; 08.30–12.30 Sat.
timber: 10–14 Rylston Rd, off Lillie Rd, SW6 (01–385 3851). Open 08.30–17.30 Mon to Fri.

E. Nash (Removals) Ltd
If you like rummaging through piles of junk and someone else's household rejects you'll enjoy a visit to Mrs Nash's shop. Her sons run a removal business so she has regular new supplies of 'bits and pieces'. One of many similar shops in Lillie Rd.
291 Lillie Rd, SW6 (01–385 2599). Open 09.00–17.00 Mon to Fri; occasionally Sat.

The Gilded Lily
Interior designer/consultant Ray Liberatori uses his shop The Gilded Lily as an incentive to potential clients. It's frequently changed around and used as a 'set'. He specializes in furniture and furnishings of the 1850–1930 period and aims to appeal to young, first-time home owners/renters who have little money to spend but favour the Art Deco/Nouveau look. Much of his stock is original and includes reproduction aeroplanes; dancing girl and back-to-back clown lamps. He regularly stocks standard lamps, teasets, mirrors, china ornaments, single, heavily embroidered, lace and machined lace curtains and sets, and gets the lace made up into pretty scatter cushions.
293 Lillie Rd, SW6 (01–385 6153). Open 11.00–18.00 Mon to Sat; closed Thurs.

Euroframes
For the past eight years Michael Scarber has been supplying everything required for all types of picture framing. They cut glass, metal, wood and perspex to size for DIY and undertake all types of framing including block and dry mounting themselves. No ready made kits.
127 Munster Rd, SW6 (01–736 2167) Open 09.30–17.30 Mon to Fri; 10.00–13.00 Sat.

Naylors
Gay Naylor's eye for the unusual makes this shop a regular port of call for those who enjoy novelty bric-à-brac. Stock, bought from country auctions and secret sources, is always a bit quirky; she regularly finds old tin boxes, walking sticks, cheese dishes, jelly moulds, all sorts of clothes and bits of lace.
131 Munster Rd, SW6 (01–731 3679). Open 10.00–18.00 Mon to Fri; closed Thurs; 10.30–16.45 Sat.

Danish Pâtisserie
Although it's called the Danish Pâtisserie, Mr Vadillo, who runs

it is French and his recipes are French. Croissants, French stick loaves, *petits fours,* cream cakes, tarts; pastries and cakes made to order.
156 Munster Rd, SW6 (01–731 3877). Open 09.00–17.30 Mon to Sat.

Christopher Antiques
This pretty shop which overflows onto the pavement sells authentic Victorian and Edwardian bamboo furniture of all types and sizes from an occasional table to a bed. They restore everything meticulously on the premises, reckon to stock 500 pieces at any one time and specialize in Lloyd loom furniture.
213 Munster Rd, SW6 (01–381 3524). Open 09.00–18.00 Mon to Fri; 09.00–14.00 Sat.

Whiteway and Waldron
Whiteway and Waldron salvage architectural fittings and stained glass from wrecked houses and defunct churches. Much is Victorian, though their stocks range from 1820 to the turn of the century, and includes balustrading, carved wood, church and domestic wood and a changing variety of period details. They offer a glass restoring service and spend a lot of time advising young couples who wish to return their house/flat to its original character.
305 Munster Rd, SW6 (01–381 3195). Open 10.00–18.00 Mon to Fri; 11.00–15.00 Sats.

North End Rd Market
Since it was established in 1877 this general market has moved up the road from Jerdan Place to fill the entire length of North End Rd. The 91 stalls are a mix of (predominantly) fruit and vegetables, fish, dairy produce, pre-packaged foods and a sprinkling of the rag trade, including a very good haberdashery stall. Half a mile long, the market is a comfortable size for a wander to compare prices. The road is a busy shopping centre in its own right; there are several butchers; a Marks and Spencer, a Sainsbury, a Woolworth, and many cheap clothes shops. Like most street markets, this one is at its peak on Saturday and particularly busy on Fridays, with a less reliable complement of stallholders on other days.
North End Rd, SW6. Open 09.00–17.00 (approx) Mon to Sat; closed Thurs afternoon.

Secondhand City
The ghost that's reputed to wander around in the early evening at this vast old church hasn't deterred John James and Michael Bates 'buying, selling and part-exchanging anything' for the past 13 years. They sell furniture mostly; chests of drawers, beds, tables and chairs,

which are usually modern and bought from bankrupt stock and hotel clearance sales. They sell 'anything to do with indoors' and regularly have mattresses, blankets and crockery.
Entrance North End Rd, W14 (01–385 7711). Open 10.00–18.15 Mon to Sat.

Crowthers
The Crowther family have been running this business from their impressive, late Georgian building for over 100 years. Their speciality is antique garden ornaments, fireplace accessories, 18th-century English furniture and English oak and pine panelling. Much stock is displayed just inside the big old gates and at the back of the house in a walled garden.
282 North End Rd, SW6 (01–385 1375). Open 09.00–18.00 Mon to Fri; closed Sat.

Bicycle Revival
Three- and ten-speed bikes for hire, the daily charge decreases for longer hires. All bikes are regularly overhauled and insurance is available.
28 North End Parade, W14 (01–602 4499). Open 10.00–18.00 Mon to Sat.

PARSONS GREEN

The Gimmick
This tiny shop wedged between a framer and a cobbler specializes in 'the complete wardrobe' of old clothes, mainly those of 1940s, for women. They also make up new designs in old fabrics, and are a reliable source of old velvet curtains; fabric, knitted, quilted and patchwork bedspreads; chenille tablecloths and old lace.
117 and 119 Harwood Rd, SW6 (01–736 2053). Open 11.00–18.30/19.00 Mon to Sat.

The Shop For Painted Furniture
Dan Dunton, Ray and Wendy Newell, Jill Harding and Roy Glover are a group of ex-art students who decorate furniture to their own designs or to commissions. They use oil-based paint, finish with varnish for durability's sake and between them offer a variety of styles including traditional designs made to look old. They work on the premises, and charge on time spent.
94 Waterford Rd, SW6 (01–736 1908). Open 10.00–18.00 Tues to Sat.

Van der Fransen
Seven years ago sisters Snoo and Mimi Van der Fransen set up shop selling 20s to 50s women's clothes. They also use a mixture of these fabrics to make up their own designs, which are loose and easy to wear, usually made of cottons and so best for the summer. These days fewer old fabrics are incorporated into

their clothes because of the difficulty of finding good stuff. They also stock silk-screened cushions, hand- and machine-knitted jerseys, chenille curtains and stylish quilted coats.
96 Waterford Rd, SW6 (01-736 3814). Open 10.00–18.00 Tues to Sat.

Waterford Road Garden Centre
Stocks a vast choice of herbs, shrubs, conifers, trees, window boxes, pots and house plants.
110–116 Waterford Rd, SW6 (01-731 4717). Open 09.00–18.00 Mon to Sat; 09.30–16.00 Sun.

Bonham's Chelsea Galleries
This is the 'junk' end of Bonham's where their less valuable stuff is sold. Victorian, Edwardian and reproduction furniture, bric-à-brac, carpets and rugs are sold every Tuesday at 10.00 with viewing on Mon from 08.30–07.00. Every two weeks paintings of no particular period or style are sold.
75 Burnaby St, SW10 (01-352 0466).

Artesiana
Artesiana sells modern Spanish furniture and ceramics. All furniture is hand made and rustic looking and designs date back over 300 years. Many pieces incorporate elaborate carvings, and all are wax finished and made from close grained, dark brown alderwood. There are chairs, tables, bedheads, dressers, stools and so on. The brightly painted traditional designs on the china date back hundreds of years and are made in a historic centre called Talaverna de la Reina.
507 Kings Rd, SW10 (01-352 2468). Open 10.00–18.00 Mon to Fri; 10.00–17.00 Sat.

Furniture Cave
A group of twelve traders sublet to 200-odd stallholders at this four-floor antiques market which has been operating for 16 years. Of the 3250 sq m (35,000 sq ft) of space, some is devoted to restoration workshops and a transport company but most is used by dealers. The basement sells 18th- and 19th-century English furniture; the ground floor English and Continental objets d'art and furniture; unusual period arts and crafts; and architectural artefacts like wrought iron staircases, brass taps and even roundabouts. The third and top floors specialize in pine, both very old and stripped; reproduction oak and English country furniture.
533 Kings Rd, SW10 (01-351 3870). Open 10.00–18.00 Mon to Sat.

London Car Stereo Centre
The London Car Stereo Centre sells, installs and repairs car radios, stereo systems, electric windows, radio telephones, sky-

port (see-through) sun roofs and mobile fittings. They keep stocks from a wide range of manufacturers including Pioneer, National Panasonic, Sanyo and Blaupunkt.
559 Kings Rd, SW6 (01-736 8351). Open 08.30-18.00 Mon to Sat.

Christopher Wray's Lighting Emporium
It was on 14 September 1966 that Christopher Wray carved his first niche in the King's Road. Now anyone could be excused for thinking he's taking over the whole street with his colourful Lighting Emporium, Lamp Workshop, Tiffany Shop, Pot Shop and Terra Cotta Pots. Originally Christopher restored and sold decorative lighting of the period between 1880 and 1914. The shop's popularity was instant, and so was the demand for spare parts, which led to the evolution of the Lamp Workshop. Next came the Tiffany Shop, selling grand lampshades made from pieces of coloured glass, usually in Art Deco designs. These are all reproduction, made either from glass or plastic to original designs. A 100-page fully illustrated catalogue of stock is available for approximately £1 (ring for exact price). Original lamps range in price from approximately £20 to £100 and wallbrackets sell from approximately £15. Reproductions are approximately two-thirds the price of originals. The Pot Shop and Terra Cotta Pots are the latest venture, selling hand-thrown terra-cotta gardening pots, and antique and old terra-cotta pots respectively.
Christopher Wray's Lighting Emporium 600-602 Kings Rd, SW6; Christopher Wray's Tiffany Shop, 593 Kings Rd, SW6; Christopher Wray's Pot Shop, 606 Kings Rd, SW6; Christopher Wray's Terra Cotta Pots, 591 Kings Rd, SW6 (for all branches phone 01-736 8008/5989.) All branches open 10.00-18.00 Mon to Sat with the exception of the Tiffany Shop and Pot Shop which are closed on Mon.

And So To Bed
Keith Barnett and family search out original English brass and brass and iron bedsteads, restore them and sell them in as near mint condition as possible. They scour the outposts of what was the British Empire and have imported beds from as far afield as Portugal, Spain and India. They stock an average of 150 beds at the shop, which are all in tip-top condition, but shoppers can also view and buy the beds in various states of repair at the workshop (see end of entry). The bedstead is only a frame and for it to be of any use for sleeping, you'll need to buy a bed base (like a divan without the legs) and a mattress. And So To Bed can fix all that for you – they have their own little

industry. Most of the frames are standard size so you might pick up a secondhand bed base to cut the outlay. Renovated original brass bedsteads sell from £250; brass and iron combinations from £80. Reproduction all-brass headboards cost from £100; all-brass bedsteads from £200. The shop always keeps a selection of old and new patchwork quilts and white crochet bedspreads which they can get made to particular designs/ colour combinations. Number 59 specializes in wooden beds: mahogany and oak four-posters. They range in price from £300 up to £3000 depending on the age and quality of the wood.
7 New Kings Rd, SW6 and 59 New Kings Rd, SW6 (01–731 3593). Open 10.00–18.00 Mon to Sat.
Renovation work is done at their workshop: 404 High Rd, NW10 (open 08.00–18.30 Mon to Fri and 08.00–14.00 Sat) where they also make copies of original designs.

Luigi's
Luigi opened this small, cramped but well-stocked Italian deli in 1973. He sells a range of delicious home-made salads, chicken Kiev and other re-heatable dishes, cheesecakes and pâtés, and always has ham on the bone, roast beef, various salamis and continental sausages. The shelves are lined with high class groceries, nine different olive oils and every kind of pasta imaginable. At this branch a fine selection of (named and priced) cheeses is displayed in the centre of the shop. They sell 145 different Italian wines.
60 New Kings Rd, SW6 (01–731 4994). Open 10.00–21.00 Mon to Sat; 12.00–14.00 Sun. Closed 12 August to 29 August.

The Merchant Chandler
Terence Donovan and Peter Gillbanks opened this home and kitchenware shop set in a converted Victorian house ten years ago. Unmistakable from the outside with its brick walls covered with plates, inside is a pleasant higgledy-piggledy array of French and English kitchen- and homeware. Downstairs houses basketware, the first floor displays kitchenware, and at the back is a room packed with seconds in china. Upstairs houses cane furniture, matting and linen baskets.
72 New Kings Rd, SW6 (01–736 6141). Open 08.45–17.30 Mon to Fri; 08.45–14.00 Thurs; 08.45–17.00 Sat.

Lunn Antiques
Stephen and Janet Lunn specialize in old linen, ranging from pre-war synthetic fibres and hand-made tablecloths to embroidered sheets, bedspreads and pillowcases. They regularly sell period clothing, including christening gowns and baby clothes, and also have elaborate

textile wall-hangings, oriental embroidery and lace-covered pillows.
86 New Kings Rd, SW6 (01–736 4638). Open 10.00–18.30 Mon to Sat.

Garden Crafts
For 52 years the Dimmock family have been selling garden ornaments and furniture, both originals and copies. They buy up life-size cast stone and marble figures from old manor houses and import smaller pieces from Spain, Italy and France. They manufacture a range of cast aluminium Victorian-style garden furniture, but don't undertake individual commissions.
158 New Kings Rd, SW6 (01–736 1615). Open 09.00–18.00 Mon to Fri; 10.00–15.00 Sat.

Fulham Pottery
Established in 1670 to make bottles and drinking vessels and modernized by the installation of a brick bottle kiln in 1841 (still standing). Today the pottery confines itself to selling all the equipment needed for potting, including kilns. A resident potter gives advice; mail order details are sent on request.
210 New Kings Rd, SW6 (01–731 2167). Open 09.00–17.00 Mon to Fri; 09.00–12.00 Sat.

Just Sofas
This shop buys and sells sofas and armchairs of all periods and in all states of repair. It is worth checking regularly and lodging a particular request.
216 New Kings Rd, SW6 (01–731 5606). Open 10.00–16.30 Mon to Sat.

Cobra
Cobra sells Art Deco and Art Nouveau furniture, carpets and occasionally objects. Everything is original, and some pieces are signed by their designers.
220 New Kings Rd, SW6 (01–736 4710). Open 10.30–17.00 Mon to Sat; closed Thurs.

Resista Carpets
Resista specialize in cords, heavy duty, meraklon broadloom carpets and Persian-type rugs. It is a small company which offers a personal service, buys in massive quantities so sells at very good prices. All the shops are painted bright red, and they provide a delivery service and aim for a 24-hour fitting service.
255 New Kings Rd, SW6 (head office) (01–731 2588). Also at 584 Fulham Rd, SW6 (01–736 7551); 148 Wandsworth Bridge Rd, SW6 (01–731 3368); all open 09.00–18.00 Mon to Sat.

Fiona Campbell
Fiona Campbell provides an enormous international collection of wallpapers and fabric

pattern books. She makes up bed covers, cushions, curtains, bedheads and valances to order and is particularly good on stylish finishes with lots of trimming and detail. As a sideline to use up remnants, she makes lovely soft dolls and toys which are displayed in the window.
259 New Kings Rd, SW6 (01–731 3681). Open 09.30–17.30 Mon to Fri.

Casa Mia
Casa Mia keeps a small selection of most delicatessen foods: free range eggs, wholemeal breads, English and Continental cheeses, pâtés, cider and honey roast ham on the bone, pastramis, salami, high class groceries, coffee beans ground to order, and Italian biscuits. They are an off-licence, too, and have regular special offers on magnums and 2-litre French and Italian wines. They keep some of the less usual beers, including Guinness brewed in Ireland.
275 New Kings Rd, SW6 (01–731 5810). Open 10.30–22.30 seven days a week.

Dee Harrington
Gazing into Dee Harrington's shop is like looking inside a giant box of chocolates. A vast ribbon tied in a bow covers the ceiling and the decor is pale pink. Dee deals in period clothes, especially 30s, 40s and Victorian 'special' clothes like lace camiknickers, fringed shawls, nighties, embroidered tablecloths, fans and kimonos. She hires out anything on request, including antique/old wedding gear – veils etc. Downstairs designer Gilly Vogler makes ultra-feminine clothes to order, and there are also some off-the-peg clothes; all colourful and highly individual.
279 New Kings Rd, SW6 (01–736 0037). Open 11.00–18.00 Tues to Sat.

Chelsea Trading Discount Store
Chelsea Trading Discount Store import 400 different lines made in rattan or cane from pot holders to three-piece suites. They have something for every room in the house. Despite its name, prices seem comparable with similar stockists.
421 New Kings Rd, SW6 (01–731 3131). Open 09.30–18.00 Mon to Sat.

Richard Morris
Richard Morris is one of many stripped pine furniture dealers in and around Wandsworth Bridge Road. He has extensive stocks which are spread on to the pavement and he specializes in unusual pieces like corner cupboards with glass-etched doors, chests and dressers. Everything is stripped, treated and restored at his Putney workshops.
142 Wandsworth Bridge Rd,

SW6 (01-736 1448). Open 09.00–18.00 Mon to Sat.

Kickback

Last year the directors of the English Kicker company decided they would do away with sales at their many London branches. Instead they opened Kickback where all Kicker discontinued lines, model shoes, samples and slightly damaged footwear are sold at half the normal retail prices. They reckon to regularly carry 20,000 cut-price pairs for children, women and men.

156–158 Wandsworth Bridge Rd, SW6 (no phone). Open 10.00–18.00 Mon to Fri; 10.00–16.00 Sat; open until 19.00 Thurs.

Pierrot

Hinny Charlton and Jeannie Forman design and/or commission everything on sale at their delightful children's shop. There are hand-made clothes, wooden toys, soft toys, appliqué and hand-painted quilts, cot sets and a wide range of present possibilities for children from birth to eight years old. Quality comes first at Pierrot, and a lot of stock is personalized so making it pricey – an ideal place for doting indulgent relatives, godparents and parents who want really special gifts for a baby or small child.

174 Wandsworth Bridge Rd, SW6 (01-736 1123). Open 10.00–18.00 Mon to Sat; 10.00–13.00 Thurs.

PEOPLE LIKE US SHOP AT...
BOLLAND

THE
NATURAL
STORE
SHOE

12 CHELSEA

South Kensington, Worlds End, Chelsea.

There is little of shopping interest immediately around South Kensington Station. Nearby Bute St has the only 'village' feel, with several good food shops including two superb continental pâtisseries, delicatessen and greengrocer. The greatest density and mixture of South Kensington's shops is in Fulham Rd. They cluster around the Meridiana restaurant and further into Chelsea around Finches pub. Provençal fabric from Brother Sun, fine cheese from Crispins, coffee from Whittards, stationery from Paperchase and further on granary stick loaves from Summers, South East Asian artefacts from Ganesha and herbal delights from L'Herbier de Provence.

Somewhat less stylishly than in the 60s the Kings Rd lives on as a centre for youth and young fashions. Boutiques covering most fashions come and go and the promenading (particularly on Saturdays) continues. Peter Jones is the only department store and is the up-market branch of John Lewis, with good gift and china departments. Tasteful up-market home gifts can be found in the nearby General Trading Company. The two new wave or punk shops, Boy and Seditionaries, along with many other interesting shops, are at the Worlds End end of the road. If you make it to them, you've 'done' the Kings Rd.

Antiques and bric-à-brac can be found at Chelsea's two covered markets, Antiquarius and Chelsea Antique Market. The Kings Rd is also good for footwear.

See also Notting Hill and South of the River.

TRANSPORT

South Kensington
Tube stations: South Kensington.
Buses: 14, 30, 49.

Chelsea/Worlds End
Tube stations: Sloane Sq, South Kensington.
Buses: 11, 19, 22, 31, 49.

LOCAL OPENING HOURS

Most shops in South Kensington and Chelsea stay open 10.00–18.00 Mon to Sat; a few close on Mon or early on Sat.

REFRESHMENTS

Dacquise
20 Exhibition Rd, SW7
Open 11.00–23.30
Polish restaurant which makes delicious range of pastries on the premises. Coffee and tea with cakes.

Maison Verlon
12 Bute St, SW7
Open 09.00–18.00 Mon to Sat.
Old-fashioned tea rooms. Delicious cakes, tarts, etc., to French and Austrian recipes.

Le Boulevard
178 Fulham Rd, SW10
Open 09.00–18.00 Mon to Sat.
Patisserie belonging to the Bonne Bouche chain; a tea room is planned.

Habitat café, Top Floor
206–222 Kings Rd, SW3
Open 09.30–18.00 Mon to Sat; until 19.30 Thurs.
Wholefood cakes and snacks; very Habitat.

SOUTH KENSINGTON

Bag End
Trunks and suitcases spill on to the pavement at this three-year-old travel goods shop. They sell a wide range of trunks, suitcases (leather and synthetic) and numerous in-flight type travel bags. Bag End are particularly useful for their repair service to all travel bags. As a sideline the shop buys and sells limited amounts of secondhand silver jewellery.
6 Old Brompton Rd, SW7 (01–581 0299). Open 10.00–18.00 Mon to Sat.

Mercurious Bookshop
Mercurious keep some children's and cookery books but specialize in astrology, psychology, Eastern and Western mysticism, ecology and related subjects.
80 Old Brompton Rd, SW7 (01–589 7967). Open 11.00–20.00 Mon to Fri; 11.00–18.00 Sat.

Christies, South Kensington
At this branch of Christies they sell everything sold at the main branch (furniture, paintings, European ceramics, jewellery, silver etc.) but they specialize in the middle to lower price range with a fast turn around. They

also specialize in what they call the new collecting fields: costumes and textiles; fans and militaria; dolls, toys and games; cameras and photographic equipment; scientific instruments; domestic and other machines; tools; mechanical music; motoring; aeronautical and railway art and literature; cigarette cards and ephemera. They also organize collectors' cars sales, which are usually held at Beaulieu. Sales are advertised every Monday in *The Daily Telegraph; Art and Antiques Weekly* and, by subscription only, the *Antiques Trade Gazette*. Viewing takes place at least one day in advance of the sale.
85 Old Brompton Rd, SW7 (01-581 2231). Open 09.00-17.00 Mon to Fri; viewing only until 19.00 Mon.

Mend-A-Bike
Apart from providing a full repair service, Mend-A-Bike overhaul old bikes which they sell with a three-month guarantee.
3 Kendrick Mews, off Reece Mews, off Old Brompton Rd, SW7 (01-581 2044). Open 10.00-18.30 Mon to Fri; 11.00-16.00 Sat.

Allison's Wonderland
Mrs Allison sells cut-price dressmaking fabrics. Her permanent sale includes broderie anglaise, trevira, cheesecloth, some sari materials, and a wide range of jerseys, needlecords, ginghams and other cottons. The small jumbled shop also sells haberdashery, tea towels, towels and tights.
7a Harrington Rd, SW7 (01-589 8429). Open 09.00-18.00 Mon to Fri; 09.00-17.30 Sat.

Môme
Clothes at this tiny canopied corner shop are either imported from France, Italy, Germany and Holland (the Olly range only) or hand-made in this country. Although it is a children's clothes shop, it will undertake adult-size commissions from Môme hand-made designs to order. From the subtle-coloured babygrows to the smart outfits for 14-year-olds, everything sold at Môme is 'special'. It is beyond most people's price range and particularly appeals to our wealthy foreign visitors.
27 Harrington Rd, SW7 (01-589 8306). Open 10.00-18.00 Mon to Fri; 10.00-16.00 Sat.

Monsoon
A delightful range of Indian clothes. See page 11-12 for full details.
54 Fulham Rd, SW3 (01-589 9192). Open 10.00-18.00 Mon to Sat; 10.00-19.00 Wed.

Parrots
Three floors of ideas for presents to suit all tastes and all pockets: photograph frames,

pottery, ashtrays, jewellery, lighters and keyrings, traditional toys, copies of Victorian games, books and stocking-fillers and lots more.
56 Fulham Rd, SW3 (01-584 5699). Open 10.00-18.00 Mon to Fri; 10.00-17.30 Sat.

Conran
Most people know that Terence Conran is the man behind Habitat and a well respected designer. His collection at this shop is based on quality and style in modern design and rare antique objects. Furniture, fabrics, floor coverings, lighting, household linens and virtually everything to do with cooking, eating and drinking. Seasonal brochure on request.
77 Fulham Rd, SW7 (01-589 7401). Open 09.30-18.00 Mon to Sat.

Chelsea Glassworks
The friendly neighbourhood glassworks where no customer is too big or too small. Ready cut and polished mirrors, perspex, do-it-yourself picture frames, and glass cut to any size. Barrie Semmens claims they are the 'last bastion of free enterprise glazing in London'.
105 Fulham Rd, SW3 (01-581 2501). Open 08.00-17.30 Mon to Fri; 08.00-12.00 Sat.

Whittards
Established in 1886, Whittards retains a delightful olde worlde atmosphere despite recent attempts to modernize the place. They roast 19 different blends of coffee on the premises, sell over 60 blends of tea, including China, Indian, Ceylon, Darjeeling and Green teas, which are sold loose. They also stock a range of exotic tinned foods, honeys and chocolate, including Charbonnel et Walker. They run a mail order service, and will send a price list on request.
111 Fulham Rd, SW7 (01-589 4261). Open 08.15-17.00 Mon to Fri; closed Sat.

Pan Bookshop
The exceptionally long hours of this bookshop make it worth remembering for last minute gifts and boring Sunday afternoons. They stock all Pan books in print, plus a selection from 30 different paperback publishers, some large format coffee table books and a good range of children's books.
158 Fulham Rd, SW10 (01-373 4997). Open 10.00-22.30 Mon to Sat; 14.30-18.30 Sun.

Paperchase
The quieter branch of this superb stationers and paper merchants. Downstairs at this branch artists' materials, glues etc. and specialist papers. (See page 14.)
167 Fulham Rd, SW7 (01-589 7839). Open 10.00-18.00 Mon to Fri; 10.00-19.00 Sat.

Brother Sun

This pretty but pricey shop sells French provençal cotton print fabric by the metre, as well as made into various garments, quilted and patchwork bags of all sizes, and covering a range of stationery items including cheque book covers, photograph frames, notebooks, diaries and even coasters. They also sell authentic French espadrilles for both men and women (downstairs). Thankfully they hold two genuine sales each year.

171 Fulham Rd, SW7 (01-589 6180). Open 10.00-18.30 Mon to Sat.

London Lighting Co Ltd

Every available inch of Geoffrey Harris' shop is taken up with lights and lamps of every conceivable type, size and shape. He also sells bulbs, switches and lighting accessories.

173 Fulham Rd, SW3 (01-589 4270). Open 09.30-18.00 Mon to Sat.

Butler and Wilson

Small canopied shop with an extensive range of old and new Art Deco jewellery, 1920s scarves, bags, bracelets, boxes, bangles, cigarette cases, brooches, ivory, enamel and silver jewellery.

189 Fulham Rd, SW3 (01-352 2045). Open 10.00-18.00 Mon to Sat. Also at Libertys. (See West End, Regent St.)

Spanish Shop

This quaint-looking shop staffed by Spaniards sells classical Spanish guitars and equipment. Usually it stocks Spanish records and sheet music, which were unavailable as we went to press because of the political situation in Spain. There are also Spanish perfumes, dancing dolls and souvenirs. They have two teachers who give guitar lessons.

226 Fulham Rd, SW10 (01-352 8285). Open 10.30-15.00 Mon to Sat.

Chelsea Catering Co

Over 50 different English, French and Italian cheeses can be bought at this long-established delicatessen, which caters for private functions. Amongst the fare from their kitchens are many different quiches, pork sausages, pastries, and six pâtés, as well as various sweet pies. They should be noted for selling ice in 10-lb bags, and a wide range of luxury biscuits, chocolates and groceries.

305 Fulham Rd, SW10 (01-351 0538). Open 08.15-17.30 Mon to Fri.

Summers

From an unremarkable, cluttered, small and very busy shop, Mr Freeman bakes a wide range of pastries, fresh cream gateaux,

cakes, florentines and rum babas, but those in the know call for his unrivalled granary stick loaves and croissants. He also bakes regular croissants and plaited chola.
323 Fulham Rd, SW10 (01–352 8286). Open 07.30–19.30 Mon to Fri; 07.30–18.00 Sat.

L'Herbier de Provence
Huge white sacks of dried herbs grown and imported by the Caussade brothers in St Remy, Provence, are stacked on the floor and sold loose in this delightful shop. Over 100 herbs and flowers are on sale – some gift packaged – and French manageress Françoise Subyin is a mine of information about all of them. There are also speciality teas, a range of French honeys, vinegars and pure olive oil soaps.
341 Fulham Rd, SW10 (01–352 0012). Open 10.00–19.00 Tues, Wed, Fri, Sat; 14.30–19.00 Mon, Thurs.

Lesley Hodges
Lesley Hodges specializes in antiquarian and modern books on all aspects of costume and fashion including needlework and textiles. She publishes a catalogue of books and magazines four times a year.
Queen's Elm Parade, off Fulham Rd, Old Church St, SW3 (01–352 1176). Open 10.00–18.00 Mon to Fri; 10.00–13.00 Sat.

Hundred Acre Farm Shop
All the frozen meat on sale at this unique farm shop has been reared, slaughtered, butchered and fast-frozen at David Holmes' Yorkshire farm. The beef, pork, lamb, chicken and game on sale are of top quality and prices undercut regular butchers. Best savings are made on bulk purchases which are sensibly packaged for the freezer. The shop also sells free range farm eggs, smoked salmon and a small range of frozen vegetables. Price list available on request.
51 Hollywood Rd, SW10 (01–351 1053). Open 09.00–17.00 Mon to Sat; 09.00–19.00 Tues and Fri.

Zella 9
Zella 9 claim to keep the largest selection of limited editions and inexpensive contemporary prints, as well as the latest framed and unframed works from many British artists. They have a framing service.
2 Park Walk, SW10 (01–351 0588). Open 11.00–21.00 seven days a week.

Ganesha
Anne and Maarten Timmer who used to live in South-east Asia run this delightful shop. They select and import everything on sale. Most goods are unobtainable elsewhere and are not mass produced for the export trade. While the wide

range of artefacts comes from all over S.E. Asia, most come from Indonesia and Thailand and include wood carvings, musical instruments, shadow puppets, traditional basketware, textiles, lacquerware, paintings, records and books. They specialize in the ingredients (particularly spices) and utensils for Indonesian and Thai cooking. An ideal source of unusual gifts.
6 Park Walk, off Fulham Rd, SW10 (01–352 8972). Open 11.00–19.00 Mon to Sat. Late and Sunday opening at Christmas.

WORLD'S END

Tamesa Fabrics
Tamesa manufacture all their fabrics which are exclusive to this shop and display them in lengths at their spacious showroom/shop. They specialize in furnishing fabrics and work mainly with designers and architects, although they welcome the general public. Their range is extensive and varied, concentrating on modern as opposed to traditional designs. Most fabrics are made from natural fibres and the range includes weaves, sheers and prints of all sizes both geometric and pretty patterns.
343 Kings Rd, SW3 (01–351 1126). Open 09.00–17.00 Mon to Fri.

Dress Pound
Women's nearly-new clothes shop, where clothes in decent repair and not dated are sold on a sale and return basis. At this branch nearly-new clothes for children in the basement called Kids Pound and a play area with a sand pit. Also a noticeboard for sale of big items like carry-cots, prams etc.; Dress Pound take 10%. See Notting Hill for more details.
396 Kings Rd, SW10 (01–351 2232). Open 10.00–18.00 Mon to Sat; 10.00–19.00 Wed.

Miracles
Miracles sell modern and unusual furniture and soft furnishings. Everything sold has to have a unique quality – 'all are a little miracle' say the shop. Heart-shaped and rainbow neon lights, hand-painted blinds and screens, tables with secret drawers, etc.
436 Kings Rd, SW10 (01–352 0828). Open 10.30–18.30 Mon to Fri; 10.00–17.30 Sat.

C. T. Strangeways
This is the original branch of Strangeways (also see Holland Street, Notting Hill) which was set up to sell the work of a group of ex-RCA students. Today, as then, everything sold at the shop has a bizarre quality, like their famous life-size plaster sheep, outside deckchairs and a range of quirky ceramics.
502 Kings Rd, SW10 (01–352

9863). Open 10.00–18.00 Mon to Sat.

Tibet House
The first London shop to specialize in Tibetan goods, the Tibet House can be relied on for colourful woven wool jackets, embroidered felt boots, a range of cotton and cotton/synthetic mix shirts and dresses, a limited range of jewellery, books and prints and several different types of woven shoulder bags. The shop has a distinctive façade and is run by Tibetans.
490a Kings Rd (entrance in Langton St) SW10 (01–352 1080). Open 10.00–18.00 Mon to Sat.

Oxus
Tribal rugs, textiles and embroideries made by nomads from Persia, Afghanistan, Turkey, Morocco, Russia and Asia are sold from this informal showroom. Most are antique and cost on average £200, but they may cost up to £1000.
11 Langton St, SW10 (01–351 1925). Open 10.00–19.00 Mon to Fri; ring on Sats.

Hobby Horse
One of the most attractive and well-stocked craft equipment suppliers in London. The two-room shop is particularly good for beginners' kits in most crafts and lately specializes in beads, most sold pre-packaged, imported from many countries and of many sizes. A catalogue is supplied on request, ring to check the price.
15 Langton St, SW10 (01–351 1913). Open 10.00–17.30 Mon to Sat.

CHELSEA

Jane Halkin
For the past 25 years Jane Halkin has provided a very carefully chosen selection of fine quality fabrics at her shop. Her specialities include English wool tweeds, prints of all kinds, mainly on cottons, and Swiss voile. She also stocks ready-to-wear seasonal skirts, silk squares, ties and cravats.
45 Sloane Ave, SW3 (01–589 2919). Open 10.00–17.00 Mon to Fri; 10.00–13.00 Sat.

Meeney's
Colourful, fun sporty clothes for children and adults imported from America. Cowboy shirts, T-shirts, basketball and sweat shirts with the team name printed on the back; dungarees and lots of work jeans. Also playwear – baseball outfits, cowboy hats and boots. Range of pretty clothes for girls up to 6.
162 Draycott Ave, SW3 (01–581 2163). Open 10.30–18.00 Mon to Fri; 10.30–16.00 Sat. Also at 241 Kings Rd, Chelsea and 197 Kensington High St, W8.

The Richard Smith Shoe Company
Richard Smith has been designing boots and shoes for women for 17 years for various shops and companies but is particularly known for his association with Chelsea Cobbler. Ironically his own shop, where his small and exclusive range of pricey but well made women's footwear is on sale, is the original Chelsea Cobbler premises.
165 Draycott Ave, SW3 (01-581 2375). Open 10.00-18.00 Mon to Fri; 10.00-17.00 Sat.

Mary Fox Linton Ltd
Interior designer Mary Fox Linton sells a smattering of decorative bits and pieces for the house. Samples of fabrics for curtains (complementary wallpapers also available) and cushions are a mainstay but her most stunning stock is a range of dhurrie rugs. Imported from India, made in 100% wool or cotton, and available in a variety of sizes, the rugs are made in superb strong colours in geometric designs. Orders can be taken to exactly match colour schemes but that takes six months.
1 Elystan St, SW3 (01-581 2188/01-584 4803). Open 09.30-18.00 Mon to Fri; 10.00-16.00 Sat.

Rafael
This Italian delicatessen daily prepares several large trays of different re-heatable Italian-inspired dishes - stuffed peppers, a pasta dish - as well as quiches, taramasalata, a giant cooked rib of beef and various salamis. There's a good cheese counter with French and Italian favourites; a variety of packaged pastas; olive oils; French bread and croissants. Service comes with a bit of Italian bravado and a straw hat and outside they have a special doggy hook to tie up all those poodles and afghans that live around here.
4 Elystan St, SW3 (01-584 7906). Open 09.00-18.30 Mon to Fri; 09.00-15.00 Sat.

Sign of the Times
Cathy McGowan, who made a name for herself in the 1960s introducing *Ready Steady Go*, runs this nearly-new clothes shop. She opened several years ago with clothes from the likes of Gary Glitter, Elton John and Adam Faith, but today her stocks are far more down to earth and include anything and everything for men, women and children. The shop is small and all available space is crammed with clothes so plenty of time is needed to sift through the rails.
17 Elystan St, SW3 (01-589 4774). Open 10.00-17.30 Mon to Sat.

The Fabric Shop
The owners have samples of thousands of crisp, light mater-

ials in bright, fresh colours. They like pretty, small patterns (like the Greenfield Village collection with matching wall-papers) and don't go in for silks, damasks and brocades.
6 Cale St, SW3 (01-584 8495). Open 09.30-17.30 Mon to Fri; 10.00-13.00 Sat.

Chelsea Fish and Poultry Shop
The proprietor of this small fishmongers is cheerful and helpful. Whatever fish are in season will be found on the slab, plus smoked fish, chicken and other poultry and game in season.
10 Cale St, SW3 (01-589 9432). Open 07.30-16.00 Tues and Wed; 07.30-16.30 Fri and Sat.

Cookshop Caterers
Small, somewhat chaotic (the fact that the door handle is on upsidedown characterizes the place) and very popular delicatessen, grocers and breadshop. A team of competent cooks prepare a delicious array of pâtés, taramasalata, quiches, pies, tarts (their treacle tart is superb), cooked meats and sausage rolls and Scotch eggs (for which they are locally famous), which can be bought in the shop or ordered for private functions. Also good breads (some home made), home-made pickles, marmalades and jams, cheese and pricey gift-style groceries. They serve hot soup to take away.
16 Cale St, SW3 (01-589 8388). Open 09.00-14.00, 15.00-17.30 Mon to Fri; 09.00-13.00 Sat.

Walton St Stationers' Co
Beautiful writing papers in a choice of styles and colours, coloured writing inks, their own 100% cotton writing paper in a choice of seven colours, two sizes and borders with matching correspondence cards. Also a selection of Curwin Press wrapping papers.
97 Walton St, SW3 (01-589 0777). Open 10.00-18.00 Mon to Fri; 10.00-13.00 Sat.

Joan Price's Face Place
All the department stores have beauty departments who'll do facials, give cosmetics advice, do leg waxing and a whole range of different beauty treatments. The difference with Joan Price's Face Place is that she offers a choice of 18 different companies' cosmetics which can all be tried and bought after impartial advice has been given. Appointments are essential for treatments, but with a bit of organization, what a nice way to unwind from a shopping spreee. Cosmetic advice, facials, body massage, leg waxing, sun lamp treatments, ear piercing and electrolysis.
33 Cadogan St, SW3 (01-589 9062). Open 10.00-18.00 Mon to Fri; 10.00-13.00 Sat. Appointments essential. Also at 31 Connaught St, W2.

David Mellor
Like Divertimenti and Elizabeth David's shop, David Mellor is a high quality specialist cookery and kitchenware shop. He imports largely from France and stocks include ironmongery as well as kitchen equipment and tableware. French café-style coffee cups, earthenware crocks, cooking equipment, glass, cutlery, etc., are all well designed and laid out for easy viewing on large ground and basement floors. David Mellor has a connection with Sheffield and designed some of the cutlery in the shop.
4 Kings Rd, SW3 (01–730 4259). Open 09.30–17.30 Mon to Sat.

Beaton's
Still run by the Beaton family, this little-changed, old-fashioned bakers has been baking (on the premises) for over 70 years. They specialize in crusty white loaves, and make tarts, cakes and pastries to sound English recipes. Cakes are displayed on silver cake stands.
134 Kings Rd, SW3 (01–589 6263). Open 07.45–18.00.

Boy
Previously called 'Acme Attractions' and part of the clothes scene in Antiquarius (see separate entry), Boy is the pioneer of punk fashions. At the time of going to press utility, military, strap and heavy-duty wear were the rage.
153 Kings Rd, SW3 (01–351 1115). Open 10.00–18.00 Mon to Sat.

The Boot Store
London's first store to specialize exclusively in boots; for men and women. They stock many of the leading and lesser known American and Spanish boot manufacturers including the entire Frye range, also leather belts, bags and American-style boot ankle straps.
157 Kings Rd, SW3 (01–352 8092). Open 09.30–18.00 Mon to Sat.

Habitat
The larger of the two London branches (see also page 13) with three enormous floors (including a restaurant/café on the top floor). Modern furnishings, basketware, glass, china, kitchenware and cooking equipment, lighting, rugs, fabric and related gift lines.
206–222 Kings Rd, SW3 (01–351 1211). Open 09.30–18.00 Mon to Sat; 10.00–19.30 Thurs.

Givans Irish Linen Stores
This old-fashioned linen draper is delightfully out of sync with the rest of the Kings Rd. They sell top quality linens and towellings, much made in Ireland, and feature a superb, enormous unisex towelling dressing gown. They hold an annual genuine sale which shouldn't be missed.

207 Kings Rd, SW3 (01–352 6352). Open 09.30–17.00 Mon to Fri; closed 13.00–14.00 for lunch.

Tiger, Tiger

Any child would enjoy a visit to this well-stocked and colourful toy shop. The choice of toys is imaginative and the shop frequently stocks one-offs or short runs from craftsmen toymakers. It is particularly good for glove and string puppets, dolls' houses, realistic and life-size soft toys as well as an abundance of small, pocket-money toys.
219 Kings Rd, SW10 (01–352 8080). Open 10.00–18.00 Mon to Sat.

Kipling

This attractively laid-out two-floor shop imports all manner of things decorative and functional from India. Goods are tasteful, and include a range of upholstered bamboo/cane furniture, bamboo accessories including plant holders, framed mirrors, coat hangers, shelves and shelving units, towel rails, superb old patchwork quilts, Rajastani tapestries, bedspreads, tablecloths and rugs, and cotton fabric by the metre. There are also marble effect bathroom fittings to order.
306 Kings Rd, SW3 (01–352 9159). Open 10.00–18.00 Mon to Fri; 10.00–14.00 Sat.

Gas Log Fire Centre

All the fun of a coal fire without the encumbent bother: artificial and authentic-looking logs made of volcanic lava 'burn' with calor gas flames in traditional-style fire baskets. See them working and find out all about them here.
232 Fulham Rd, SW10 (01–352 2560). Open 10.00–18.00 Mon to Sat.

Chelsea Antique Market

Entering this large, rambling covered market is like entering a maze. Large and small antiques of all types including period clothes and jewellery are sold by seasoned dealers.
245a Kings Rd, SW3 (01–352 9695). Open 10.00–18.00 Mon to Sat.

Designers' Guild

The original branch at 277 specializes in pretty, co-ordinated fabrics and wallpapers with matching accessories. Designs are soft and subtle, fabrics natural but prices very high. They sell off-cuts co-ordinated for patchwork and remnants for napkin- and cushion-making. At 271 DG have expanded their accessory range to include covered sofas, dressers, cane furniture, lights, rugs, mirrors, pottery and tasteful home objects.
277 Kings Rd, SW3 (01–351 1271) and 271 Kings Rd, SW3 (01–352 5460). Open 09.30–17.30 Mon to Fri; 10.00–16.00 Sat.

Osborne and Little
Around 400 superb original wallpapers and fabric designs are hung on screens and displayed in pattern books at Osborne and Little. The range is all special and includes hand-printed papers, printed hessian, metallics and a range of friezes. Orders are ready the same day.
304 Kings Rd, SW3 (01–352 1456). Open 09.30–17.30 Mon to Fri; 10.00–13.00 Sat.

Terry de Havilland
Terry de Havilland was one of the first shoe shops to specialize in snazzy women's fashion shoes, and continues to be flamboyant and sparkly details, high heels and plenty of gold. They sell canvas boots and stiletto-heel mules.
323 Kings Rd, SW3 (01–352 9866). Open 10.30–18.00 Mon to Sat.

Kickers
The first London shop devoted entirely to the very popular French casual booties for men, women and children. They import 24 designs including the original and still popular ankle boot in two-tone suede. See Kickback, Wandsworth Bridge Rd, Parsons Green, Earls Court section for details of their permanent sale shop.
331 Kings Rd, SW3 (01–352 7541). Open 10.00–18.00 Mon to Sat. Also at 183a Brompton Rd, SW3.

Retro
Retro sell original 30s-50s clothes and accessories for men and women. The emphasis is on style and particular period changes with the fashions – currently they've got plenty of '50s clothes, mostly imported from America. They are particularly good on shoes, bags, hats and gloves and offer an alteration service.
339 Kings Rd, SW3 (01–352 2095). Open 10.30–18.30 Mon to Sat.

Zapata Shoe Co
Superb hand-made contemporary shoes, sandals and boots for men and women, all designed by top shoe designer, Manolo Blahnik. Top prices too.
49–51 Old Church St, SW3 (01–352 8622). Open 10.30–18.30 Mon to Sat.

Antiquarius
Over 200 stalls in this covered antique market sell everything from Art Deco teasets and Victorian silver jewellery to ephemera, old kitchen furniture, glass and china. There is also a large section devoted to period clothes, with many collectors' items (from 1920 to 1960).
15 Flood St (entrance Kings Rd too) SW3 (01–351 1145). Open 10.00–18.00 Mon to Sat.

Le Cochon Rose
Once face to face with this authentic charcuterie française, complete with the day's specials chalked in the window and the babble of French conversation inside the shop, it's easy to imagine you're in France. They prepare various delicious-looking salads, French main dishes and snacks which are displayed in the window. Also pâtés, French cheeses, cold meats and saucissons, breads and a variety of groceries.
83 Lower Sloane St, SW3 (01-730 2898). Open 10.00–18.30 Tues to Sat; 13.00–18.30 Mon.

Mexicana
The high prices of the beautiful clothes imported from Mexico no longer seem so outrageous when compared with a lot of the badly-made pricey fashion clothes in Kings Road boutiques. Dresses, blouses and skirts feature intricate pin tucking and lace inserts and are dyed in bright, vivid colours or black and white. Styles are plain and classic, some are vaguely medieval.
89 Lower Sloane St, SW1 (01-730 3871). Open 09.30–17.30 Mon to Fri; 10.00–13.00 Sat.

Tutto
On the site of the old Elle shop, Tutto stocks both Elle and Fiorucci clothes. Everything is exorbitantly priced. See Brompton Road, Knightsbridge for full details on Fiorucci.
27 Sloane Sq, SW1 (01-730 7050). Open 10.00–18.30 Mon to Fri; (until 19.30 Thurs); 10.00–18.00 Sat.

The Danish House
The Danish House stocks everything for the needlewoman; in fact it provides the greatest range of equipment under one roof in London. Over 1000 embroidery designs, canvas by the metre, footstool and cushion covers, DMC silks and wools, fine canvas, and books on embroidery and sewing. Also seasonal hand-made arts and crafts from Denmark which includes tablecloths, mats, napkins, place cards, hand-made quilted items for children, dried flower circlets and Danish candles.
16 Sloane St, SW1 (01-235 9868). Open 09.30–17.30 Mon to Sat.

Partridges
Its unusually (for this area) late opening hours make this high class grocery and deli a boon for everyone working in, living in, or passing through Sloane Square. They stock a wide range of cold meats and salamis and pride themselves on their whole turkey and Alderton ham baked in marmalade to an old Suffolk recipe. Ranges of freshly prepared salads, quiches, pâtés,

mousses and main dishes (prepared in their kitchens and ready for re-heating) are of a high standard. They sell French and English cheeses, kept in good condition, Loseley ice-cream, fresh cream cakes, coffee and fresh bread daily. There is also an off-licence.
132 Sloane St, SW1 (01-730 0651). Open 09.00–20.00 Mon to Sat; 10.30–19.30 Sun.

13
KNIGHTSBRIDGE

Sloane St, Montpelier St and Beauchamp Place, Brompton Rd, Knightsbridge

Nobody goes to Knightsbridge for a bargain. The area is rich in classy high fashion clothes and shoe shops from the cheaper Warehouse via up-to-the-minute fashions at Jap and Fiorucci to the very pricey chic of St Laurent Rive Gauche, Elliots, Jordans and Russell and Bromley. Most chain shoe shops are all here too.

Knightsbridge is dominated by Harrods; a must for tourists. You can buy virtually *everything* at Harrods, but the Food Hall, with its beautiful tiled ceiling and wondrous displays of fish and other food should not be missed, whether you want to buy or just look.

Many of the more interesting clothes shops are in Beauchamp Place (pronounced beecham), Janet Reger, couture lingerie, fashion clothes from Panache, Monsoon and others and men's shirts from Deborah and Clare. Also a wide range of the more exclusive shoes from Gamba, Kickers, Deliss and Shoosisima, while *very* exclusive clothes and gift shops line Walton St. The Walton Stationery Shop is worth a visit for superb stationery.

See also Notting Hill, Fulham and West End.

TRANSPORT

Knightsbridge
Tube stations: Knightsbridge, Sloane Sq.
Buses: 14, 30, 74.

LOCAL OPENING HOURS

Following Harrods' lead, many Knightsbridge shops stay open until 18.30/19.00 on Wed. A few close early on Sat.

REFRESHMENTS

Gloriette Pâtisserie Ltd
128 Brompton Rd, SW1.
Open 09.00–18.00 Mon to Sat.
Old-fashioned tea rooms with a few seats outside. Delicious Austrian konditorei pâtisserie.

SLOANE ST

Just Jane
Just Jane, maternity clothes, used to run several shops but has now retreated to this branch and to running small shops within shops. They sell everything for the mother-to-be except underwear, although they do sell bras. Clothes are pretty and fashionable but far pricier than Mothercare or the many suitable loose-fitting dresses from Laura Ashley and other ordinary dress shops. They are useful for swimwear and long evening dresses.
6 and 8 Sloane St, SW1 (01–235 6639). Open 09.30–17.30 Mon to Sat; 09.30–19.00 Thurs.

London Bedding Centre
With nearly 30 years of trading the London Bedding Centre can justifiably claim to be experts in beds and bedding. Most of their beds are made to their own specifications by leading manufacturers. These and other beds in stock are the result of research into the needs of their customers. They recommend that all beds are 'tried' in the shop, and even stock beds to accommodate partners of different weights with equal support. They also stock a variety of the latest and most novel designs in beds (round beds, etc.) the bedclothes to fit them, and they specialize in beds for people with back problems. Finally, if you want your own design made up, the London Bedding Centre is the place to go.
26–27 Sloane St, SW1 (01–235 7542). Open 09.00–17.30 Mon to Fri; 09.00–19.00 Wed; 09.00–17.00 Sat.

Laura Ashley
This branch sells the Laura Ashley range of distinctive small print furnishing fabrics and matching wallpapers. Other branches, notably Fulham Rd, sell the wide range of pretty, inexpensive, cotton clothes for women and children for which Laura Ashley has become renowned. They are especially good for cotton nighties.
40 Sloane St, SW1 (01–235 9728). Open 10.00–18.00 Mon; 09.30–18.00 Tues to Fri; 10.00–17.15 Sat. Also at 35/36 Bow St, WC2; 71 and 75 Lower Sloane St, SW1; and 157 Fulham Rd, SW3.

Bendicks
Most of Bendicks 30-odd different hand-made chocolates are sold pre-wrapped and packaged.

There is a limited range of smaller machine-made chocolates. Bendicks are best known for their bittermints, mint crisps and sporting and military chocolate.
195 Sloane St, SW1 (01-235 4749). Open 09.00-17.30 Mon to Fri; 09.00-15.30 (approx) Sat.

Truslove and Hanson
The best general bookshop in Knightsbridge, specializing in biography, fiction, children's books and current affairs.
205 Sloane St, SW1 (01-235 2128). Open 09.00-17.00 Mon and Tues; 10.00-19.00 Wed; 09.00-17.30 Thurs and Fri; 09.00-13.00 Sat.

Patricia Roberts
Beautiful designer knitwear. (See page 124 for full details.)
60 Kinnerton St, SW1 (01-235 4742). Open 10.00-18.00 Mon to Sat.

MONTPELIER ST

Bonhams
Hold auctions virtually every day selling virtually everything. Regular sales include prints, watercolours and bygones; antique furniture; oil paintings and porcelain.
Montpelier St, SW1 (01-584 9161). Open 09.00-17.00 Mon to Fri.

Janet Reger
Beautiful but incredibly expensive lingerie. (See page 6 for full details.)
2 Beauchamp Place, SW3 (01-584 9368). Open 10.00-18.00 Mon to Fri and 10.00-17.00 Sat.

Deliss
Deliss make imaginative boots, shoes and handbags in their basement workshop. Their greatest claim is to be able to make a pair of boots in 24 hours!
41 Beauchamp Place, SW3 (01-584 3321). Open 09.30-17.30 Mon to Fri; 12.00-16.00 Sat.

The Map House
The Map House sell a selection of modern maps but are moving further into the specialist field of antique maps and prints. Some date back to the 16th century. They have a wide range of 18th- and 19th-century prints and old brass instruments such as telescopes.
54 Beauchamp Place, SW3 (01-589 4325). Open 09.45-17.45 Mon to Fri; 10.30-16.00 Sat.

Gamba
Famous and long-established shoemakers who are particularly known for their ballet shoes. Also bar ones, tap shoes and shoes of all periods made to order. At this branch they concentrate heavily on their other range of smart, pricey men and women's fashion shoes,

sandals and leather slippers.
55 Beauchamp Place, SW3 (01-584 4774). Open 09.30-18.00 Mon to Fri; 10.00-17.00 Sat.

BROMPTON RD

Fiorucci
When it opened, Fiorucci was hailed as Italy's answer to Biba. Clothes and accessories are made in garish, unlikely colour combinations in either witty or high fashion (to date, new wave and 50s style) designs. Prices are exorbitant and all clothes feature the Fiorucci label which has snob appeal. Mainly for women, some clothes are OK for both sexes: shirts, jackets, T-shirts, trousers, jeans (supposed to be really well-fitting), dungarees, skirts, blouses, and dresses. Also at Bond St, West End; and Tutto, Sloane St, Knightsbridge.
15 Brompton Rd, SW3 (01-584 4095). Open 10.00-18.30 Mon to Fri; 10.00-19.30 Wed; and 10.00-18.00 Sat.

Charles Jourdan
Beautiful looking and beautifully made high-fashion shoes for men and women, from Jourdan's French factory. There is also a full range of accessories for women, including hats, gloves, watches and pens. Despite the exclusive aura of the shop, not everything on sale at Charles Jourdan is exorbitantly priced.
47-49 Brompton Rd, SW3 (01-584 3258). Open 09.30-18.00 Mon to Sat; 09.30-19.00 Wed.

Miss Selfridge
Miss Selfridge sells a wide range of reasonably priced fashion clothes and accessories for women. Along with the Warehouse Utility Clothing Co, Miss Selfridge brings a spot of cheap clothing to the otherwise pricey Knightsbridge.
75 Brompton Rd, SW3 (01-584 7814). Open 09.30-18.30 Mon to Sat; 09.30-19.00 Wed.

Gloriette
There's a pleasant, old-fashioned quality to these tea rooms serving and selling a range of Austrian konditorei, croissants, Danish pastries and cream cakes. There is limited seating outside on a small raised pavement overlooking the bustle of Knightsbridge.
128 Brompton Rd, SW1 (01-589 4750). Open 09.00-18.00 Mon to Sat.

Forces Help Society and Lord Robert's Workshops
Lacquer bedtrays, basketwork, tables, garden furniture and household brushes are made by men disabled during the First and Second World Wars.
122 Brompton Rd, SW3 (01-589 3243). Open 09.00-17.00 Mon to Fri.

Scandinavian Shop
The ground floor of the Scandinavian Shop is devoted to clothes, glass and giftware while downstairs houses the food. Clothes include a range of Finnish Marimekko label cotton dresses, hand-knitted garments featuring the traditional Fair Isle-type patterns and Norwegian knitting yarn. Food includes herring prepared in many different ways; cheeses; round, square and odd-shaped rye and crisp breads; Finnish sausages, jams and liqueurs.
170 Brompton Rd, SW3 (01-589 7804). Open 09.30–17.30 Mon to Sat.

Feltons
This 80-year-old company take great pride in the flowers and plants they sell. They only ever use a knife to cut flowers; treat them with great respect; sell only the very best quality blooms and always advise customers how to look after their purchase. Everything sold is seasonal so they never sell forced plants. Their produce may be expensive but Feltons make sure customers get good value for money. Delivery service and two other City branches.
220 Brompton Rd, SW3 (01–589 4433). Open 08.30–17.30 Mon to Fri; 08.30–12.00 Sat.

Midnight Shop
The only food shop open really late in Knightsbridge. They stock general provisions, frozen meat, a limited range of fresh fruit and vegetables and soft drinks. The nearest other late food shop is Partridge's delicatessen in Sloane St, and any number of mini-supermarkets in Earls Court Rd.
223 Brompton Rd, SW3 (01–589 7788). Open 10.00–24.00 seven days a week.

Reject Shop
This is the original Reject Shop (see also Tottenham Court Rd, West End) where they sell a wide range of reject kitchen and homeware at less than normal prices. Also end of lines samples and slight seconds. They deal with large manufacturers and can provide continuity of stock. Furniture, basketware, glass, china, and kitchen equipment with gift items.
245 Brompton Rd, SW3 (01–584 7613). Open 09.45–18.00 Mon to Sat; 09.45–19.00 Wed.

KNIGHTSBRIDGE

Harrods
Amazingly Harrods began life as a simple double-fronted grocery shop in 1849. The present building (dating from 1901 and elaborately lit up on winter evenings) covers a space of 2 hectares (5 acres) and employs a staff of over 6,000.

You pay a bit more for everything at Harrods but the (usually) old-fashioned reverential service sometimes makes it worth it. Harrods delights in being able to provide almost anything. There are designer rooms and up-to-date fashions in Way In; sportswear, animals; a bank; groceries, cosmetics; haberdashery; silver; babies' and children's equipment, to name a small selection of departments. Their food hall is superb and worthy of a special visit. Beneath the beautiful elaborately decorated ceilings, the very best meats, poultry, game, fresh and smoked fish (don't miss the daily prepared display), cheese, breads and groceries can be found.
Knightsbridge, SW1 (01–730 1234). Open 09.00–17.00 Mon to Fri; 09.30–19.00 Wed; 09.00–18.00 Sat.

Harvey Nichols
Knightsbridge's other store confines its stock to fashion and accessories; clothes, perfumery, a Cartier boutique, a Hardy Amies boutique, model hats, suedes and leathers, a Jean Varon boutique and the 21 shop – smart young fashion designs, linens, lingerie and all the year round cruise and resort wear.
Knightsbridge, SW1 (01–235 5000). Open 09.30–18.00 Mon to Sat; 09.30–19.00 Wed.

The German Food Centre
All manner of German foods and wine can be found here. They specialize in sausages, mostly smoked, cheese, bread and tinned foods.
44 Knightsbridge, SW1 (01–235 5760). Open 09.00–17.30 Mon to Fri; 09.00–17.00 Sat.

Bradleys
Bradleys is the place to go for lingerie. For the past 25 years they have been manufacturing lingerie, corsetry and beachwear for women of all shapes and sizes. They do a wide range of styles for those with the perfect model figure up to the DD and E cups; also nursing bras, mastectomy bras and underwear for 'difficult' shapes.
83 Knightsbridge, SW1 (01–235 2902). Open 09.00–17.30 Mon, Tues, Thurs, Fri; 09.00–19.00 Wed; 10.00–17.30 Sat.

14 VICTORIA

Pimlico/Belgravia, Victoria, Piccadilly/St James's/Westminster.

St James's is the home of some of London's oldest established gentlemen's tailors, hatters and bespoke shoemakers. James Lock for hats (they invented the bowler) and John Lobb for shoes are two examples. Nearby Jermyn St is *the* place for exclusive gentlemen's shirts and suitings, fine pipes and toiletries. Somewhat out of sync, there is Paxton and Whitfield, arguably London's finest cheese shop.

Burlington Arcade houses fine cashmeres, and this part of Piccadilly has several old-established sporting shops like Swaine, Adeney and Brigg and, of course, Lillywhites for all sporting equipment and clothes. Sporty fashions can be had from Simpsons. Swan and Edgar, the only department store, has an old-fashioned, more traditional image.

Superb chocolates, high class groceries and out of season fruit and veg can be had, at a price, from Fortnum and Mason. Victoria itself has little to offer and is almost entirely taken over by the station, air and bus terminals. Its only department store, the Army and Navy, has a superb food hall and wine department and a little of everything else.

Victoria does have many excellent, lively, small food markets; notably Strutton Ground and Tachbrook St – also a mini-Italian centre with fine delicatessen and Wrights the fishmonger. The interesting shops border on the edges of Victoria. Pimlico Rd and Elizabeth St have the greatest density of shops. The former has become a smart antiques and interior decoration centre, not forgetting the superb Elizabeth David shop in off-shoot Bourne St. Elizabeth St is notable for Justin de Blank's two shops and Inca, the Peruvian shop.

See also Chelsea, West End, Bloomsbury and Southwark.

TRANSPORT

Pimlico/Belgravia
Tube stations: Pimlico, Sloane Sq.
Buses: 11.

Victoria
Tube stations: Victoria, St James's Park.
Buses: 29, 38, 52, 70.

Piccadilly/St James's/ Westminster
Tube stations: Green Park, Piccadilly, Westminster.
Buses: 9, 14, 19, 22, 38.

LOCAL OPENING HOURS

Shops in Piccadilly, Westminster and Pimlico tend to close half-day on Sat; some follow the West End traditions of staying open late on Thurs.

REFRESHMENTS

Ceylon Tea Centre
22 Lower Regent St, SW1
Choice of several pure Ceylon teas, sandwiches, cakes, etc.

PIMLICO/ BELGRAVIA

Meadow Herbs Shop

For years this family-run cottage industry has strived to revive the old skills of making herb pillows, sachets and other aromatic products, and has sold them wholesale all over the country. This is their retail outlet where their entire range of both ready-made and kits and ingredients for pot pourris (including an Elizabethan herb garden type), herb pillows, spices, aromatic herbs and natural skin care products are sold. They choose pretty botanical fabrics for coverings.
47 Moreton St, SW1 (01-821 0094). Open 09.00–17.30 Mon to Thurs; 09.00–17.00 Fri.

Guernseys Galore

This shop 'grew' out of a successful mail order business. The owners import a range of machine-knitted and hand-finished traditional guernseys (in a variety of colours and sizes) from Guernsey and reckon to be the cheapest source outside the island. Also Breton-striped French knitwear (the sort with buttons across one shoulder). They still run a mail order service (for children, too).
49 Moreton St, SW1 (01-834 6141). Open 09.00–18.30.

Bicycle Revival

Three- and ten-speed bikes for hire; daily charge decreases for longer hires. All bikes overhauled and insurance available.
17–19 Elizabeth St, SW1 (01-730 6716). Open 10.00–18.00 Mon to Sat.

Justin de Blank Provisions Ltd

Justin de Blank opened this grocery/delicatessen/wine shop (his first) 11 years ago. Specialities are French cheeses, which are bought in France and laid down over here to mature. The finest farmhouse Cheddars, French butter, hams, cured meats, fresh exotic vegetables and fruit, honey, French and English bottled fruits and condiments are also available. A delicious array of home-made savoury and sweet foods is prepared daily (also private catering) and there's a selection of deep frozen gourmet foods. Also wines, ciders and fruit liqueurs. High prices.

42 Elizabeth St, SW1 (01-730 0605/6). Open 09.30-19.30 Mon to Fri; 09.30-14.00 Sat.

Inca

Peruvian Luisa Porras and her English partner Isobel Norman began in a small way importing a range of Peruvian knitwear and crafts. Today they've moved to spacious two-floor premises, enlarged their stock and sell wholesale all over the world. Brightly coloured and beige/grey/cream alpaca knitwear (jerseys, gloves, hats and scarves) for children and adults are their mainstay, but they also sell alpaca hand-spun vegetable-dyed wool in muted shades by the gramme, colourful basketware, hand-woven clothes, hats, rugs and a variety of decorative and home-related crafts upstairs.

45 Elizabeth St, SW1 (01-730 7941) Open 10.00-18.00 Mon to Fri; 10.00-13.00 Sat.

Justin de Blank Herbs, Plants, Flowers

There is always a pavement display of plants, herbs and cut flowers at Justin de Blank's specialist herb and seed shop. Over 100 different dried and growing herbs are stocked, with a wide range of seeds, spices, exotic vinegars and oils, herb teas and tisanes as well as seasonal cut flowers. Quality and reliability are good but, as at all J de B shops, prices are often outrageous. Knowledgeable staff give advice.

114 Ebury St, SW1 (01-730 2375). Open 09.30-18.30 Mon to Fri; 09.00-15.00 Sat.

Elizabeth David Shop

Tucked away in Bourne St and with a tiny fraction of stock on display at pavement level, this shop holds a superb range of cooking utensils and equipment. With her knowledge of cooking, Elizabeth David is well-equipped to stock such a shop; the basement is crammed to capacity with French kitchen equipment, china, and every culinary device imaginable. Her

sale, generally held in October, shouldn't be missed.
46 Bourne St, SW1 (01-730 3123). Open 09.30-17.30 Mon to Sat.

The Upstairs Shop
The Upstairs Shop sells furnishings for the bedroom to give a pretty co-ordinated look. The shop will arrange to furnish your bedroom for you or you can choose one or more items from the range of bedspreads with matching valances, over-pillow cases, scatter cushions, curtains, lampshades and bases, and even fabric covered tissue-boxes, all in a co-ordinated range of pretty, small pattern cotton fabrics. One of several up-market and pricey interior design shops in Pimlico Road.
22 Pimlico Rd, SW1 (01-730 7502). Open 09.30-17.30 Mon to Fri.

Rain Fabrics and Decoration
Another of the smart interior design type shops that have sprung up in Pimlico Rd over the last few years. Rain is a houseware shop, selling bamboo furniture and basketware, glassware and china, lamp shades, cushions, etc., in complementary and matching pretty fabrics. Fabrics are sold by the metre, there is matching wallpaper, and a mass of gift items from the Far East, particularly at Christmas.
42 Pimlico Rd, SW1 (01-730 3318). Open 10.00-18.00 Mon to Sat.

Just Gingham
Just Gingham stocks approximately 180 different lines in, you guessed it, gingham. Household soft furnishings for the bedroom, bathroom, nursery and kitchen include lined moses baskets, lampshades, sheets, duvet covers, wallpapers and matching tiles.
44 Pimlico Rd, SW1 (01-730 2588). Open 09.30-18.00 Mon to Fri; 10.00-16.00 Sat.

Casa Pupo
Saved from demolition a few years back and with a sister branch in Chelsea, this shop keeps to the cheaper lines and has a large reject section. Casa Pupo is best known for its Spanish, Portuguese and Italian ceramic bowls, plates, dishes, plant pots, animal and fruit ornaments, lamp stands and containers. These are arranged in colour themes in large, airy, white-painted rooms. There is also a small range of their distinctive thick pile, patterned Spanish rugs, a large lighting section and The Black Room – a gift shop within the main shop selling things like Crabtree and Evelyn soaps, jams and preserves; candles, basketware and cooking equipment.
56 Pimlico Rd, SW1 (01-730

7111). Open 09.30–18.00 Mon to Sat.

Hippo Hall
A superb new shop specializing in furniture and interior design for children's rooms. The highlight of the shop is hand-painted furniture (chairs, tables, desks, bookshelves, screens etc.) designed and painted by mural artist Annie Sloan. The shop also sells Alresford soft toys, pricey party clothes by Emma Goad, French bootees and a hoard of gift items. Murals sell from £100. An indulgent parent's paradise.
65 Pimlico Rd, SW1 (01–730 7710). Open 09.30–18.00 Mon to Sat.

WHI Tapestry Shop
Sells a full range of tapestry wools and canvas, catering for the novice and expert alike. Their staff will design to order as well as selling designs from stock. A note for perfectionists: everything is hand-painted.
85 Pimlico Rd, SW1 (01–730 5366). Open 09.30–17.00 Mon to Fri.

VICTORIA

Holland and Barrett
Part of a large chain, this is the only health food shop for miles. They stock a wide range of health foods, vitamins and herbal remedies, wholemeal and high protein breads.
10 Warwick Way, SW1 (01–834 2711). Open 09.00–17.30 Mon to Sat.

R. E. Wright & Sons
Established in 1876, fishmonger Wright's now have a large, brand-new corner shop built in the traditional style with tiled walls and marble slabs. All fish and shellfish in season, poultry and eggs. There is always a wide variety, but Mr Wright can get special requests within 24 hours.
10a Warwick Way, SW1 (01–834 7702). Open 08.30–18.00 Mon to Sat.

The Scripture Gift Mission
The Scripture Gift is busy keeping up with worldwide demand for bibles and distributing scriptures in over 400 languages. From their solemn Home Sales department they sell bibles, various scriptures and give away numerous leaflets on evangelism.
3 Eccleston St, SW1. Open 09.00–16.30 Mon to Fri.

Bovingdons
Bovingdons is a general delicatessen/food shop. It is unmistakeable with its giant champagne bottle sign, although parking is a bit tricky in this busy one-way street. They make up quiches, salads, pâtés, etc., on the premises, always have a York

ham, a selection of French cheeses and do business lunches to order. Other groceries include pastas, jams, biscuits and coffee, herbs and wines.
9 Eccleston St, SW1 (01–730 1375). Open 08.30–19.00 Mon to Fri; 09.00–13.00 Sat.

American Children's Shop
Stephanie Callan and Barbara Garrard import a range of American children's clothes which are guaranteed to delight the kids but probably horrify you. Superman, Batman, Wonderwoman and Donald Duck outfits, Mickey Mouse gift sets of underwear, and horror of horrors, baby bottles shaped like animals. Also funky babygrows, rain- and sleep-wear and gift items.
18 Eccleston St, SW1 (01–730 0714). Open 10.00–18.00 Mon to Sat.

Axfords
Axfords have been selling good quality men's clothing since 1880. For the past few years they've split their window space with their new business of selling flashy, sexy women's underwear. The men love it!
306 Vauxhall Bridge Rd, SW1 (01–834 1934). Open 09.00–17.00 Mon to Fri; 10.00–17.00 Sat.

Costa Coffee Boutique
The coffees roasted and blended by Costa's factory in Lambeth are sold at this boutique. Here customers can sample the blends (standing room only) before buying. Also a wide range of European coffee-making equipment.
324 Vauxhall Bridge Rd, SW1 (01–828 5215). Open 08.30–18.00 Mon to Sat.

Tachbrook St Market
Fruit and veg, seafood, plants, cut flowers and secondhand bric-à-brac can be had from this small and popular long-established market. Price comparisons are strongly advised. Unusual vegetables can be found opposite the fishmonger from a Cypriot stall.
Off Vauxhall Bridge Rd, SW1. Open 09.00–17.00 Mon to Sat. Best days Fri and Sat.

Cornucopia
Cornucopia is like an Aladdin's cave of clothes and accessories from 1900 to 1960. The shop does not specialize in any particular style but most of the clothes are for women with odd things like top hats and dancing shoes for men.
12 Tachbrook St, SW1 (01–828 5752). Open 10.30–18.00 Mon to Fri; 11.00–18.00 Sat.

Scootabout
Anyone with a full or provisional car licence can hire a fully automatic kickstart Puch moped from Scootabout. Prices include everything – even a helmet. The

deposit, which is not cashed but held as a security, is fairly hefty and depends on age – under 25s pay the most.
17 Tachbrook St, SW1 (01–821 5177). Open 09.00–18.00 Mon to Fri; 09.00–14.00 Sat and Sun.

The Army and Navy Stores
The now enormous Army and Navy Stores has a history that has always attracted the patronage of the services. Victoria's only store was founded in 1871 by a small group of army officers wanting to buy wine at a cheaper rate. So successful was their little venture that they soon had a thriving import business on their hands. By 1930 the store went public and a couple of years ago it doubled in size. Like all department stores it sells a little of everything, but is particularly noted for its food hall which keeps excellent international groceries and cheeses, cold meats and pâtés and even haggis. They grind freshly roasted coffee to order, have a Gloriette pâtisserie counter and bake bread on the premises.
Victoria St, SW1 (01–834 1234). Open 09.00–17.30 Mon, Wed, Thurs; 09.30–17.30 Tues; 09.00–18.00 Fri and Sat.

Piklik
This tiny shop imports women's clothes from Thailand and China. All are hand-made, hand-embroidered or crocheted. Prices are very reasonable.
199 Victoria St, SW1 (01–828 1070). Open 10.00–19.00 Mon to Fri; 10.00–18.00 Sat.

Strutton Ground Market
One of Victoria's oldest markets, happening at lunchtimes only Mon to Fri (when the street is closed to traffic). It's a boon to nearby office workers and locals alike. There are always plenty of fruit and veg stalls, several clothes stalls, household goods and a lot of stuff of dubious origin sold from big boxes. Delicious oven-hot bread from Stiles the local baker.
Off Victoria St, SW1. Open 11.30–15.00 Mon to Fri.

Bonne Bouche
Run by next-door English restaurant 'Bumbles', this small shop specializes in English farmhouse cheeses and English wines, as well as a variety of middle-price French, German and Spanish wines. Cheeses are bought in vast sizes – up to 27 kilos (60 lbs) – and sold from manageable pieces. Their range includes Stilton, Blue Cheshire, Blue Vinny and a range of Cheddars, Lancashires and Derbys.
14 Buckingham Palace Rd, SW1 (no phone). Open 10.30–19.00 Mon to Fri.

Girl Guides Association and Scout Association
These shops are next door to each other and both sell all the

bits and bobs of scout and guide uniform (classic style green scout shirts with button-down pockets and blue guide blouses wear well and are reasonably priced) as well as a seemingly comprehensive range of camping equipment. Served by uniformed members of the Association.
17–19 Buckingham Palace Rd, SW1 (01–828 1448). Open 09.00–17.30 Mon to Fri; 09.00–13.00 Sat.

Kemp and Co
Kemp and Co was established in 1870 and is a 'free house' artists' materials shop: brushes, watercolours, oils, papers, etc. and they also specialize in framing. Their stationery section is very good for unusual postcards and greetings cards.
28 Buckingham Palace Rd, SW1. Open 09.00–17.30 Mon to Fri; 09.00–12.30 Sat.

J. A. Allen & Co
An equestrian bookshop selling books on all aspects of horse breeding, management, showing, riding, racing, driving and polo.
1 Lower Grosvenor Place, SW1 (01–828 8855). Open 09.00–17.30 Mon to Fri; 09.00–17.00 Sat.

PICCADILLY/ ST JAMES'S/ WESTMINSTER

Charbonnel et Walker
Charbonnel et Walker, Royal Warrant holders, have been making chocolates since 1875. One special feature of their chocolates is that each is numbered on the bottom and the number corresponds to a list of fillings. Assortments of customers' favourites are then made up, sold loose or packed in superb presentation boxes; including hand-made ones. One special idea for presentation boxes: C et W make gold foil covered chocolate letters to spell out a name or message when the box is opened. Luxury prices.
28 Old Bond St, W1 (01–629 4396/5149). Open 08.30–17.30 Mon to Fri; 09.30–13.00 Sat.

Scott Adie Ltd
Scott Adie have been kilt and tartan specialists for nearly 140 years. They make kilts to order for men and women and know all the varieties of proper Highland dress, including evening wear. They also stock kilt pins, tartan by the yard, traditional Scottish jewellery, rugs, cashmeres, lambswool, scarves, etc.
14a Clifford St, Bond St, W1 (01–629 6331). Open 09.00–17.30 Mon to Fri; 09.00–12 30 Sat.

Fortnum and Mason
The Queen's grocery, where assistants in tail coats serve high class international groceries and condiments. Speciality fruit and veg out of season, cheeses, teas, coffees, superb hand-made chocolates, game and other pies; game, including dressed boar's heads, to order. Much frequented by window shoppers.
181 Piccadilly, W1 (01-734 8040). Open 09.00–18.00 Mon to Sat.

Hatchards
With its wooden-framed bow windows, this is London's 'smart' bookshop. Hardback copies of all the new 'good' fiction and a reliable standing stock of classics. There is a strong children's section and a paperback department in the basement.
187 Piccadilly, W1 (01-439 9921). Open 09.00–17.30 Mon to Fri; 09.00–13.00 Sat.

Chubb
The range of Chubb locks, security fittings for doors and windows, wall safes and deed boxes can be seen at this Chubb showroom. They have a key cutting service at this branch and can arrange repairs to Chubb locks and installations with their Bromley-by-Bow, E3, branch who operate a fitting service.
68 St James's St, SW1 (01-493 5414). Open 09.30–17.00 Mon to Fri.

Turnbull and Asser
Turnbull and Asser is one of many bespoke tailors and shirt and tie makers in Jermyn St and its immediate surrounds. Established in 1885, today they are reckoned to be marginally trendier than the others and keep well up with the fashions. They will hand-make shirts, jackets, suits, slacks and accessories in a variety of fabrics (a large percentage of which are exclusive to T&A), but today they sell mostly ready-made. Everything is beautifully made in sound, well-wearing natural fabrics; service is from another era and prices befit the upper echelons.
71/72 Jermyn St, SW1 (01-930 0502). Open 09.00–17.30 Mon to Fri; 09.00–13.00 Sat.

J. Floris Ltd
Floris, a peaceful sanctuary of delightful fragrances imported from all over the world, dates back to 1730. Aside from perfumes and toilet waters, Floris make every kind of bath luxury from soaps and bath essences to scented sachets and perfumed powders, mouth washes, hair sets, traditional hand-painted china pomander balls, ceramic jars of country garden pot pourri, and a large range of preparations for men. Also ivory hairbrushes; pure

bristle tooth and nail brushes, natural tortoiseshell combs of all sizes and natural sponges which are piled in the window.
89 Jermyn St, SW1 (01-930 2885). Open 09.30-17.30 Mon to Fri.

Paxton and Whitfield
In a street renowned for quality gentlemen's clothing, Paxton and Whitfield seem a little incongruous. They are perhaps London's most famous cheese shop, selling to many leading restaurants, and have regular customers who travel from far and wide for their cheeses. They keep 300 different English and European cheeses both soft and hard but are famous for their Stiltons (one of the few places where customers are encouraged to sample). They sell their cheeses whole or in very small portions and if they haven't got what you require, they will get it for you within 10 days. They also sell York hams and Jacksons' range of speciality teas. The staff are respectful and very knowledgeable about everything they stock.
93 Jermyn St, SW1 (01-930 0259). Open 08.30-17.00 Mon to Fri; 08.30-12.00 Sat.

Astley's
Founded in 1862, Astley's has become a temple to pipe smokers. The Victorian shop, complete with a museum of rare antique pipes from all over the world, specializes in briar pipes and has 30 different shapes (both bowl and stem) on view. They stock antique pipes of all styles, sell their own tobacco, and provide a pipe-repairing service.
109 Jermyn St, SW1 (01-930 1687). Open 09.00-18.00 Mon to Fri; 10.00-13.00 Sat.

Herbert Johnson
Herbert Johnson are superior hatters and have been since 1895. Their specialities are sporting and country hats but they also make straw boaters, panama hats and any hat to order – even using customers' own materials. They have extensive stocks in the shop, and make service caps for the Armed Forces. For men and women.
13 Old Burlington St, W1 (01-439 7397). Open 09.00-17.30 Mon to Fri; 09.00-12.30 Sat.

Burberry's
Renowned for the classic British raincoat as well as a pricey range of tailored and classic clothes for men and women.
18 Haymarket, SW1 (01-930 3343). Open 09.00-17.30 Mon to Sat; 09.00-19.00 Thurs.

Design Centre
A government-aided concern with the double aim of improving and encouraging design in industry and informing custom-

ers in England and abroad about available and well-designed products. The Centre holds regular exhibitions and maintains an index of this country's designers. It also has a small retail shop with a selection of items bearing the Design Centre kitemark for good design.
28 Haymarket, SW1 (01-839 8000). Open 09.30-17.30 Mon to Sat; 09.30-21.00 Wed and Thurs.

Fribourg and Treyer
Georgian bow-fronted shop complete with oak panelling and period fittings (*circa* 1720), selling a wide range of snuffs, cigars and their own brand cigarettes, long old-fashioned matches and tobacco-related gift items including plain and spotted snuff handkerchiefs.
34 Haymarket, SW1 (01-930 1305). Open 09.00-17.00 Mon to Sat.

15 SOUTHWARK

Vauxhall, Waterloo, Lambeth, Southwark, Oval/Stockwell.

Much of the original Southwark, at least in the North, has got mown down underfoot by the planners and the long distance lorry drivers. Trying to get to the other side of the road and reach *that* shop can be a daunting experience and the impression is that some of the older shops only remain standing as the result of an oversight on the part of the powers that be. The Elephant and Castle remains the shopping capital of the Borough, but if you look carefully you can still stumble across traces of the village shops, down the side streets of Stockwell, Kennington and Lambeth, although the old Lambeth Walk has been completely modernized into a streamlined shopping precinct.

See also City, Bloomsbury and Chelsea.

TRANSPORT

Vauxhall
Tube stations: Elephant and Castle.

Vauxhall
Tube stations: Vauxhall.
Buses: 44, 77, 185.

Waterloo
Tube stations: Waterloo, Lambeth North.
Buses: 70, 171, 188.

Lambeth
Tube stations: Elephant and Castle.
Buses: 63, 95, 133.

Southwark
Tube stations: Waterloo, Borough.
Buses: 44, 70.

Oval/Stockwell
Tube stations: Oval, Stockwell.
Buses: 45, 88, 118.

LOCAL OPENING HOURS

The traditional half-day closing in Southwark is Wed for Kennington and the Oval, and Thurs for Vauxhall. Many of the more interesting shops ignore the half-day and work a six-day week.

REFRESHMENTS

Cafés pepper the area; there are no 'special' tea places.

VAUXHALL

New Covent Garden

Now in its custom-built walled-in building, New Covent Garden fruit, vegetable and flower wholesale market is not as accessible to casual onlookers as it was when it occupied its central West End location. They actively discourage non-buying visitors, but proper group visits can be arranged by ringing. Bulk sales only.

Nine Elms, Vauxhall, SW8 (01-720 2211). Open 04.00–11.00 Mon to Sat.

Fish and Tackle

Mr and Mrs Groves' shop is lined from floor to ceiling with tanks containing many varieties of tropical and cold water fish, together with accessories. The Groves also specialize in coarse fishing tackle, but not game tackle, including maggots, worms and other bait.

19 Wilcox Rd, SW8 (01-622 0138). Open 09.30–17.30 Mon to Sat.

The Chair Doctor

Mr Stevenson does not carry any stock but offers a first-class modern and antique chair restoration and upholstery service. He specializes in buttoning; gives prompt efficient service, quotes and advice.

20 Wilcox Rd, SW8 (01-720 0840). Open 09.30–17.30 Mon to Fri; 10.00–15.00 Sat.

Heels and Wheels

This incongruously named junk shop with a strong line in secondhand furniture offers a knife and scissor sharpening service. They also cut keys.

50 Wilcox Rd, SW8 (01-720 3413). Open 09.30–17.30 Mon–Sat; 09.30–13.00 Thurs.

WATERLOO

Drury Tea and Coffee Co

Twenty-two different blends of coffee ground to order, speciality teas, wine and beer, tea and coffee making equipment, etc.

1–3 Mepham St, SE1. Open 08.30–18.00 Mon to Fri.

F. W. Evans

New bicycles, plus cycling

accessories and occasionally secondhand bikes.
77–79 The Cut, SE1 (01–928 4785). Open 09.30–17.30 Mon to Fri; 09.00–17.00 Sat; closed 13.45–14.30 daily; closed Thurs.

The Cut Market
At its peak at lunch-time, this general food, fruit and veg, plant and cut-price clothes market is a boon for Waterloo workers. There is a good bread shop diagonally opposite The Old Vic, a fishmonger halfway down the market and numerous butchers. Many of the shops lining the Cut sell at discount prices, and there are bargains to be had in stationery, plants, dress fabrics, and changing 'quick sale' merchants.
Lower Marsh St, off Waterloo Rd, SE1. Open 09.00–17.00 Mon to Fri.

LAMBETH

East Street Market
A long market closely packed with stalls selling fruit and veg, household goods, clothes, toys and their speciality, plants. The plant market is halfway down East St in a side turning. Bedding plants and houseplants are very cheap, with special 'bulk' bargain trays sold auction style. Busiest towards the end of the week and particularly on Sunday when even the traffic wardens turn out.
Off Walworth Rd, Elephant and Castle, SE17. Open 08.00–17.00 Tues, Thurs, Fri and Sat; 08.00–13.00 Sun.

Baldwins
Bottles line the walls at this delightful and old-fashioned herbalists who sell over 200 varieties of dried herbs, numerous seeds for growing and a range of herbal products, lotions, potions and remedies.
173 Walworth Rd, SE17 (01–703 5550). Open 09.00–17.30 Tues to Sat.

Soldiers
Would-be field marshals can marshall their troops here. John Turnstill's shop has dozens of drawers all full of tiny soldiers of all ranks and nationalities. Mr Turnstill keeps all the leading manufacturers' as well as his own design soldiers and will even make up other people's designs. He also stocks a full range of military books.
36 Kennington Rd, SE1 (01–928 7479). Open 11.00–17.00 Mon to Sat; closed Wed and Sun.

A. Leete's & Co Sales Ltd
Established in 1826 and still retaining many original features, this shop is the retail outlet for Leete's and Co's range of industrial and household paints. Aside from carrying all Leete's paints the shop regularly has sales of discontinued colours at half-price.

129–130 London Rd, SE1 (01–928 5283). Open 08.30–17.00 Mon to Fri.

O. Bellusci & Son (Tony's English and Continental Delicatessen)
Ottorino Bellusci's English and Continental delicatessen compensates for the lack of good quality food shops in this area. He keeps a wide range of salamis, Continental cheeses, olives and olive oils, pastas, pâtés and wines. Also fresh vegetables, tinned groceries and coffee ground to order.
39 South Lambeth Rd, SW8 (01–582 0766). Open 08.30–19.00 Mon to Sat.

SOUTHWARK

South London Leisure Centre
Over 730 square metres of tents and camping equipment can be viewed at this leisure centre, along with garden furniture, hammocks, ski-wear and calor gas heaters. Also at the Camping Centre London, Kilburn.
309 Borough High Street, SE1 (01–403 0989). Open 10.00–18.00 Mon to Sat.

Tattoo Studio
Mr Bryant will tattoo virtually any part of your body any day of the week. His spotlessly clean studio displays hundreds of different designs to choose from, or he will work to particular requests. Tattoos take between five minutes and one hour to complete depending on size and design. Also ear piercing.
113 Borough Rd, SE1 (01–928 4701). Open seven days a week.

Crafty Elephant
Crafty Elephant is the retail outlet for locally made crafts as part of the Elephant Job Creation Scheme. The standard of work and styles varies enormously; crafts include earthenware, pottery, leathergoods, puppets, macramé and woodwork.
116 Borough Rd, SE1 (no phone). 09.00–17.00 Mon to Fri.

OVAL/STOCKWELL

Bob White
This extremely busy shellfish shop has a high reputation. Lobsters, crabs, winkles, whelks, cockles, prawns and shrimps are all available; also jellied eels, turkeys, geese and ducks at Christmas. Bob White's run a Sunday shellfish stall at the Oval from 10.00–15.00.
1 Kennington Lane, SE11 (01–785 1931). Open 09.00–17.00 Tues to Fri; 08.30–17.30 Sat; 08.00–18.00 Sun; closed Mon.

Bits and Pieces
Mr Lindsay deals in men's

secondhand suits, shirts, shoes, jackets and pyjamas, and reckons he can do a complete rig-out for under a fiver. Also bedding and curtains, bric-à-brac and some clothing for women and children.
320 Kennington Lane, SE11 (01–735 4502). Open 09.00–18.00 Mon to Sat.

Antique Centre
This shop opened just as we went to press and showed such a fine selection of stripped pine furniture and old clocks that it warrants inclusion. The MacMillan family, who run the shop, undertake repairs to antique clocks and also offer a stripping service.
190 Wandsworth Rd, SW8. Open 09.00–18.30 Mon to Fri; 09.00–16.00 Sat.

Flowerfayre
Mr King and his daughter Deborah offer a most unusual service at their flower and plant shop. They create flower sculptures for special occasions and keep an impressive selection of photographs to show potential customers. Taxi cabs, football pitches, cats, dogs and teddy bears are amongst their accomplishments. The Kings also sell a wide range of dried flowers, plant pots and accessories.
236 Wandsworth Rd, SW8 (01–720 4196). Open 09.00–17.30 Mon to Fri; half-day closing Thurs.

The Sportsman
The Sportsman is a good all-round sports shop. They are particularly strong on fishing gear, training shoes, all the usual sports equipment (tennis racquets, footballs, etc.) and clothing. They repair racquets and engrave (and sell) sports trophies.
461 Wandsworth Rd, SW8 (01–622 2214). Open 09.15–17.45 Mon to Fri; 09.15–13.30 Wed.

E. Allen and Sons (Clapham) Ltd
This family firm dates back to 1860. They sell baby hardware: prams, nursery furniture, baths, high chairs, Maclaren buggies (also service and repair buggies) and a variety of baby toys.
463–465 Wandsworth Rd, SW18 (01–622 7700). Open 09.00–18.00 Mon to Sat; 09.00–13.00 Wed.

Marenghi and Sons
Mr Patel's delicatessen keeps a good selection of cheeses, herbs and spices, cold meats, quality groceries and Italian olives.
8 Claylands Rd, SW8 (01–735 1497). Open 08.00–19.00 Mon to Sat; 09.00–13.00 Sun.

Earth
This tiny shop is crammed with pottery, leather bags and belts, soft and wooden toys, jewellery and other hand-made gift items. It's arranged in a higgledy-

piggledy fashion and a long browse is needed to take it all in. The pottery is made on the premises behind the shop and commissions are taken for specific sets, etc. Also greetings cards and wrapping papers.
5 Windmill Row, SE11 (01–582 0096). Open 10.00–18.00 Mon to Sat.

Edwardes' (Camberwell) Ltd
Mr Edwardes aims to give a sound, all-round service to the locality's bike owners and potential bike owners. He keeps bikes from all leading manufacturers (including children's) which are stacked for easy surveillance. A full range of accessories and a repair service.
240–242 Kennington Park Rd, SE11 (01–735 5176). Open 08.00–17.30 Mon to Fri; closed Thurs.

Generation Game
A wide range of leading British and European manufactured children's clothes is on sale at this lively shop. Emphasis is on children choosing their own clothes and everything is displayed round the room. Generation Game covers from birth to age 12 in everything except shoes. A playpen and toys are provided for the very young. Fashion knitwear is made to order.
330 Kennington Park Rd, SE11 (01–735 4330). Open 09.30–17.30; half-day Thurs.

16 SOUTH OF THE RIVER

Battersea, Clapham, Wandsworth, Putney, Brixton.

The many Londoners who think civilization stops at the north bank of the Thames would be surprised at the wide variety of excellent shops to be found south of the river. As this section covers such a large area, it is only possible to mention comparatively few names.

Putney has lots of antique and secondhand furniture shops, two street markets and a surprising number of good clothes shops. The rather grimy streets of Battersea are synonymous in many people's minds with the Dogs' Home – it also boasts a number of interesting food shops and old-fashioned specialist shops.

Shopping in Wandsworth is dominated by the Arndale Centre which houses branches of most well-known chain stores, but those prepared to seek beyond the Centre will find interesting oddities like Colin Renwick's kite and balloon shop.

The final area to be covered in this section, Brixton, is to be recommended for a number of shops selling camping gear and for its lively, vibrant market.

See also Fulham, Chelsea and Worth a Visit.

TRANSPORT

Battersea
Buses: 19, 39, 49, 88, 137.

Clapham
Tube stations: Clapham North, Clapham Common, Clapham South, Clapham Junction (BR).
Buses: 45, 77, 88.

Wandsworth
Buses: 22, 47, 78, 149.

Putney
Tube stations: Putney Bridge, East Putney; Putney (BR).
Buses: 22, 39, 85, 93.

Brixton
Tube stations: Brixton.
Buses: 50, 159.

LOCAL OPENING HOURS

Half-day closing in Battersea, Brixton, Wandsworth and Clapham is Wed; in Putney it's Thurs.

REFRESHMENTS

Di's Larder
62 Lavender Hill, SW11
Open 10.00–19.00 Mon to Sat.
Wholefood shop and bakery with seating inside and out for delicious home-made cakes.

BATTERSEA

Battersea Dogs' Home
Lost dogs handed in to police stations or found roaming the streets by police are sold from the dogs' home if they are not collected within seven days. Dogs (and cats) may be cheap but are often emotionally disturbed by their stay in Battersea.
4 Battersea Park Rd, SW8. Open 14.00–16.00 seven days a week to collect lost dogs.

All Manna
The success of All Manna's natural food store in Richmond prompted the opening of this far larger branch with its own flour mill and bakery behind the shop. They mill only the Organic Farmers' and Growers' Association's highest standard of grain, which they stone-grind and bake immediately. Apart from their range of wholesome breads and cakes, All Manna stock a wide range of beans, grains, pulses, stone-ground flour, dried fruit, nuts, over 150 culinary and medicinal herbs, dairy produce (including goat cheese) and a range of inexpensive kitchen implements like woks and cast iron and pottery crocks. Discounts are given on bulk purchases, and they provide a private catering service.
250 Battersea Park Rd, SW11 (01–223 9211). Open 10.00–19.00 Mon to Fri; 09.30–18.30 Sat and 11.00–15.00 Sun.

J. Mist and Sons Ltd
This fishmonger has been in the same family for over 80 years and is known locally for its friendly service and advice. They sell most fresh fish in season, including shellfish, and smoke their own haddocks and bloaters. They'll get anything (in season) on request.
254 Battersea Park Rd, SW11 (01–228 6784). Open 07.30–17.00 Tues to Sat; half-day Wed.

Leisure Crafts
A general craft equipment and artists' materials shop specializing in glass, ceramic and wooden beads.
123 Falcon Rd, SW11 (01–228 0140). Open 09.00–17.30 Mon to Sat; 09.00–13.00 Wed.

Davy
This small shop is jam-packed with antiques and curios. Everything is priced (very reasonably) and it is the kind of place where hours slip by while a lot of browsing is done. Mrs Bradley runs the shop now and it has been in her family for over 100 years. Here is an example of what you will find: glove stretchers, propelling pencils, painted silk flowers, jet and mother-of-pearl buttons, cigarette cards, postcards, military medals and hat badges, crockery, paintings, glass, linens, and sewing and bead accessories. Mrs Bradley offers two services: bead threading and converting pierced ear fittings to screws.
3 Battersea Rise, SW11 (01–228 0466). Open 14.00–18.00 Mon to Sat; 10.00–14.00 Thurs.

Puddledocks
Besides being a very good delicatessen with a wide range of cold meats, pâtés, home made salads and cheese and fudge cakes, Puddledocks stock deep-frozen home-prepared meals. Prices are very reasonable; choose from a menu including chicken chasseur, Hungarian goulash, and devilled chicken livers.
4 Battersea Rise, SW11 (01–228 2231). Open 09.00–22.00 Tues to Sun.

Acquired Taste
John Thorogood's shop is a godsend locally for its superb range of 80-odd cheeses all in perfect or near-perfect condition. There is also real ale, rough cider, and a full range of delicatessen foods including coffee, home-made pâtés and herbs.
9 Battersea Rise, SW11 (01–223 9942). Open 10.00–21.00 Mon–Sat; 12.00–14.00 Sun.

Northcote Rd Market
Sells seasonal fruit and veg with West Indian and Asian specialities sold from stalls and the permanent shops which line the market. A good place for bulk purchases of beans, rice, and so on.
Northcote Rd, Battersea Rise, SW11. Open Thurs, Fri and Sat; not so good on Tues and Wed.

Curls Bakery
Battersea's excellent local bakers, who bake superb crusty loaves in a variety of shapes; delicious doughnuts, apple puffs and buns. They make wedding cakes to order.
12 Northcote Rd, SW11 (01–228

2995) Also at 94 Northcote Rd and 1 Battersea Rise. Open 08.00–18.00 Mon to Sat.

A. De Marco Ltd
De Marco's make superb Italian ice-cream in 50 different flavours. They sell it in cones and tubs of all sizes suitable for the freezer.
60 Northcote Rd, SW11 (01–228 8108). Open 07.30–18.00 Mon to Sat.

CLAPHAM

Clapham Crafts
An enterprising group of women recently opened this retail outlet for their crafts and all work on the premises. Naine Woodrow and Mary Neville pot at the back of the shop and fire downstairs and Suzanne Leverington stitches away at her quilts in the shop. Pottery is Japanese influenced (from Naine) and traditional English tableware (from Mary) and there's always a seconds basket. Suzanne's quilts can be commissioned. She prefers working in natural fabrics, particularly Liberty prints, and works by hand and/or machine. There is also an ace horticulturalist who gives plant advice and sells a range of well-tended plants.
24 North St, SW4 (01–622 0681). Open 11.00–19.00 Mon to Sat.

Stringers Freezer Centres
All the staples for freezer living are stocked here: pre-packaged meat, ice-cream, vegetables, bacon, pizzas and fish, as well as fresh eggs, cheese and bacon. The Centres have been operating for six years and prices are very reasonable for this kind of food.
8 Lavender Hill, SW11 (01–228 6624). Open 09.00–17.00 Mon to Sat. 32 Clapham High St, SW4 (01–622 6329). Open 09.00–17.30 Mon, Tues, Wed and Sat; 09.00–18.00 Thurs; 09.00–20.00 Fri. 4 York Rd, SW11 (01–228 0535). Open 09.00–17.00 Mon to Sat.

Lavender Hill Pottery
You can watch the pottery being made in the back of this shop – stoneware glazed with green, blue and yellow with a line-daisy pattern. There are extensive stocks in the shop, but personalized pottery can be made to order. They carry a range of other crafts including macramé hanging pots, jewellery, painted wooden mirrors, cards and wrapping paper.
27 Lavender Hill, SW11 (01–223 7003). Open 10.00–18.00 Mon to Sat.

Norman and Robinson Gas Ltd
Fully reconditioned gas appliances, mainly cookers and fires, can be found here. The shop is over 10 years old and can be

relied upon to supply working equipment. They do repairs and take in part-exchange.
50 Lavender Hill, SW11 (01–228 2114). Open 09.00–17.30 Mon to Sat; 09.00–13.00 Wed.

Di's Larder
Di's Larder sells natural foods and home-made breads. They carry extensive stocks of honey, grains, pulses, dried fruit, nuts, flours, juices, oils, cheeses and their own yogurt and muesli. Their delicious home-made cakes, pastries and snacks can be sampled on the premises, or the daily-prepared soups, seasonal salads and hot dishes make superb carry-out meals. They have a good selection of cheeses and the breads are outstanding and include Irish soda bread, granary, sesame, wholewheat and caraway loaves on Saturdays. Everything is prepared on the premises so there is always a delicious smell wafting round this lively shop. Seating for teas inside and out.
62 Lavender Hill, SW11 (01–223 4618). Open 10.00–19.00 Mon to Sat.

Town and Country Antiques
Town and Country specialize in pine furniture. They strip and polish most of it themselves and are a regular source of chests of drawers, dressers of all sizes, tables and wardrobes. Free delivery and reasonable prices.
119 Lavender Hill, SW11 (01–228 4093). Open 09.30–18.00 Mon to Sat.

George Malyard
Mr Malyard is a hatter. For 25 years he has made hats for men and women on the premises. His own or customers' designs take on average two weeks to make, but the more common hats like trilbys, stetsons, panamas and caps can usually be fitted from stock. The shop also carries a stock of quality men's shirts.
137 Lavender Hill, SW11 (01–223 8292/228 5276). Open 10.00–17.30 Tues to Sat.

The Patio Scene
The Patio Scene is the place to visit for reproduction Victorian patio furniture, castings, balust-trading and decorative metal-work. Everything is made from non-rust cast aluminium, and is available in black, white, pink, gold or unpainted. They undertake designs to order and also stock a selection of Chinese Chippendale-style chairs, various bamboo hanging baskets and outside lanterns.
171 Lavender Hill, SW11 (01–228 2595). Open 10.00–18.00 Mon to Fri.

B. Reading and Sons Ltd
John Reading sells records and musical instruments at discount prices. He also carries sheet music, and a wide range of styluses. His range of acoustic guitars is particularly good, and

he also sells recorders, tambourines and harmonicas, plus accessories for guitars and other instruments.
258 Lavender Hill, Clapham Junction, SW11 (01–228 0956). Open 09.00–17.30 Mon to Thurs; 09.00–18.00 Fri and Sat; 09.00–13.00 Wed.

The Lock Centre
The Lock Centre is one of the few places which operates a 24-hour lock-out service. They can cut door and car keys and carry a stock of Chubb, Yale, Union, Ingersoll and Banham locks. They also stock all the various accessories including door chains, bolts, window locks and Yale burglar alarms.
285 Lavender Hill, SW11 (01–223 5533; 24-hour 01–228 3220). Open 09.00–17.30 Mon to Sat; closed lunchtime and Wed.

Debris Antiques
Debris Antiques always carry slightly unusual pieces, not all of which are antique. Furniture of all ages is their mainstay, particularly stripped and polished pine chests of drawers and seamen's chests, but there is also crockery, bric-à-brac and old lamps. They operate a wood-stripping service.
584 Wandsworth Rd, SW8 (01–720 9172). Open 09.00–17.00 Mon to Sat.

J.J. Contract
J.J. Contract sell Victorian and Edwardian tiled and wrought iron fireplaces with grates. All stock is cleaned up and ready for working use. There are also fenders, fire-irons, railings and wrought iron candelabra.
787a Wandsworth Rd, SW8 (01–622 9604). Open 10.00–16.00 Sat only.

Alan's Cycles
Alan Forster specializes in new and secondhand children's and adults' Viscount bikes. He takes in old cycles in part-exchange, offers a 10% discount for cash sales, does repairs and sells a wide range of cycle accessories. There is also a key-cutting service.
791a Wandsworth Rd, SW8 (01–622 9077). Open 09.15–18.15 Mon to Sat.

Cash and Carry China Warehouse
Mr Asghar's shop is known for its cut-price sets of domestic china. He carries a wide variety of patterns, does a smart line in imitation French chunky coffee cups, and sells loose plates very cheaply in lots of one dozen. Discounts are given on very large orders.
19a Clapham High St, SW4 (01–720 3401). Open 10.00–18.00 Mon to Sat; closed Wed.

Rainbow Groceries
Richard Bluestone's wholefood shop has its own bakery on the premises which produces a

superb range of breads. He prepares hot lunchtime snacks like vegetarian sausage rolls, rissoles, pies and pizzas with no real meat, fish or egg ingredients. He sells delicious cakes: carrot, chocolate and vanilla, carob, banana, flapjacks and walnut brownies, as well as all the usual wholefoods: nuts, oils, beans and grains, honeys, jams, chutney, soya protein, etc.
153 Clapham High St, SW4 (01–622 1230). Open 10.00–17.30 Mon to Thurs; 10.00–18.00 Fri and Sat.

Here Is Food
Pamela Price's specialist food shop and delicatessen is a good place for food presents. There are shelves of tempting-looking jars, tins and presentation packs of French specialities (including sweets), and home-made jams and pickles; the kind of stuff you would have to be feeling very self-indulgent to buy for yourself. Superb but pricey seasonal salads are prepared daily, as are cakes, pâtés, and a range of delicious eatables made by local housewives. Also good bread.
The Pavement, Clapham Common, SW4 (01–622 6818). Open 10.00–21.00 seven days a week; open bank holidays and 11.00–15.00 on Christmas Day.

WANDSWORTH

General Auctions
General Auctions have a concession on all unclaimed bicycles, lost or stolen, which are recovered by the police. They hold regular weekly sales, well-attended by dealers and private buyers alike. The number and quality of the cycles varies from week to week. Viewing is possible on Fridays, but prompt arrival for the sale is advised.
53–65 Garratt Lane, SW18 (01–870 3909). Viewing 09.00–17.00 Fri; sale 10.00 Sat.

Gatto
A large, warehouse-style, cut-price tool shop which stocks all types of carpentry hand tools, motor and general engineering tools, most portable power tools (no bench tools), and a range of motor accessories.
206 Garratt Lane, SW18 (01–874 2671). Open 09.00–17.00 Mon to Fri; 09.00–13.00 Sat.

The Kite and Balloon Co
Colin Renwick reckons to supply anything involving wind power. This includes an enormous range of kites and all types of balloons from 200 10-inch ones at a 'special' price to full-size hot air balloons (for the person who has everything, of course). There is also a balloon printing service – how about balloon Christmas, moving or party cards?
613 Garratt Lane, SW18 (01–947 8505). Open 09.00–18.00 Mon to Sat; half-day Wed.

Rostronics Computer Centre
John Barton and John Penrick describe themselves as being 'a bit nutty; quite nice nutty'. They deal in computers of all sizes and for all imaginable situations, as well as computer manuals, components, software (programmes and games) and magazines. They will happily ladle out advice on building your own.
115–117 Wandsworth High St, SW18 (01–870 4805). Open 09.00–18.00 Mon to Fri; 09.00–13.00 Sat.

Monster Music
John Turner, Doug Ayvis and David McLatterty sell music equipment for bands: guitars, amplifiers, drums, synthesizers, speakers, PA equipment and all the necessary accessories. They buy and sell both new and secondhand and will hire out anything in the shop. They also have three rehearsal studios for hire, either with or without a 250-watt PA system.
134 Wandsworth High St, SW18 (01–870 6584 or 01–870 4048). Open 09.30–18.00 Mon to Sat.

Ruffler and Deith
Want a fruit machine, video game, pool or snooker table? Mr Deith and Mr Ruffler are waiting to sell you a new or secondhand model. They also sell pinball books, and hire out equipment, reluctantly.
152 Wandsworth High St, SW18 (01–870 5224). Open 09.00–18.00 Mon to Fri.

PUTNEY

Small Fry
Gail Parmigiani specializes in knitted clothes for children up to six. She keeps samples and some stock of all her designs in the shop and garments are made to order if she hasn't the right size. Regular favourites include knitted dungarees with Liberty print padded bodices, knitted dresses with white collars, and satin jackets with knitted sleeves.
33 Felsham Rd, SW15 (01–785 9153). Open 10.00–17.00 Tues/Wed/Thurs/Fri; closed 13.00–14.00 for lunch.

Peppermint
Peppermint is an excellent women's clothes shop. Fiona Dickson and Sally Fisk are very interested in fabrics and cuts and choose stock accordingly. Everything is mix and match and very reasonably priced. Guernseys, track suits, French and Italian casual wear and accessories form the basic stock. They buy mostly from small French firms.
18 Putney High St, SW15 (01–789 0854). Open 10.00–18.00 Mon to Sat.

Jigsaw
John Robinson's women's clothes shop aims to save Putney-ites a trip into the West End. He stocks leading names like French Connection, Hardware Clothing Co, Mulberry, Fiorucci and Ronald Sassoon.
114 Putney High St, SW15 (01–785 6731). Open 09.30–18.00 Mon to Sat.

Importers Ltd
A delicious aroma of coffee proclaims that beans are roasted on the premises here. They import, blend and roast all the coffees on sale, as well as stocking coffee-making equipment from all the leading manufacturers, including the original Spong cast-iron hand grinder. They also stock specialist teas and give discounts on bulk purchases.
167a Putney High St, SW15 (01–789 0942). Open 08.30–17.30 Mon to Sat.

Putney Flea Market
Browsers will enjoy this small market with its reasonably priced old clothes, jewellery, bric-à-brac, crockery, cookers, books and farm eggs.
Putney Hill, near the junction with Putney High St. Open Mon–Sat 09.00–17.00.

Icor Interiors Ltd
Icor has been making simply-designed solid pine furniture for 12 years. All pieces are hand-finished and melamine-lacquered. A full catalogue is available on request, and designs include square and round tables, bench seats, chests of drawers, kitchen and shelf units, beds and sofas. All designs pack flat.
195 Upper Richmond Rd, SW15 (01–788 0982). Open 10.00–17.30 Mon to Sat; closed Thurs.

The Home Wine Centre Ltd
Everything needed for home brewing can be found at Miss Studley's help-yourself shop, including the necessaries for making English wines and wines ready for drinking in three weeks!
222 Upper Richmond Rd, SW15 (01–785 9299). Open 09.30–18.00 Mon to Sat; closed 13.30–14.00 for lunch.

Romaine's
A highly revered, old-fashioned and family-run fishmonger which sells most fresh fish in season from the modest mackerel to expensive salmon.
1a Lacy Rd, SW15 (01–788 1366). Open 07.30–16.30 Tues to Sat; half-day Thurs.

Nimbus
Actress Katy Butler runs this clothes shop where the emphasis is on the feminine look. Many of the clothes are designed for the shop but others are imported from India,

Morocco and Afghanistan. There are pretty clothes for four- to twelve-year-old girls, and a range of Edwardian-style underwear: camisoles, bloomers and petticoats. Very reasonable prices.
3a Lacy Rd, SW15 (01-789 3535). Open 09.00-18.00 Mon to Sat.

Gavin's
Nick Taylor, Simon Gavin and Gavin Barlow run this high class food shop. Much of the prepared food - cakes, quiches, pâtés and salads - is home-made. There's a good selection of cooked meats, salamis and cheese, as well as Loseley products and several real ales. They can arrange outside catering.
5a Lacy Rd, SW15 (01-785 9656). Open 09.30-19.00 Mon to Fri; 08.30-17.30 Sat.

Spice
Rona Cooper, who had designed and made up clothes from her home for five years, runs Spice by keeping a selection of fabrics and designs in the shop, and then taking orders. She adapts her designs to suit customers' preferences. Prices are fairly high, but attention to detail, use of trimmings and quality of fabrics warrant the outlay. Rona keeps a selection of Peruvian and Welsh knitwear and a range of ready-made clothes in the shop. Stock is interesting and highly individual.
20 Lacy Rd, SW15 (01-789 5771). Open 10.00-17.00 Tues to Sat.

Putney Market
A general street market with the usual plethora of fruit and veg stalls; also household goods, hardware, shoes, clothes and meat auctions.
Off Putney High St in car park; Fri and Sat all day.

BRIXTON

Tarpaulin and Tent Co
Aside from a complete range of camping equipment, walking shoes and a limited stock of army surplus equipment, this shop carries an extensive range of tents. They are the main dealers for the Maraschal range and keep a large stock of Europleasure tents; both ranges include family frame tents, ridge tents, and back-packing tents. They also stock original bivouac tents; army marquees (20′ x 29′ and 20′ x 47′) and feature a 'special price' 14′ x 14′ x 7′ tent. There is also a branch at Clapham High Road.
101-103 Brixton Hill, SW2 (01-674 0121). Open 09.00-18.00 Mon to Sat.

Bits of Cloth
This shop features a regularly changing selection of a wide

range of end-of-line dress-making fabric at discount prices.
34 Electric Ave, SW9 (01–274 0224). Open 09.00–17.30 Mon to Sat; half-day Wed, late opening Sat.

Brixton Market
Brixton Market is an experience. It's a vast maze of open market stalls and covered market halls. Non-stop reggae music beats out and virtually everything on sale caters for West Indians. There's an excellent English fish stall and an abundance of places selling tropical fruit and vegetables.
Adjacent to Brixton Station, SW9. Open 08.00–18.00 Mon to Sat; half-day Wed.

Arthur Collier (Brixton) Ltd
For the past 98 years the Collier family has been selling an extensive range of hand- and electrical carpentry tools, hand-engineering tools (large electrically-run items like lathes can be ordered), butchers' cutlery, and plumbing tools of their own and others' manufacture. Their stocks are extensive – their display of spanners alone is valued at £1300–£1400!
423 Coldharbour Lane, SW9 (01–274 2042). Open 09.00–17.30; closed 12.30–13.30 Mon to Sat; closed 13.00 Wed.

Continental Food Stores
This warehouse-like store with goods sold from cardboard boxes specializes in Chinese, Nigerian and West Indian food. It is particularly notable for bulk buys of rice, beans, pasta, spices and pickles.
435/437 Coldharbour Lane, SW9 (01–737 2645). Open 09.00–17.30 Mon to Sat.

Caseys
Casey's have been camping specialists for 20 years. They cover the entire range of equipment including an extensive selection of tents (ridge-, trailer-, frame- and folding caravans), everything necessary for equipping a tent, and a full range of back-packing gear. They guarantee all products and give a full after-sales service – all repairs are carried out in their own workshops.
374 Brixton Rd, SW9 (01–733 1199). Open 09.00–18.00 Mon to Sat; closed Wed except during June, July and August.

17
RICHMOND

One of London's few real villages, Richmond offers a little of everything. Most shops are tasteful and quality conscious. Close to the park, and within a stretch of 200 metres on Richmond Hill, you can find several antique shops, an excellent modern furnishings store, a shop specializing in coffee beans, a good delicatessen and an Austrian Konditorei, both the latter open on Sunday. The numerous little alleyways leading to Richmond Green are full of fascinating shops selling antique and modern jewellery, antique furniture, paintings and crafts, and are always worth exploring. Further into the busy, confusingly one-way centre, there's a shop selling craft materials, a branch of Dickins and Jones, several excellent bookshops, shoe shops, exclusive fashion shops and Crocks, a place to buy cheap china.

TRANSPORT

Tube stations: Richmond (also BR).

LOCAL OPENING HOURS

Several shops open on Sun and work seven days a week in Richmond; early closing is Wed if it's not ignored.

REFRESHMENTS

Original Maids of Honour
228 Kew Road, Surrey
Open 09.00–17.30, half-day Mon.
Traditional English teas!

Crocks
Crocks carry 80 tonnes of china at any one time. 75% of their stocks are rejects, so prices are low. They are also a good source of casseroles and glassware.
2 Quadrant Hse, The Quadrant, Richmond (01–940 0466). Open 10.00–17.30 Mon to Sat; closed Wed.

Sellar Bros (Fastenings) Ltd
Fastenings and tools. (See page 132-3 for full details.)
27b The Quadrant, Richmond (01-948 1504).

Kramer
Austrian Konditorei: specialities made and baked on the premises include Black Forest gateaux, strawberry flan, German apple strudel and fresh cream cakes. Breads are made by another bakery. Good for tea-time treats on Sunday.
Duke St, Richmond (01-940 1844). Open 08.30-18.00 Mon to Sat; 12.00-18.00 Sun. Also at 20a Richmond Hill.

Bazaar
Stylish ethnic clothes for women. (See page 90 for full details.)
6 Duke St, Richmond (01-948 3626). Open 10.00-18.00 Mon to Sat.

Quelque Chose
Hand-made British crafts; natural skin and hair care products; soft toys; crochet; pottery; lots of cards and wrapping papers. Also children's clothes (0-11), and gift items like English country soaps in fabric bags, peg dolls in Liberty prints, herbal dolls which duplicate as pin cushions and pyjama dolls with faces.
9 King St, Richmond, Surrey (01-948 3036). Open 10.00-18.00 Mon to Sat.

Magic Bus Bookshop
Books on art, astrology, comparative religion, cookery, fantasy, fiction, gardening, humour, health, sci fi, mysticism and related subjects.
10 King St, Richmond, Surrey (01-940 1802). Open 10.00-18.00 Mon to Sat; 10.00-20.00 Fri.

Lion and Unicorn Bookshop
Lively children's bookshop with books catering for the up to twelves. There is a wide range of fiction and non-fiction, plenty of picture books and titles from all the popular paperback publishers. They run a Saturday Bookworms Club.
King St, Richmond, Surrey (01-940 0483). Open 09.30-17.30 Mon to Sat.

Laskys
Hi-fi equipment. (See page 12 for full details.)
32 Hill St, Richmond, Surrey (01-948 1441). Open 09.00-18.00 Mon to Sat.

Richmond Tea and Coffee Co
Particularly useful for its Sunday opening hours, the Richmond Tea and Coffee Company sell 14 blends of coffee and 14 kinds of China and Indian teas, as well as a full range of coffee making equipment. They serve tea, coffee and cakes at the back of the shop.
9 Hill Rise, Richmond (01-940

0855). Open 09.00–18.00 Mon to Sat; 09.00–14.00 Wed; 11.00–18.00 Sun.

Trend Interiors
Set back from the Hill, this exclusive furnishings store sells everything that homemakers with a taste for modern design could want. There are chairs, tables and sofas; china, pottery and glass (including many items of Scandinavian manufacture that are difficult to get hold of over here); plus lots of small, unusual gift items and cards.
8 Richmond Hill, Richmond (01–940 7261). Open 09.00–18.00 Mon to Sat.

Doll Shop
Most of the dolls on sale at Amy Bailey's shop are original from all periods. If the dolls need redressing, great care is taken to make exact reproductions of the period costumes, where possible using period fabrics, lace and ribbons.
18 Richmond Hill, Richmond (01–940 6774). Phone for appointment.

Richmond Hill Delicatessen
Its late and Sunday opening hours make the Richmond Hill Delicatessen a boon to locals and visitors to Richmond. They sell 60 different English and continental cheeses, a range of home-made pâtés, salamis, olives, bread; and salads.
22 Richmond Hill, Richmond (01–940 3952). Open 10.00–21.00 Mon to Sun.

Tridias
Large and imaginative selection of children's toys: soft toys, masks and toy theatres, dolls' houses and lots of little pocket money items.
6 Lichfield Terrace, Sheen Rd, Richmond (01–948 3459). Open 09.00–17.30 Mon to Sat.

Kew Books
Mary Bland runs this general bookshop which, with its close proximity to Kew, specializes in old books on natural history, botany and gardening. Ms Bland will help find any book on request.
9 Mortlake Terrace, Kew (01–940 2512). Open 10.00–17.30 Mon to Sat; closed Wed.

Antique Wardrobe at Camille
Period clothes (especially 1930s) in immaculate condition at very competitive prices.
5 Station App., Kew Gdns, Richmond (01–948 3990). Open 10.00–18.00 Mon to Sat.

Original Maids of Honour
Probably the area's most famous tea place serving a traditional English tea. They also sell bread and cakes to take away.
Kew Road, Kew, Surrey (01–940 2752). Open 09.00–18.00 (shop) 09.00–17.30 (tea room) Tues to Sat; closed Mon afternoon.

18
WORTH A TRIP

This short section looks at places which are outside the areas covered in depth in this book. All are worth a trip for specific shopping needs.

Brent Cross Shopping Centre
The first 'out of town' shopping complex designed on American lines to have been built in this country. As well as branches of the big Oxford St department stores like John Lewis, there are many other shops, plus snack bars, restaurants and a pub in this ultra-modern, air-conditioned shopping plaza. If you are staying in North London, why not try it as an alternative to the long trek to Oxford St?
Located where the North Circular Rd meets the M1 and Hendon Way. Hendon Central is the nearest tube.

The Hire Shop
The main South West London depot of this 20-year-old general hire company. A free colour catalogue is available on request, and stocks cover access towers; ladders; concrete mixers; building, decorating and plumbing equipment; emergency heating; power tools (including floor sanders); car maintenance tools; gardening equipment; floor and carpet cleaners; household and leisure equipment; nursery gear; beds; TVs and tape recorders. Also a full range of catering equipment.
183 Horn Lane, Acton, W3 (01-992 0101). Open 08.30–17.30 Mon to Fri; 08.30–13.00 Sat. See Yellow Pages for other branches.

Stork Reject Shop
Every mum should know about Toni Smith's marvellous shop. Toni stocks both reconditioned secondhand, and manufacturers' seconds in children's equipment. All is sold with a year's mechanical guarantee and the manufacturers' seconds come with the normal guarantee. Stock includes cots, high chairs, bikes and trikes, nappies, sheets, carry cots and push chairs. Stork also operate a part ex-

change system, a baby buggy repair and maintenance service and a pram hood and apron recovering service.
192 Horn Lane, W3 (01-992 4573). Open 10.30–17.30 Mon, Tues, Thurs and Fri; 10.00–17.00 Sat.

Joker
Circus master Gerry Cottle and show producer Max Butler have opened this colourful mask, joke and novelty shop. It is crammed with jollities, all clearly priced, and has caused a sensation with local children. The main feature of the shop is fancy dress/costume hire. Over 3000 different costumes are available and most of them hang from the ceiling in the two-floor shop. Costumes reflect the owners; many are bizarre and circus-style and include clown costumes. They are available for hire for both adults and children.
97 Chiswick High Rd, W4 (Turnham Green tube station) (01-995 4118). Open 10.00–19.00 Mon to Sat.

Renubath
Renubath re-surface pressed steel and cast iron baths in a range of 20 different colours. They can also remove cracks and stains. If pushed, they will re-surface basins and lavatories but if these are worn it's hardly worth the expense.
596 Chiswick High Rd, W4 (01-995 5252 Ansaphone 24 hours a day). Open 09.30–18.00 Mon to Fri; definite price quoted on phone.

Harrods Auction Galleries
Sales of objets d'art, carpets, rugs and antique and modern furniture are held every two weeks on Wed and Thurs at Harrods Auction rooms. Sales start at 10.00 and viewing is on the previous Mon and Tues. Every Thurs at 14.00 there are specialist sales of either paintings; silver and jewellery; books; toys and models; or costumes and textiles. Although the Rooms attract mainly Harrods-type buyers, there are plenty of cheap lots covering a wide range of furnishings.
Arundel Terrace, Barnes, SW13 (01-748 2739).

New Caledonian/ Bermondsey Market
Open air dealers' antique market where tourists and occasional visitors are spotted a mile off and have to work hard (barter) for a bargain. Small antiques.
Tower Bridge Rd, and Bermondsey St, SE1. Open 05.00–13.00 Fri only.

John Bennett & Co
John Bennett is a general sports accessory and equipment shop selling everything from a lilo to a fishing line! They make a point

of keeping several new and secondhand billiards tables in stock. These come from various sources and are of all ages, in varying states (from a pub reject to an antique table from a baronial home), and in all price brackets.
157 Old Kent Rd, SE1 (01–237 4411). Open 09.00–17.30 Mon to Fri; 09.00–16.00 Sat.

Austins of Peckham
These huge premises, full of good, fairly priced secondhand furniture, are almost an institution. Austins have been in the business for years, and are an excellent source of beds, chairs, sofas, tables and all the less glamorous furnishing essentials.
41 Brayard's Lane, SE15 (01–639 0480) and 19 Peckham Rye, SE15 (01–639 3163). Open 09.00–17.30 Mon to Sat; 09.00–12.00 Thurs.

Sagbags/Mike Enright's Warehouse
Mike Enright was one of the first people to make sagbags and sell polystyrene granules for top-ups and DIY. He still makes a wide range of different shaped and covered sagbags, and sells the polystyrene beads. Most of his business is wholesale but he is happy to sell slight seconds to the public.
4 Elephant Lane, SE16. (01–237 8818/2211). Open 09.30–18.00 Mon to Fri.

Waterside Workshops
An enterprising group of young craftsmen and women have adapted this vast waterside warehouse to suit their workshop needs. All are happy to take direct commissions and have samples of their work available for viewing. Currently knitters (of several styles), shoemakers, potters, musical instrument makers and printers are using the workshops.
Rotherhithe St, SE16 (01–237 0017). Occasionally hold 'Open Day' sales at weekends. Wise to ring first.

Aeonics
Now expanded into the mail order gift business (catalogue on request), Aeonics began life as a do-it-yourself duvet-kit firm. They now sell sophisticated bedding and ready-made duvets, as well as the kits (with or without filling), which are simple to make, cheap and available by mail.
92 Church Rd, Mitcham, Surrey (01–640 1113). Open 08.00–18.00 Mon to Fri; 09.00–17.30 Sat.

Hardwick Textiles Limited
Graham Paffey boasts a superb selection of cut-price fabrics at this shop. He's particularly strong on woollens, including worsted suitings, worsteds and terylene mixes. Fabrics come in dress and coat weights, and there are a variety of cottons,

crimplenes, treviras, linings, remnants and haberdashery.
369 Green St, E13 (01–472 1284). Open 09.00–17.30 Mon to Sat; closed Wed. Upton Park tube.

Handweavers Studio and Gallery
In 1973 a group of highly enthusiastic amateurs and teaching weavers set up this novel venture. Under one roof anyone interested in weaving can feel, see and buy a variety of yarns, looms, drying rollers and books on all aspects of hand weaving, as well as a changing collection of finished products. The studio also holds regular classes for beginners and experts and there is always plenty of advice available.
29 Haroldstone Rd, E7 (01–521 2281). Open 10.00–17.00 Tues to Sat; 10.00–21.00 Fri. Blackhorse Road tube, close to Walthamstow street market.

Paint and Paper Shop
This do-it-yourself shop stocks a little known North Country paint brand called Johnstons. They keep the entire BS range of colours in gloss and emulsion, all at discount prices. They also offer 33% off all manufacturers' vinyl wallpapers and 20% off all ordinary papers. With reductions like that, it is worth the journey to Walthamstow.
34 Queens Rd, E17 (01–521 0704). Open 08.00–17.30 Mon to Sat; 08.00–13.00 Thurs. Walthamstow Central tube.

Comet
Comet have several warehouses dotted around the edge of London, all of which are advertised in the national press along with details of the Comet range of discount goods. They concentrate on fridges, washing machines, TVs, audio equipment, photographic gear and a range of household appliances like irons and kettles. When you visit a Comet warehouse, you fill in an order form and goods are produced from stock. Reductions vary, but most goods carry a guarantee.
190 London Rd, Hackbridge, Surrey (01–669 4321). Open 09.00–20.00 Mon to Fri; 09.00–17.30 Sat. Hackbridge station (BR). Also at Old Book Centre Building, North Circular Rd, NW10 (01–459 8877); Rainham Rd South, Dagenham (01–595 5111); Silverdale Rd, Hayes, Middx (01–573 1841); 278 Upper Richmond Rd, SW14 (01–785 9891).

SHOP INDEX

SUBJECT INDEX

(London University's bookshop) and chains like Words and Music which mix current paperbacks and remaindered stock. There are also a large number of antiquarian and specialist dealers.

Since the design explosion of the 1960s (Mary Quant, Ossie Clark, Bill Gibb), the London clothes scene seems quieter. At the top end of the market come Brown's, Wardrobe, Bombacha, Piero di Monzi, as well as fun places like Fiorucci, Mrs Howie, Swanky Modes and more. London is still the home of Laura Ashley, famous for her distinctive, inexpensive country styles.

For men, outside the classic bespoke tailors on Savile Row, the pace continues to be set by French and Italian styles at Brown's, Bugatti's (Kensington Church St), Yves St Laurent. Blades combines Savile Row quality with the younger look. But many men plump for the compromise between style and classic quality offered by Austin Reed, Aquascutum and Burberry's (for men's and women's raincoats).

Punk fashion has been a grassroots movement that, over the last couple of years, has reached designer-status (and prices) at shops like Seditionaries and Boy on the Kings Rd.

London is famous for knitwear. Plain, classic designs are cheapest from Marks and Spencer; Scottish classics from Westaway and Westaway and more centrally from the Scotch House; and more unusual designs from Scottish Merchant, Tomlinson and Tomlinson, Ritva and Holborn Village Crafts.